Yeats and The Theatre

Design by Charles Ricketts for the King
in a revival of *The King's Threshold*, June 1914.

Yeats Studies Series

Yeats and The Theatre

EDITED BY

Robert O'Driscoll and Lorna Reynolds

First published in Canada 1975
First published in the U.S.A. 1975
First published in the United Kingdom 1975

Published by
THE MACMILLAN PRESS LTD
London and Basingstoke
Associated companies in New York
Dublin Melbourne Johannesburg and Madras

SBN 333 18564 1

Printed in Canada by
The Hunter Rose Company
Toronto, Ontario

Contents

List of Illustrations

Acknowledgements

Without the generosity of Michael and Anne Yeats this volume would not have been possible in its present form. We express our deep gratitude to Michael and Anne Yeats for permission to quote from their father's published works and for permission to present Yeats material that is published here for the first time. We are also grateful to the following:

Faber and Faber Limited and New Directions Publishing Corporation, agents for the Trustees of the Ezra Pound Literary Property Trust, for permission to publish YŌRŌ by *Motokiyō*, translated by Fenollosa.

The Society of Authors on behalf of the George Bernard Shaw Estate for permission to use Shaw's summing up at the end of Yeats's lecture, "Contemporary Irish Theatre," which appears here for the first time.

H. E. Robert Craig, as administrator of the E. Gordon Craig Estate, for permission to reproduce the Craig illustrations and to quote from Gordon Craig's published and unpublished works.

Jean Townsend, Toronto, for permission to reproduce her engraved portrait of W. B. Yeats which illustrates the jacket of this volume.

University College, Galway, and the Arts Council of Ireland for subventions to assist in the publication of this work.

J. M. Kelly, CSB, and L. K. Shook, CSB, of St. Michael's College, University of Toronto, for their sound advice.

The editors acknowledge the assistance of the following distinguished advisors:

Russell K. Alspach
Suheil Bushrui
David R. Clark
Eric Domville
Denis Donoghue
Richard Ellmann
Ian Fletcher
René Fréchet
George M. Harper
A. Norman Jeffares
John Kelly
Brendan Kennelly
F. S. L. Lyons
Norman H. MacKenzie
Desmond Maxwell
Georgio Melchiori
William M. Murphy
Shotaro Oshima
Kathleen Raine
Balachandra Rajan
Ann Saddlemyer
Michael Sidnell
Francis Warner

Introduction

This volume, devoted to "Yeats and The Theatre," explores the one
absorbing concern of Yeats, that which gives coherence to his literary career, the expression of personality, whether in lyric or dramatic form, of "blood, imagination, intellect running together." The
unpublished lectures, presented here for the first time, reveal the
aesthetic and philosophical bases for his beliefs. It is clear that the
nature of Yeats's genius was inescapably dramatic. He first realized,
he tells us, how personality could be expressed in poetry when his
father read to him as a schoolboy parts of *Coriolanus* and the opening passages of *Prometheus Unbound*: "I came to think, and thought
for years, that the only noble poetry was dramatic poetry, because
it always put human life, tumultuous, palpitating, behind every
thought." His next revelation came from reading the verse of an
obscure Irish patriot, verse expressive of entire sincerity of feeling,
without subterfuge, without elaboration, which, though it was bad
poetry, he found moving, even "to tears." This confession of sincere
feeling he came to call "personal utterance." Later, when he went
to London, he discovered that there were others there who thought
in the same way, the poets with whom he formed the Rhymers' Club.
All of them believed in "personal utterance" as the function of
poetry.

In this, Yeats and his friends were, of course, at one with the
Romantics. It meant rejecting the rhetoric of the Victorians and the
conventional attitudes and morality behind that rhetoric, as the "per-

sonal utterance" of the Romantics had meant rejecting the rhetoric of the eighteenth century. Yeats, like the Romantics, saw style, not as a ready-made dress put on to cover the self, but as the revelation of self, of personality, of the mysterious essence unique to a particular human being: "To bring back the arts of personality, the personality of the lyric poet or the dramatic personalities of plays—that was our thought, consciously or unconsciously. But a great deal follows from it. It involves a change . . . from an impersonal contemplative culture to a culture that could only be attempted in action." By a culture of action Yeats means a culture which allows men to put their lives into their work.

Dramatic expression, it is clear, did not constitute for Yeats an entry into a new path, but a following of his original bent: drama was merely another form of "personal utterance." "Personal utterance" through drama, however, ironically demands oblique, non-realistic techniques: it demands a rejection of the realistic imitation of the surfaces of life, the accepted mode of the Victorian stage. As early as the 1880s Yeats had been interested in poetic drama; during the nineties he was experimenting with symbolic presentation, and in the first decade of this century his theories seemed confirmed and encouraged by the living proof of Synge's genius, who was "pure artist" and expressed in drama "a life that had never been expressed before."

The articles in this volume trace Yeats's search for the techniques through which he could realize his philosophy of theatre: his interest in Gordon Craig's experiments and his revision of his early plays to bring them into line with Craig's concept of stage space and movement; his discovery of Noh drama; and his recognition of certain figures, such as Swift and Oedipus, because of their powerful, violent, indeed, bizarre personalities, as metaphors for his own thought.

The unpublished materials presented for the first time in this volume demonstrate the importance of Yeats's unpublished writings in the establishment of definitive texts and in the understanding of his finished work. The lectures on personality and the notes for these lectures represent a first draft of Book IV of *The Trembling of The Veil*, antedating considerably the *Memoirs* of 1915–16. The manuscript revisions of *Oedipus at Colonnus* appear to advance the text of the play printed in *The Collected Plays of W. B. Yeats*. The unpublished Noh play, made available to us by the late Ezra Pound, is one of the possible sources for *At The Hawk's Well*.

With the wealth of surviving manuscript material not only of W. B. Yeats but of his father and the other members of the Yeats family, scholars have an opportunity to study the creative processes in greater detail and depth than ever before in literary history. This is possible because of Mrs. W. B. Yeats's vision and wisdom in preserving the manuscripts of almost everything her husband wrote, her generosity in presenting much of this material to the Irish nation, and the generosity of the Yeats heirs, Michael and Anne Yeats, in allowing scholars access to this material.

Parke Cottage   LORNA REYNOLDS
Eyrecourt   ROBERT O'DRISCOLL
County Galway
Ireland

A poet is by the very nature of things
a man who lives with entire sincerity,
or rather the better his poetry
the more sincere his life;
his life is an experiment in living
and those that come after
have a right to know it.

W. B. YEATS

from the notes for a lecture
"Friends of My Youth"
published here for the first time.

How Yeats
Influenced My Life
In the Theatre

Micheál MacLiammóir

I understood Wilde, but never as far as I can tell has he influenced my life, my thoughts, my actions. Yeats was the only writer who did that. I have described in *An Oscar of No Importance* how on my return to London from Spain, when I was fifteen, my entire being was overwhelmed by two opposing passions. On the one hand I was obsessed by the brilliance and shadow of Spain, and of the tapestry of sights and sounds and smells and ideas and manners and prejudices known as *cosas de España*; and on the other by a rediscovery of my own country in a new light. A painter I had met at an English friend's house had given or lent me (if he lent it he never got it back; it is still in my possession) a copy, already battered and thumbworn, of Yeats's *Ideas of Good and Evil* and it excited my imagination as deeply as my first reading of *The Happy Prince* had done in the days of the *Peter Pan* tours long ago.

"The Greeks," Yeats had written in "Ireland and the Arts," the essay in the volume that moved me most and either made or wrecked my life, "the only perfect artists in the world, looked within their own borders, and we, like them, have a history fuller than any modern history of imaginative events; and legends which surpass, as I think, all legends but theirs in wild beauty . . . while political reasons have made love of country, as I think, even greater among us than among them."

Ireland, then, was not just a place one remembered with a sort of resigned affectionate regret, a place one went away from when life

1

with all its fantasies loomed ahead, went away from as inevitably as a child goes away from its nursery or its school or its mother's breast. Ireland was the "garden of the future." It was there we must live again; it was to the mountains and the lakes and the legends that haunted them we must turn for inspiration. It was Dublin, degenerated by history into a provincial town, that we must remould into a capital city.

"I might have found more of Ireland if I had written in Irish, but I have found a little, and I have found all myself." . . . If *he* had written in Irish! Oh, and *a great deal more besides! If he had written in Irish* . . . .

A week or so later, after an introduction from my father to a friend of his who wore a kilt, which caused much consternation in the London streets, I joined the Gaelic League. I tried to write in Irish after my first year, stories and sketches and various odds and ends, although my chief ambition still was to be a painter, and it was as a painter, not as an actor—my own profession—or as a writer, that I decided to return to Ireland. And so George Moore was possibly right when he said, in some words that were half tribute, half bitter disillusion, that the whole of "the Irish movement had sprung from Yeats and really returned to him." This naturally referred only to Yeats's movement in Anglo-Irish literature which took the form, when all is said and done, of an intellectual anti-emigration scheme, and as that it has had astonishing results.

I am quite aware that it has been the chief force in my own life. I said the other day to a friend, Professor Lorna Reynolds, that if it had not been for Yeats, she and I would not be lunching in the Dublin house I have shared for so many years with Hilton Edwards; that if it had not been for Yeats, Hilton Edwards would certainly not have been in Dublin either, nor would our Gate Theatre ever have existed! Were it not for the same remarkable man, I would never have learned the language my grandfather spoke naturally, and certainly I would not have published seven books in it. Had Yeats made or wrecked my life? From the point of view of a successful English-speaking actor, probably he had ruined it: London or New York are the rational centres for our tribe, not Dublin with its already established National Theatre, its regularly supplied importations, its small and often inexperienced groups of players and directors working against indescribable odds, or its brilliant and unexpectedly numerous comics and variety artists. The poet himself, as I have pointed out on more occasions than one, turned his back at last upon the very theatre he had created and took refuge in the cultivated drawing-room, and one is more and more aware that the Ireland of which he dreamed and for which Pádraic Pearse died would be, I am convinced, a bitter disillusion to them both.

Still, my own life, for good or ill, has been shaped by him and never as long as I live can I turn away from it.

There are many of us in the theatre under this same debt or bearing this same grudge: Siobhán McKenna, Cyril Cusack, Eithne Dunne and a host of others would long ago have followed the foot-steps of other Irish players and left forever for Broadway or Hollywood or for that magical city where the sun rises and sets in the West End, but for the opposing magic of Yeats who, like the Goddess in his own poem, never failed to call:

> Away, come away:
> Empty your heart of its mortal dream.
> The winds awaken, the leaves whirl round,
> Our cheeks are pale, our hair is unbound,
> Our breasts are heaving, our eyes are agleam,
> Our arms are waving, our lips are apart;
> And if any gaze on our rushing band,
> We come between him and the deed of his hand,
> We come between him and the hope of his heart.
> . . .
>
> And brood no more where the fire burns bright
> Filling your heart with a marshal dream
> For breasts are heaving and eyes are agleam.
> Away, come away to the dim twilight.

Yeats on Personality:
Three Unpublished Lectures

Robert O'Driscoll

CRITICAL INTRODUCTION

"All three lectures have worked themselves out as a plea for uniting literature once more to personality, the personality of the writer in lyric poetry or with imaginative personalities in drama."[1] So Yeats wrote to his father on 23 February 1910, while preparing these lectures in which he claims he was articulating the "convictions of the last ten or twenty years."[2] In the same letter to his father he also wrote:

> In the process of writing my third lecture I found it led up to the thought of your letter which I am going to quote at the end. It has made me realize with some surprise how fully my philosophy of life has been inherited from you in all but its details and applications.[3]

What is clear here, and what is more abundantly clear in the unpublished correspondence between the two, is that Yeats's father played a far greater part in the shaping of his son's thought than is generally recognized. With his father's philosophy carefully articu-

1. *The Letters of W. B. Yeats*, ed. Allan Wade (London 1954), p. 548.
2. Yeats states this at the beginning of the first lecture. It would be cumbersome to identify quotations from the lectures in my introduction; consequently I have only identified quotations from other sources.
3. *Letters*, p. 549.

4

lated in correspondence and conversation, with his own non-naturalistic theatrical experiments, and with the example of John Synge, in whom he could see the living embodiment of the philosophical principles he was discovering in Nietzsche, Yeats in the early twentieth century became preoccupied with understanding what is meant by *personality*.

By *personality* Yeats means something similar to what he had meant by symbolism during the 1890s. His concept of symbolism had been built on a belief in the uniqueness and sacredness of all living forms; a symbol he saw as the physical manifestation of a thought or emotion. By the end of the 1890s, however, symbolism had become associated in his mind with an unreal spiritual art, a world of intellectual essences and impossible purities, and an artistic belief that the ideal can be achieved only when the light of the manifest world has been snuffed out. Subsequently, in the first decade of the twentieth century, Yeats becomes intensely interested in *personality*, in that energy that emanates not merely from the brain, imagination, or sensations, but from *the whole man*, of "blood, imagination, intellect, running together,"[4] a literature that celebrates the energies of the body as well as the energies of the mind, which captures the intensity of personal life that moves a man who is free from fear and dependence on external circumstance.

Yeats explores these matters indirectly in the essays he wrote for *Samhain* and *The Cutting of an Agate*, and directly in this series of drawing room lectures delivered in London,[5] before a distinguished audience that included George Bernard Shaw, Ezra Pound, William

4. *Essays and Introductions* (London 1961), p. 266.
5. The lectures were delivered to raise money for the Abbey Theatre after Miss Horniman had withdrawn her subsidy. According to William Carlos Williams, they were delivered at the Adelphi Club: "Another night we had been given tickets for a benefit lecture by W. B. Yeats, at the Adelphi Club, on the work of some of the younger Irish poets. It was a very fashionable affair, to be presided over by Sir Edmund Gosse, who, it appears, hated the Irishman's guts. The tickets were a guinea each" (*Autobiography*, London 1968, p. 115). Certainly Sir Arthur Birch and his daughter had something to do with the arranging of the lectures. On 10 December 1909 Yeats wrote to Lady Gregory, saying that he was going to call on Sir Arthur Birch "and arrange about lectures" (*Letters*, p. 543). Edmund Gosse, who chaired the second lecture, refers to Arthur Birch's daughter. Yeats has written underneath the title of the first lecture "as delivered at Old Burlington Street."

Carlos Williams, Edmund Gosse, Herbert Trench, and others.[6]

Personality, Yeats suggests, is the living essence that animates individual thought and action, whether in life or in literature. It is a force that is constantly exploding habitual forms, the force that animates words on a page, or an individual face or form when that individual is most truly himself: "I have always come to this certainty," Yeats writes in 1906, "what moves natural men in the arts is what moves them in life, and that is, intensity of personal life, intonations that show them, in a book or a play, the strength, the essential moment of a man who would be exciting in the market or at the dispensary door."[7] Or as John Butler Yeats put it in a letter to his son when Yeats was preparing these lectures: "Personality to

6. Carlos Williams gives a rather self-indulgent account of the lectures many years afterwards:

> I sat alone, Ezra and his crowd being at some other section of the hall. I was fascinated by the proceedings, listening closely to what was being said. The hour was drawing to a close when Yeats began to speak of those young men, Lionel Johnson among them, who had been consistently denied an audience in England though in his opinion they well merited it and more.
>
> What was there left for them to do, then, but to live the decadent lives they did? What else, neglected as they found themselves to be, but drunkenness, lechery or immorality of whatever other sort?
>
> He got no further, for Sir Edmund, to everybody's consternation, at that point banged the palm of his right hand down on a "teacher's bell" on the table beside him. Yeats was taken aback, but after a moment's hesitation went on or tried to go on with what he was saying. Again Sir Edmund rudely whammed his bell—and again Yeats tried to continue. But when it happened the third time, Gosse, red in the face and Yeats equally so, the poet was forced to sit down and the lecture came to an end. My own face was crimson and my temples near to bursting but I had not been able to get to my feet and protest.
>
> "Why didn't you?" some of the ladies were saying to Ezra. "Why didn't you say something for your friend? None of you was up to it. You let him browbeat you—without a protest."
>
> What a chance it had been for me—but I wasn't up to it. I must have shown by my face, however, how near I was to an explosion, for a woman back of me, an extraordinary-looking woman almost spoke—but didn't, and so I sank back once more into anonymity (*Autobiography*, pp. 115–16).

7. *Essays and Introductions*, p. 265.

my mind is human nature when undergoing a passion for self-expression."[8]

Personality is, therefore, the expression, without regard to circumstance or accruing advantage, of the energy that is unique to an individual expressing himself in active life or passionate feeling. Caught up with it is a sense of individuality, identity, and an instinct which intuitively draws a person to something, before the intellectual faculties can justify that process. The literature produced by personality has nothing to do with the loud-tongued rhetoric of politician or priest, nor with the abstract unembodied beauty that had consumed Yeats during the 1890s, but is as a fountain "jetting from the entire hopes, memories, and sensations of the body."[9] It is sensuous and rises from the body and soul "as the blade out of the spear-shaft, a song out of the mood, the fountain from its pool."[10] It bids us "touch and taste and hear and see the world," and moves us to the point where our thought rushes out "to the edges of our flesh."[11]

With a literature produced by personality it is the process rather than the product that matters. Artists create not for ulterior motives: to please an audience, make money, tell anecdotes, win the favour of friends, provide evangelical or moral maxims, express the abstract thoughts of the age, or to offer humanitarian solutions to social problems. Instead they create for the intrinsic joy of the process of creation, or to satisfy some inner energy that compels them to express their individual personalities. Art becomes for them the compulsive cry of a man as he passes through nature to eternity. And yet, courage and ingenuity are needed as well as sincerity, courage to reveal one's inner emotions to others, and ingenuity to embody these emotions in some appropriate myth.

Personality, therefore, is the overflow of passionate energy, and style is the energy that remains in a work after the dictates of logic and necessity have been satisfied.[12] When personality is expressed in art, however, when the artist makes visible to the senses of an

8. *J. B. Yeats: Letters to his son W. B. Yeats and others 1869–1922*, ed. Joseph Hone (London 1944), p. 125.
9. *Essays and Introductions*, pp. 292–93.
10. *Ibid.*, p. 295.
11. *Ibid.*, p. 292.
12. See Yeats's essay, "Poetry and Tradition," *Essays and Introductions*, pp. 253ff.

audience something he has felt in the depths of his own soul, some way must be found to temper the outflow of expression, to preserve dignity of artistic movement and thus exclude from the work "the animation of common life."[13] Great schools of drama, Yeats argues, are distinguished by the device they have chosen to check the rapidity of dialogue and expression. The Greeks discovered it by excluding action from the stage and by the constant presence of the Chorus before whom characters had to "keep up appearances" while expressing the most vehement of passions. Shakespeare achieved this check on expression by the "slow, elaborate structure" of his blank verse and by his use of the psychological soliloquy.[14] Most modern dramatists, Yeats contends, by picturing an external reality on the stage, made expression of a deeper reality impossible. John Synge, however, was able to give direct expression to his personality and yet retain dignity of dramatic movement because he found in the material world, and particularly in the life and language of the west of Ireland, the "metaphors and examples"[15] by which he could express his own emotion and thought.

Before Yeats gave Synge his famous directive: "Go to the Aran Islands. Live there as if you were one of the people themselves; express a life that has never found expression;"[16] before this, Synge's work, Yeats contends, was brooding and morbid because he was attempting to express his emotions directly in the poems he was writing. He had not yet found a mask, or an "objective correlative" (Yeats articulates this concept long before Eliot coined the term), a concrete way of making a personal emotion objective and dramatic. In the character of the people on the Aran Islands, however, in "the harsh grey stones" and the "hardship of the life there,"[17] in the seasonal changes and nuances of light and shade, Synge found a concrete correspondence for the emotions that permeated his own soul: he was, Yeats writes, "a drifting silent man full of hidden passion, and loved wild islands, because there, set out in the light of day, he saw what lay hidden in himself."[18] The Aran Islands satisfied "some necessity"[19] in his nature and when he observed the life of the islanders or collected their sayings he was discovering in these stories and sayings two ways by which the subjective elements in his own

13. *Essays and Introductions*, p. 333.

14. *Ibid.*   16. *Ibid.*, p. 299.   18. *Ibid.*, p. 330.

15. *Ibid.*, p. 277.   17. *Ibid.*, p. 331.   19. *Ibid.*, p. 325.

mind could find objective and dramatic expression: first, by his use of the actual physical life and geographical features of the west of Ireland; and second, by the language he placed in the mouths of his characters, the concrete meditative cadences of Kerry and Aran, which lacking "definition" and "clear edges," and being "full of traditional wisdom and extravagant pictures,"[20] was a perfect medium for the "drifting emotion, the dreaminess, the vague yet measureless desire"[21] characteristic of both the author and island people.

Art, Yeats suggests, must use the external world as a symbol "to express subjective moods,"[22] and in Synge he found a perfect example of the type of synchronization possible between an artist's mood and the external experiences he presents in his work. Art, therefore, is not an imitation or extension of nature. Nature, to true artists, has no independent reality but is the embodiment or expression of the inspired intuitions of the mind. Analytic science, the observation or study of the laws of nature, merely corroborates what the mind intuitively knows. As Yeats puts it in his book on Blake in 1893, nature provides the "symbols or correspondence whereby the intellectual nature realizes or grows conscious of itself in detail."[23] Or as he puts it in a poem thirty years later:

> For Nature's pulled her tragic buskin on
> And all the rant's a mirror of my mood. . . .[24]

Artists, indeed all human beings, are drawn, either unconsciously or consciously, to the external scene that corresponds to their inner emotions.

John Synge had broken the mould of modern drama. The Rhymers had altered the form of the lyric; consequently Yeats chooses them as the second example of how personality can be expressed in art. The Rhymers were a group of nervous highly-strung artists held together by their faith in the lyric as a mode of self-expression:

> Lyric poetry also could be made personal, it would reach a new poignance or rather it would recover its old poignance again if we could speak once more simply and naturally as Velong [Villon?] spoke, expressing the emotions that came to us in life, thinking

20. *Ibid.*, p. 334.   21. *Ibid.*, p. 299.   22. *Letters*, p. 607.
23. *The Works of William Blake* (London 1893), I, p. 237.
24. *Collected Poems* (London 1961), p. 275.

nothing for the sake of literature, everything for the sake of life, writing our poems as if they were letters to some dear and intimate friend.[25]

The lives of the Rhymers were full of personal tragedy, and yet they were able to express dissipation and despair in their art, to give to the world "life as it presents itself to a rare and delicate organization," without losing their dignity as human beings living on the edge of a dark abyss. To do this they turned away from those abrasive, strident, marching rhythms of the Victorians, rhythms which, the Rhymers believed, straitjacketed emotion and shattered the delicate impulses of the artist: "When a man is approaching a truth," Yeats suggests in his second lecture, "or a notion for himself he approaches it timidly, shyly . . . full of hesitation, of doubt of the discovery." The Rhymers created, through the delicate interplay of assonance and half-rhyme, new forms for the lyric, creating out of the struggles in their own soul an art that was in no way self-indulgent, but a compulsive cry made impersonal by the form the artist has chosen to communicate his emotion. In this process the artist sees all that he does from without, and allows "his intellect to judge the images of his mind as if they had been created by some other mind."[26] The Rhymers presented to the public a mask of serene accomplishment that gave no betrayal or hint of the emotions tormenting their troubled hearts. Yeats admired their courage and courtesy, their achievement of personal dignity.

In addition, the Rhymers attempted "a culture of action," a culture which allows men to put their lives into their work:

> . . . our form of poetry could only be made by men living some
> kind of active, passionate life. Man knows himself by action only,
> by contemplation, never; and this mysterious thing, personality,
> the mask, is created half consciously, half unconsciously, out of
> the passions, the circumstance of life.[27]

Behind every line of lyrical poetry produced by the Rhymers, Yeats states in the second lecture, one can feel the presence and the pressure of the artist's life "as if he were a character in a play of Shakespeare's."

25. See below, Joseph Ronsley, "Yeats's Lecture Notes for 'Friends of My Youth,' " p. 71.
26. *Autobiographies* (London 1961), p. 345.
27. See below, Ronsley, p. 77.

In this lecture on the Rhymers, Yeats suggests that he survived perhaps because he belonged "to a country still lost in mere rough energies,"[28] but more probably because he renounced the lyric mode before it had destroyed him as well as his contemporaries:

> I can understand that generation, for I was of it. I almost shared its curse without any excess to help the strain of the emotion which was the foundation of our work. The only thing in life that we valued left me at last worn out with a nervous excitement. I renounced a lyrical mood that I might remake myself.[29]

Having renounced the lyrical mode and mood, Yeats sought to remake himself through drama, and the theatre is the third example he explores in these lectures as to how personality can be expressed in art. Yeats, of course, had long been interested in drama. He reveals in his second lecture that before the Rhymers Club had been formed he came to think, as a consequence of his father's reading of dramatic passages in *Coriolanus, Manfred,* and *Prometheus Unbound,* "that the only noble poetry was dramatic poetry, because it put human life, tumultuous, palpitating, behind every thought." He had been fascinated by the poetic drama created by his friends during the 1880s, and during the nineties he had written plays himself. With his renunciation of the "lyrical mood," however, and his consequent founding of the Irish National Theatre, he turned a more critical eye on the plays then being presented on the stage. He discovered that he had to fight a similar battle to the one which the Rhymers had had to fight against the popular literature of their time: the battle between the hollow realistic recipes for success and a more sincere way of presenting emotion on the stage.

The realistic dramatist, Yeats contended, is concerned with the exposition of characters and circumstances in the external world, with copying the surfaces of life, and presenting on the stage the merely clever and mimetic. Because he must be popular to be successful, he follows set formulas for success; he plays to the predictable, panders to topical interests, humanitarian emotion, accepted social and political doctrines, and a morality that no one ever questions. He is more interested in his audience than his subject; he substitutes abstract generalizations for individual life, and fills his plays with "average" men and women sustained by habit, routine, the fear of public opinion: in short with characters filled with the

28. *Ibid.*, p. 67.   29. *Ibid.*, p. 69.

"ceremony of timidity and the fear of life." On the stage, words are spoken in such a way that the natural music of their rhythm is distorted or lost; because the actor must speak as he does in daily life his language is habitual, joyless, sterile. The actor is the puppet of the stage manager; voice and movement are studied and smothered by sensational scenery which, like bad paintings, reveals the story without thought.

Realistic drama was, therefore, in Yeats's mind an extension of what happens in daily life. What he wanted, and what, with the help of his friends, he got, was a new type of drama, "distinguished, indirect, and symbolic,"[30] plays behind which an artist could put his own "passionate personality," and in which artist, actor, and audience could "rejoice in every energy, whether of gesture, or of action, or of speech, coming out of personality, the soul's image."[31] Characters should be created more full of energy and vitality than those we meet in the streets, "men and women living in a more splendid and passionate world than our eyes have seen, and speaking a loftier language than our ears have heard."[32] The theatre, therefore, becomes "abundant, extravagant, poetical and joyful, as the old literature was joyful,"[33] a place where the mind goes to be liberated, to escape the "arbitrary conditions" of material life.[34] Its action is not limited, as in realistic drama: it can concentrate the "whole of a lifetime in an hour." Nor is its beauty external, "not in pasteboard or in anything else," but in the "movement of men's bodies and the sweetness of their voices."[35] Everything must be subordinated to voice and movement. Scenery should serve as background: the natural limitations of the stage, the fact that it is an artificial medium, should be accepted;[36] the stage designer should suggest rather than represent a natural scene. A scene should never be complete in itself, "should never mean anything to the imagination until the actor is in front of it."[37] The audience's attention,

30. *Essays and Introductions*, p. 221.
31. *Explorations*, ed. Mrs. W. B. Yeats (London 1961), p. 170.
32. Unpublished Yeats lecture on the Irish Theatre (1903). The manuscript is in the possession of Senator Michael Yeats.
33. *Ibid.*
34. *Explorations*, p. 96.
35. Unpublished Yeats lecture on the Irish Theatre (1903).
36. *Explorations*, p. 178.
37. *Ibid.*, p. 179.

therefore, is directed toward the actor, and the actor is free to follow his own instincts; he loses all consciousness of individual character and becomes a medium, a clear transparent vessel through which the emotion that is embodied in words or in moments of passion can pass. Words may be accompanied and interpreted with gesture, but gesture never, as it does in realistic drama, becomes "an irrelevant and competing interest;"[38] consequently, in order to give proper emphasis to the words, actors must move "slowly and quietly, and not very much, and there should be something in their movements decorative and rhythmical as if they were paintings on a frieze."[39]

The personal emotion the artist seeks to express on the stage is made dramatic and impersonal through these oblique, nonrealistic stage techniques. The choice of ancient legend as subject and the interrelating of the arts was integral to this design. Personal emotion is objectified through myth, or through an artist's belief in the recurrence of myth, the belief that human beings constantly re-enact the great myths that have been articulated in the past. Through the interrelation of the arts also, through verse, music, song, and dance, the poetic dramatist could attain the distance from life that makes credible strange events, elaborate words, and could excite in one visionary but vulnerable moment the radical mystery and innocence that existed before man desecrated the stage with mimicry, naturalism, and a mechanical sequence of ideas.

EDITORIAL INTRODUCTION

The manuscripts of these lectures, published here for the first time, survive in the hand of a stenographer and are in the possession of Senator Michael Yeats, to whom we are deeply grateful for permission to publish them. At a later date, with the stenographer's transcript before him, Yeats went through the manuscript and made certain minor revisions, chiefly in ink, but a few in pencil. We have printed these revisions in italics, and recorded in the notes all significant phrases the revisions replace. What phrases or words the stenographer has underlined we have printed in Roman type and underlined them.

In general the stenographer's punctuation has been preserved, as in all likelihood it represents the natural pauses in Yeats's voice. At

38. Unpublished Yeats lecture on the Irish Theatre (1903).
39. *Explorations*, pp. 176–77.

various points the stenographer recorded the reactions of the audience, and in order to capture the tone of the lectures I have preserved these reactions. The stenographer, however, does not indicate where the paragraphs should fall, and this need I have supplied. I have also regularized spelling, expanded abbreviations, inserted apostrophes, completed quotation marks, supplied terminal punctuation, and completed the punctuation of parenthetical phrases.

Interestingly enough, the notes which Yeats dictated before delivering the second lecture also survive and are edited in this volume by Professor Joseph Ronsley, who writes:

> His habit when lecturing was not to read but to speak semi-extemporaneously, with casual references to his notes. Thus the notes do not present a record of the lectures he gave, but provide a record of the genesis of it, and, more important, at times a clearer statement than the recorded lecture itself.[40]

Professor Ronsley is correct, I think, in considering this material as "perhaps the earliest version of much of the material in *The Trembling of the Veil*, antedating considerably the 'Memoirs' of 1916–17."[41] Professor Ronsley is also on safe ground when he suggests that Yeats first articulates in these notes important principles later developed in *A Vision*.

We are fortunate to have both drafts, because even though the notes are obviously more deeply considered and more elaborately worked over, what Yeats had to say was animated by the living audience before him. With the record of the lecture as it was given we have too an example of how the poet presents his own personality before his friends.

Some of the lectures and notes contain material that has been incorporated in another form in Yeats's published writings. There are also repetitions of familiar stories with which he illustrated what he had to say, his denigration of *Justice* and of *Mice and Men*, the story of Colonel Martin, quotations from Lady Gregory and Synge, etc. But there is much that is new and valuable in these lectures and notes. A thought or phrase, which seems opaque in one context, or so well known that it has become a cliché in another, suddenly explodes with meaning and light. Yeats too, being that pure artist who articulates with honesty what is presented to his perceptions at a particular time, circumstance, or place, is never content to remouth

40. Ronsley, p. 60.   41. *Ibid.*, p. 61.

unchanged a phrase he has used before. The emotion or thought may not change, but the words and examples he uses to illustrate that thought or emotion do change. It is also deeply moving to consider how thoughts, which appear as but the tip of the iceberg in one context, become suddenly meaningful in others. Compare, for example, the following stanza from "Lapus Lazuli" with some of the ideas Yeats expresses in his lecture on the Rhymers; in the poem, however, he uses the theatre rather than the Rhymers as an example of what he means:

> All perform their tragic play,
> There struts Hamlet, there is Lear,
> That's Ophelia, that Cordelia;
> Yet they, should the last scene be there,
> The great stage curtain about to drop,
> If worthy their prominent part in the play,
> Do not break up their lines to weep.
> They know that Hamlet and Lear are gay;
> Gaiety transfiguring all that dread.
> All men have aimed at, found and lost;
> Black out; Heaven blazing into the head:
> Tragedy wrought to its uttermost.
> Though Hamlet rambles and Lear rages,
> And all the drop-scenes drop at once
> Upon a hundred thousand stages,
> It cannot grow by an inch or an ounce.[42]

Even though the curtain is about to fall on a play, as a curtain inevitably falls on life; even though some of the actors must die on the stage, they do not break up their lines and weep, but accept the roles in which they have been cast, and in that acceptance retain their dignity as actors and human beings.

Consider too the following passage from the second lecture as a gloss on "The Statues" and "Under Ben Bulben" (the "Measurement began our might" section), poems written almost thirty years later:

> Two great movements have taken place in painting—two great facts, two great revolutionary things. One of these has been the attack on academic form in painting. What we call academic form is form based originally on certain measurements. These measurements were discovered at the Renaissance. They were taken from classic statues, and from living men and so was created a standard of form, which has passed on to the present time. It has become a

42. *Collected Poems*, p. 338.

formal and cold thing; it has become academic, and painters have rebelled against it. It was once part of the heroic life and character, but it has become a popular convention, so that it is found copied and painted on every chocolate box.

Consider the way the idea is expressed in the notes, a passage which Yeats later cancelled:

> Sincere life, that is to say passionate life, must I thought take always some new shape, have something strange and startling about it. These academic morals had they not some correspondence with the academic form of the popular painter against which the new painters were beginning to protest. That academic form which now covered our chocolate boxes had also come down from the Renaissance and had its root in classical learning.[43]

This becomes in the revised notes:

> I see today analogies between this traditional morality and the academic form of the popular painter. That too was once an enthusiasm, a discovery. It came from the Greek statues, it was reduced to measurements by the Renaissance, and at last it became a lifeless code and painters had to rebel against it often with a reckless extravagance perhaps.[44]

When we consider these examples we have some idea of the necessity of making available to students of Yeats all the drafts of his writings. Never before in literary history have we had such rich material with which to study the process of literary creation.

43. Ronsley, p. 70.   44. *Ibid.*, p. 72.

THE THEATRE[1]

[Herbert Trench presiding.]

In recent years, I am sorry to say, I am more used to talking to students than to an audience of this kind. If I get very diffuse in dealing with my subject, or if I say savage things about writers I do not approve—things as savage as you say about politicians (laughter)—you must remember the natural ferocity of artists. When a

1. The title has been inserted by Yeats at a date later than the transcription; it replaces an earlier title, "Contemporary Poetry," which Yeats had inserted and cancelled. Yeats has written underneath the present title "as delivered at Old Burlington St." The Chairman for the first lecture is not indicated in the text, but according to Hone it was Herbert Trench (*W. B. Yeats*, p. 251).

little boy I used to sail *boats on the Round Pond*[2] with another *little*
boy, *to whom I tried to be kind* [in] *a condescending way.*[3] I knew
his father had done something disgraceful, but I did not know what
it was until years after, when I found his father was an eminent
Academician whose *statues*[4] were disliked by the artists who came
to my father's studio (laughter). Generally we have a charming
subterfuge: we say we like the man though we dislike his products.
We artists cannot do that. If we dislike a man's art we set to work
and trace its effect on his character; we find all the most horrible
things in his character. That is why we are so fierce. I will try to
moderate my language today (laughter). I hope I may succeed, but
I may get carried away.

Last week when I was thinking how I was to arrange my thoughts
for this afternoon I saw two plays which may help me to express my
meaning—the Sicilians[5] and "Justice."[6] One night I saw the Sicilians,
the next night I saw "Justice," and I went back to Ireland next day.
I could not see two plays which would have brought more clearly
before me all the things I had been thinking for years, two plays
which would have made more clear to my mind the convictions of
the last ten or twenty years. In the Sicilians you saw life leaping like
a fountain. In the other you saw a wonderful thing, a marvellous feat
of skill, but the stage manager was dominant over all, the actor was
at no moment free. Between those two plays there seemed to me to
have passed centuries: that one should see them side by side was an
astonishing thing. It gave one enough thought to last one for years.

The Sicilians—and I must say I think Grasso the greatest actor
in the world—the Sicilians had learned their art, as you know, in
the outline: improvised comedy. Often and often when in their own
country they have performed some play in which nothing is given to
the actors except a scenario—the merest sketch and plot. Often they
had to invent the play as well as the action. All depended upon the
joyous spontaneity of their art: they did the right thing because their
instincts are right. The other is an art of a complex period, where

2. This phrase replaces "a boat off the coast of Ireland."
3. This phrase replaces "against whose example I was repeatedly warned."
4. This word replaces "studies."
5. Yeats is referring to the group of players from Sicily, led by the actor
   and director Giovanni Grassi, who created a sensation in Europe and
   America between 1908 and 1910.
6. *Justice* was first produced in London on 21 February 1910.

people do nothing right unless taught to do it, intonation by intonation, movement by movement. You felt also as you looked at the Sicilians that these players were showing their whole natures. They had confidence in themselves; they poured themselves out; you felt they went home exhausted because they had expressed themselves so completely. In the other you felt the player was using only a little of himself. He was depressed. You watched him with a feeling of depression. The thing that was most applauded by the audience was a dark scene—a prisoner in a cell: you can hardly see him, it is so dark. He is getting restless, walking up and down. In the distance someone is battering at the door of the prison cell. The beating gets louder and louder. You see him then getting restless and excited. He rushes at this door and begins beating on it with his fists. This scene is applauded again and again. The curtain is rung up again and again. It is a wonderful scene, but one wondered that the actor was called for. Anybody could beat on a door in the dark! (laughter). It was Mr. Barker we wanted to see. If the actors had all died we could have found other actors to do it all just as well. One had to look at the programme only through the force of habit.[7] The audience are in a most revolutionary state of mind. I heard people round me discussing, not the artistic question, not the character of the people represented, but the question whether the legal position is sufficiently humane. No, there was one exception: two girls near me were discussing for a long time this problem—whether it was or was not right to eat chocolate during the performance of a really serious play (laughter), I admire Mr. Galsworthy: I haven't admired anyone so much for years. But I detest him. It may be a question of personality: I am blind to it, I am deaf to it. I dislike this sort of thing because I hate the condition which produces it. Mr. Galsworthy is going to be a great and famous man because he is going perfectly to express the whole civilization in his work.

Then when one comes to the plays themselves, is there not there as great a difference, and precisely the same difference. There is only one theme in these Sicilian plays—human nature, simple ex-

7. Yeats has inserted in the top margin at this point: "insert passage beginning at bottom of page 6." Then at the bottom of page 6 he has inserted in the side margin, "This should come on page apropos of Justice," and in the side margin of page 7 is inserted "come on page 4." I have transposed the relevant section to the point where Yeats indicates it should come in the text.

positions of that. One feels that people are too interested in life to care for listening to any kind of argument as to whether law is right or wrong, institutions right or wrong. All the makers of these plays have the old theme—the exposition of human life in human forms, for the sake of human life. When you get to "Justice" you get to a play in which human life is simplified away to almost nothing. You know nothing of the hero's character except that he is a sensitive young man and has a weak will. The barristers are like whole troops of barristers. The characterization is of the most external kind. But you have marvellous pictures of the prison cell, of things. The whole thing is an explanation of circumstances; human life is fading and dwindling away in a vast play of circumstance. The eternal theme is going out of sight when one watches it with wonder. It is a miraculously skilful work of art.[8] I look at it with the wonder I feel when I look at some complex[9] machine. But the heart goes out in understanding of the Sicilians at every moment. For the other you want the man of science. I have no science in me. But when one gets out of sympathy with it one remembers the people for whom it is written. It is made for people who do not think about human life—the character of human love, the character of their friends, their happiness or unhappiness, their life or death. Mr. Galsworthy is writing for an age that is far more interested in commerce, business and all kinds of problems, far more interested in moral codes, revolutionary or otherwise, than in life.

I do not see many plays in England. Some years ago I had a country uncle who wanted me to go with him to all the plays which were then before the public. I began, but when I *had seen seven with* the theme *of*[10] attempted rape I refused to see any more. But I have seen two popular comedies of recent years, "His House in Order"[11] and "Mice and Men,"[12] brought to Dublin by a touring company.

8. The next sentence in the transcript Yeats has cancelled. The sentence reads: "I cannot follow it really, through with my emotions."
9. Before "complex" the stenographer has written and cancelled "complicated."
10. This phrase replaces "come to one in which the theme was an . . . ."
11. *His House in Order*, written by Arthur Pinero, was first produced in London in 1906.
12. Yeats first saw M. L. Ryley's *Mice and Men* in Dublin in 1903 after its run of five hundred nights in London, and whenever he attacked the commercial theatre he used it as his chief example (see *Explorations*, pp. 112–13).

The first was said to be a sweet and *wholesome*[13] play, and to have run for a thousand nights. I did not see much of "Mice and Men"— only an act and a half. The point at which I left was where the hero had been in love with the wife of the colonel of his regiment (I think). He goes away, is two years away. He comes back. She is represented as having been in love with him all the time and waiting for him. She writes to him. In the meantime he falls in love with the stage hoyden. On getting this letter he flings it into a basket of dirty clothes, where it is found by the husband (laughter). There was great applause in the theatre. I am told that in London it had a *like*[14] reception. In modern life the hero would have been expelled from the clubs, but he is applauded on the stage.

Then there is "His House in Order," by Mr. Pinero. There is that wonderful scene in which the brother of the hero of the play discovers that a certain little boy, always supposed to be the son of the hero and his late wife, was really the son of the wife and a certain lover. The lover was to come down and see the little boy. We might say, "It is all very sad. It happened a long time ago, and we'll say nothing about it" (laughter). But the brother sends for the friends of the family and the father of the little boy, and says to him, "Say goodbye to your son. You have five minutes to do it in, and you must then leave the country forever." You have a code of that kind insisted on in popular comedy in play after play.

In the old days personality was everything. When one reads anything about the Sicilian players in their own homes—and there is a charming book about them[15]—one finds how full they are of personal life. In the old days it was the same. You go on doing year after year something you like doing, whereas here you go on doing year after year something you dislike doing. But all our ways of life, everything, above all our system of education, are producing more and more will and less personality. When at school I had a very bad time. I was always in a state of rebellion. I thought a great deal of it. About a year and a half after leaving school I met the schoolmaster. I watched him with extreme excitement and finally was left alone! I was very shy. I said, "I know you would defend the ordinary system of education by saying it strengthened the will. But it only seems to do so, because it weakens the impulses."

13. This word replaces "humoursome" in the transcript.
14. This word replaces "big" in the transcript.
15. I have been unable to discover bibliographical details about this book.

Now I am getting to my own art: it is like a fallen king—the art of poetical drama, once most famous, now of all the most fallen. I see here friends who do not like plays in verse, and who tell me to go on writing in lyrics. But we have a pit in Ireland—just as Shakespeare had a pit in his day—and they do like plays in verse. So I go on writing them. I continually find certain misunderstandings. Whenever a verse-play of mine or anybody else is put on the stage certain complaints are made about it. It does not express certain things they are accustomed to. Complaints are made because it does not possess some quality peculiar to comedy and especially to tragi-comedy.

Congreve defines humour[16] as a singular and inevitable expression of something which is in that man and in no other man. In other words, humour is the most intimate expression of character. Comedy is the expression of character. English comedy is this in great abundance because of the freedom of the English people which enables every man to go his own way, and also, according to Congreve, because of his gross feeding (laughter). But he says that in writing comedy you cannot give character to the women, because they have too much passion. Pure tragedy is pure passion; pure comedy contains no passion. If you look at a play of sheer tragedy, Racine or a Greek play, you will see there is no character at all. The persons are defined by differing motives. It is the great glory of Shakespeare that he enriched tragedy by adding to it comedy. The question whether every poetical play should contain character is far more important than the question whether the verse form is good for plays or not. If you are looking at Falstaff[17] on the stage, or any great achievement of comedy-writing on the stage, you say, "That man is extraordinarily like himself, extraordinarily unlike me or anybody else." If you look at a typical modern play you have the same [page missing from transcript] I found that when English actors played my work they had a habit of comedy. Always at the noble moment, the great moment, when the actor must speak thinking lyrically and musically, these were the very moments when he desired to characterise. And out of this there has arisen on the English stage a perpetual over-emphasis. Listen to any passage on a London stage and you will see there is such a desire to emphasize

16. The stenographer first wrote "defends," but this she has deleted and has substituted "defines."
17. The stenographer has written "Faust," but Yeats has deleted this and substituted "Falstaff."

any important word that all the musical quality is lost. It is pseudo-comedy instead of tragedy.

In stage scenery you get painting which of course would be impossible in any picture-gallery in Europe. You get Shakespeare with a painted background not only meretricious but necessarily meretricious, for good painting takes time to get its effect. The very definition of a bad picture is one which gives everything at the first moment. You will have nothing but flashy landscape-painting. You must investigate the possibility of a background as a good painter investigates his subject. You have got to create an art of stage decoration, which would find opportunities on the stage which it cannot find in any easel painting. There are three things peculiar to the stage which must be recognised. First, there is movement. The actors are going to move about in front of any scene you put up there. Then there is light—and shade. You have real light and you should have real shadow. In the present structure of the stage, with a number of flat things at the top, you cannot get natural light, light from one point. You are limited in every way. You are practically deprived of light and shade. If you are going to reform it, to use light and shade for your effects, realism goes instantly, for you must not have painted light and painted shadow or you will have real light falling in one direction and painted light falling in another. The art of tinsel and the ridiculousness of the whole thing comes from this. You must make the stage a background for your players, but you must get your effects from simple decorative form and decorative colour.

I believe poetical drama, unpopular as it is, is going to return to the stage of Europe, and I base my conviction on nothing but this, that the stage of Europe is so altering its mechanism that it is preparing for it and nothing else. There are men working all over Europe for this object. Their work will come to very little unless there arises throughout Europe a poetical art of the stage able to make use of their work. It is Walter Pater[18] who says a change in the colour of a wallpaper makes way for changes in the mind of men.

18. The stenographer has written "Walter Paton," but Yeats is referring of course to Walter Pater. I have been unable to discover the source of this statement in Pater, and my friend Ian Fletcher writes that he doesn't think Pater ever wrote this: "It sounds more like Ruskin, or even more probably, William Morris," Dr. Fletcher concludes.

These changes are significant. Mr. Ricketts[19] and Mr. Gordon Craig[20] have made attempts in the direction I refer to. Mr. Craig has given us vast rocks and pillars, giving a sensation as if you were wandering through the streets of a marvellously romantic populace. Anything in time or space can be performed in this setting. In time we can get this extraordinary effect—the shadow of a man on the wall without the man appearing on the stage at all.

For passion and rhythm you must get rid of all realism. It is absurd if they talk passion in such a setting that you will say, "People don't talk verse in real life." I believe that in Japan they recognise that you cannot represent a natural scene—a forest, a mountain, a seashore—without landscape painting, but that you can represent a room—which they copy with extraordinary realism. When they do use the seashore they give you just a suggestion—a wave pattern for instance. For the sake of the nobility of the stage we must get rid of all meretricious painting.

In Dublin we have achieved something else. In addition to poetical drama, the heir of the ages, there is another art which builds on magnificent words—the art of extravagant comedy. When you see "Justice" you see something in which words help very little. Forced by realistic method Mr. Galsworthy must not make his people talk better than they do in daily[21] life. But if you get away from real life, or if you keep to real life and go among people who have still a vivid speech, you can get an exuberant and vivid comedy. Between the Sicilian actors and the actors in "Justice" there is the same difference in words. These Sicilians, living in an age when men delight in their own personalities and the personalities of others, used words which other people do not use. The people of whom Mr. Galsworthy writes have hardly any vocabulary. Words for them have died. In this world, where will has succeeded to personality, words, the most

19. Charles Ricketts (1866–1931), illustrator, painter, opponent of impressionism, and pioneer from 1906 onwards of a new stage design praised by Yeats.
20. The stenographer has written "Norman Craig" but the reference is of course to Gordon Craig (1872–1966), pioneer at the beginning of the century of non-naturalistic stage techniques which deeply influenced Yeats (see below, James W. Flannery, "W. B. Yeats, Gordon Craig and the Visual Arts of the Theatre").
21. The stenographer first wrote "real" but this she has deleted and has substituted "daily."

intimate expression of the soul, are getting less and less important. All the words which depend upon soul are gradually perishing away.

I believe Mr. Galsworthy's play is more perfect of its kind than any realistic play which any of us have seen on the English stage. But I feel that my own art is essentially of the theatre. By its nature it expresses itself in a theatrical way. But the spirit of the age is against it. I believe Mr. Galsworthy's art, so quiet, so essentially of the fireside, is essentially untheatrical; yet I believe it will succeed, because it is also essentially of the age. You find human life reduced almost to nothing—in his case without convention, because he is quite honest and quite sincere—and the actor has to explain himself. Ibsen would not simplify human life away to almost nothing; he would not take conventional types. The result is that from the point of view of the ordinary theatre-goer his plays are overwhelmed by their long exposition. He has to explain a play of difficult character by all kinds of little minute effects, and yet in no country of the world has he moved the mass of men. Only tragic or comic art which uses[22] all the resources of extravagant action, which concentrates the whole of a lifetime into an hour, can move large masses of men and will again in the future, I believe, move large masses of men.

Most of you know George Moore. He always struck me as most suitable for the stage—(laughter)—but put him for an hour on the stage with a perfectly realistic drama and how little would he give you! People who are happy in the world have become less and less the patrons of art. The artist becomes restless. He no longer paints beautiful and happy people. In galleries you see the artist has painted people who are unhappy. It is life under the stone—people with dwindled shoulders, people put out of shape by the struggle and stress of life. And the rich and powerful by doing this, by ceasing to be patrons of the arts, are gradually preparing the emotional substance of revolution. We really do not belong to the outcasts, to the unhappy. All the beautiful things of the world have been made by three classes of people. The poor, who have nothing to lose, who are below the fear of life, they have made and maintained all the beautiful things. Then the aristocracy have made beautiful manners, because they are above the fear of life. And the artists, who are made reckless, have made all the rest. Cowardice is sterile. I believe the

22. The stenographer first wrote "arouses" but this she has deleted and has substituted "uses."

modern codes which fill our books are the creation of timidity and the fear of life.

The Chairman (in response to a request from the audience) said: I do not agree with the judgment that modern art is devoid of joy and that ancient art is generally full of joy. I do not understand the distinction Mr. Yeats makes between quasi-scientific art and the art which aims at the expression of surfaces, as it were. The art of Mr. Galsworthy aims specially at the expression of surfaces and ideas. In its way it is extremely valuable and in no way will it militate against what we are following after—the expression of human emotion rather than the institutions of society. Barker, Galsworthy, Shaw and others are political, aiming at improved social ideals. I think the means they adopt are very well calculated for their aim. It is a kind of journalism in excelsis. But I do not think it is on the lines of the great art, and there I am with Mr. Yeats. Where the artist fails today is in the lack of his vitality. If you could get that idealistic art expressed with sufficient vital force you would get your public fast enough. The outcry is that the idealistic art requires a tenfold force of your realistic art. When all is said and done, the ideal which Mr. Yeats is trying to express, the primary and universal passions of men and the concern of man with his destiny—these big and universal questions must remain the only vital ones for the art to express. These plays on surfaces do not count in the long run.

[FRIENDS OF MY YOUTH]

Wednesday, 9 March 1910. Mr. Edmund Gosse presiding.

MR. EDMUND GOSSE: I think it absolutely unnecessary to introduce Mr. Yeats to you, but Miss Birch seems to think that it ought to be done. She has told me to do so, and I invariably do what I am told to do. It must be twenty years ago that there was put into my hand a little book called "The Wanderings of Oisin,"[1] and I said on reading it, "This new writer has nothing to do but to remain true to his own genius, to be placed in the first rank of the poetical authors of his time." That was my little prophecy. I have remained perfectly faithful to it in these twenty years, and now it has become a matter of universal acceptance. But now instead of saying anything more

1. The stenographer has written "The Wandering of Wesen (?)," but "Wesen" has been corrected to "Oisin" in the margin.

myself I am going to give a momentary antiquarian interest to this by reading to you a copy of verses. Fifteen years ago, in 1895, the late poet Lionel Johnson, who has been far more highly regarded since his death than, I am sorry to say, he ever was in his lifetime, sent to me on my birthday the first collected edition of Mr. Yeats's poems, which was then quite new, and he wrote in it these words, which have never been published, which you have never read, which Mr. Yeats has never read; and they contain all that I propose to say by way of introduction.

> Poet and friend: I send
> To you my poet friend
> Whose perfect poems are
>   Star upon star.
>
> Were gold of Ophir mine,
> That gold were far less fine
> Than his I bid you take
>   For friendship's sake.
>
> I give you of his best.
> Welcome this goodly guest
> For his sake and for mine:
>   He's of the Nine.[2]

(applause)

MR. YEATS: I might really have called these three lectures of mine Certain Definitions, for that is what I am really trying to do. I am trying to define one or two quite simple things, which things one finds in any of the arts; and if I am right about these definitions I think if one does not keep them sometimes in mind one goes very far astray.

Last time I was speaking here I used a great deal of analogies from painting, and I shall begin again with an analogy from painting.

2. The poem is included of course in Ian Fletcher's excellent edition of *The Complete Poems of Lionel Johnson* (London 1953), p. 273. I have followed the versions of the poems Yeats used to illustrate his lecture as transcribed by the stenographer; the positioning of the poems in the transcript suggests that the stenographer later recopied the poems from the text Yeats was using. Apart from some slight variations in punctuation, there is, with one exception, no substantial variation between the version in the transcript and the version in the scholarly edition published later. The one substantial variation occurs here; in the last line of the poem Gosse read, where "He's of the Nine" is in the transcript. "And for the Nine" is in the poem as presented in the Fletcher edition.

I began my own life as an art student and I am a painter's son, so it is natural to me to see such analogies. Two great movements have taken place in painting—two great facts, two great revolutionary things. One of these has been the attack on academic form in painting. What we call academic form is form based originally on certain measurements. These measurements were discovered at the Renaissance.[3] *They were taken from classic statues, and from living men and so was created a standard of form,*[4] which has passed on to the present time. It has become a formal and cold thing; it has become academic, and painters have rebelled against it. It was once[5] part of the heroic life and character, but it has become *a popular convention,*[6] so that it is found copied and painted on every chocolate box[7] (laughter). Look into any shop window and you come face to face with this kind of production.

Side by side with this there has been the idea of academic morals in poetry. It also began with the Renaissance—I should imagine *through the influence of*[8] Seneca, but I am not certain. In Milton, in the earnest passionate mind of Milton, it became a noble and wonderful thing. Then it passed on and entered into the mind of Wordsworth. Sometimes it is a noble thing, taking personal fire from him, taking his personal form and life; but more often in Wordsworth it is a very dull thing. It became an impossible thing in the ecclesiastical sonnets. And that condition of formal nobleness has gone on into the poetic art of our own day. In Tennyson, as in Wordsworth, the poet is a moralist. In Tennyson you find it in "Locksley Hall" and "In Memoriam."

Another revolt of our time in painting has been a revolt against anecdote. In the mid-Victorian period especially there was a tendency to paint pictures telling little stories, and they were selected by the Academy not because people liked the painting as a painting

3. *Cf.* "Measurement began our might" in "Under Ben Bulben."
4. Yeats has inserted this phrase at a later date and it replaces the following phrase in the original transcript: "Then got character studies, they were measured and got a sort of current form."
5. After "once" Yeats has struck out the following phrase in the original: "as Mr. Augustus John has said."
6. This phrase Yeats has substituted for the phrase, "an obsession," in the transcript.
7. It is interesting and indeed moving to see how Yeats returns to these ideas almost thirty years later in "The Statues" and "Under Ben Bulben."
8. This phrase replaces "with" in the transcript.

but because they thought there was something pleasing in the anecdote. The same in poetry. Curiously, the man to point it out was the
younger Hallam in what he wrote about the "aesthetic school of
poetry." He used that word before Rossetti was ever heard of, *for*
Tennyson had not then turned moralist. Tennyson *he said* got *his
temper*[9] from Keats and Shelley. The aesthetic school of poetry
means that a man merely puts into his poetry[10] his highly developed
perceptions and merely gives you so much life as it presents itself to
a rare and delicate organization. That is the pure poet, *Hallam
taught*, always unpopular till after his own day. Then there is the
impure poet. Wordsworth was popular in country curacies and
vicarages, and delighted papers like the "Egregious Spectator," as
Robert Louis Stevenson described it (laughter); and was also
popular with editors and journalists and others who dabble a little
in literature. He mixed in poetry popular maxims, popular morality,
all the evangelism of the day.[11] When you come to Tennyson there
is theology, humanitarianism: all kinds of things were mixed into the
pure substance of poetry. Tennyson, who was one of the greatest of
English poets, had his immense popularity not because he was a
great poet but because he used the cant phrases of the day, expressed
his time, summed up his *time*[12]—in other words flattered the mob
by stating its convictions[13] in noble and delicate speech.[14] In poetry
it is the exact equivalent of the anecdotal painting. The anecdotal
painter by accident may be a good painter, but he is popular, not
because he is a good painter but because of the anecdote.

Now both these forms tend to rhetoric, and side by side of course

9. The phrase in the transcript is "Tennyson got tone from . . . ."
10. At this point "the shape of" has been deleted in the transcript.
11. The stenographer has written "new evangelism of the day—taken from
    the people and therefore popular," but Yeats has deleted "new" and the
    phrase which originally concluded the sentence.
12. This word replaces "code" in the transcript.
13. At this point "and enquiries" has been deleted from the transcript, perhaps
    by Yeats.
14. In March 1898 Yeats had declined an invitation to write on Tennyson,
    giving as his reason: "He is in the best sense of the word the most
    English writer of the century and could not be done justice to by a
    writer, who has grown up like myself mainly among the lean kine of a
    Celtic country" (see Robert O'Driscoll, "Letters and Lectures of W. B.
    Yeats," *University Review*, III, no. 8 (Dublin 1965), p. 30). Earlier how-
    ever, in December 1892, Yeats had reviewed Tennyson's *Death of
    Oenone* for the *Bookman*, III, p. 84.

with the introduction of the *scientific*[15] speculations in Tennyson
came the carrying into poetry of the revolutionary fire of Mazzini
which gave us the rhetoric of Swinburne—again one of the greatest
of poets, but not great when he put into his poetry this revolutionary
rhetoric. In our time the rebellion came. But before I bring you to
that, before I talk about it, about my own generation, I would like
to say that I am not for one moment claiming that those of us who
helped the rebellion are in any way equal to those against whom we
rebelled. Rebellion has always been an achievement of criticism, not
of poetry.

Again I am going—*that I may*[16] escape from rhetoric—to be
biographical and tell how the new thought came to me. When I was
17 or thereabouts, on my way to school in Dublin I always break-
fasted in my father's study.[17] We lived in the country and started
very early—too early to inflict a breakfast on a servant. There my
father always read to me poetry. Looking back on it now I see that
the poetry he read to me was poetry chosen for its Pre-Raphaelitism.
He had been a Pre-Raphaelite painter. The criticism was no doubt
partly his own and of the Rossetti movement, partly the re-discovery
of William Blake and his philosophy. He hated the academic morals:
he was furious at it. He read parts of "Coriolanus" and told me the
rest of the plot—the story of Coriolanus and Aufidius. To me that
passage is the most thrilling thing in romance *where he answers that
his* home "is under the canopy." Whenever I see "Coriolanus" performed I wait for that moment and judge the performance by it; and
I have never heard it played with that Byronic melancholy with
which I heard it in my father's study. His idea was, Let us escape
from all that rhetoric, all these noble feelings, all that worthy
thought, and let us always put behind every poem a passionate
personality. He read out to me the wonderful opening passage in
"Prometheus Unbound" by Shelley—Prometheus on the rock. When
he *finished*[18] that he could not read another word. The wonderful
fifth act would leave *him* quite cold. *When*[19] Manfred says, "Oh,

15. This word replaces "wild" in the transcript.
16. The phrase replaces "to" in the transcript.
17. Somebody has written in the margin "studio," indicating that Yeats
    meant to say "studio" not "study."
18. This word replaces "got to" in the transcript.
19. Yeats has altered slightly what the stenographer has written in the type-
    script: "The wonderful fifth act would leave me quite cold. Then
    Manfred . . . ."

sweet and melancholy voices"—my father explained to me that the voices were full of melancholy sweetness because they were the voices of spirits, and they could not put off their spiritual majesty even in anger. So even with the spirit voices there must be always drama behind. And I came to think, and thought for years, that the only noble poetry was dramatic poetry, because it always put human life, tumultuous, palpitating,[20] behind every thought.

I used to go to the museum, and in the library I read the Elizabethan poets, but only cared for those wonderful Elizabethan lyrics when I knew the *imagined* men who sang them, and the incidents in which they arose. I have forgotten part of my father's ferocity against the academic poets. There was an old clergyman who came to see us, very fond *of Wordsworth* and very innocent (laughter). My father painted his portrait, and he used to say he was sure of the awful passions that man was hiding somewhere (laughter). My father used to describe them by describing the back of his head, saying that he had all the predilections of the prizefighter (laughter). Yet he had nothing against him except that the man had a taste for the dull parts of Wordsworth (loud laughter). He believed that every man who went on reading that form of morality must be a hypocrite. I believe he had the same feeling about a painter because he one day took away the character of Raphael.

Then I got a conviction which my father did not share. One day I was at the Young Ireland Society in Dublin and took up an old newspaper, and in that old newspaper I read a ballad by someone of our obscure Irish patriotic poets. A returned emigrant was describing the first sight of the hills of his own country as he came back on shipboard. I found I was moved to tears. I said, "Why is this? It is very bad writing;" and the thought came to me, "It is because it is a man's exact feeling, his own absolute thought, put down as in a letter." I said to myself, "We have thrown away the most *powerful*[21] thing in all literature—personal utterance. This poetry of[22] abstract personality has taken the blood out of us, and I will write poetry as full of my own thought as if it were a letter to a friend, and I will write these poems in simple words, never using a phrase I could not use in prose. I will make them the absolute speech of a man."

20. After "palpitating" Yeats has deleted the phrase "life full of life."
21. This word replaces "perfect" in the transcript.
22. "of" has been substituted for "which is quite open to us with" in the transcript.

Then I went to London, and I found the whole generation was thinking the same thought. The points that unite a generation together are most mysterious things. A young man once came to me from the Hudson, in America—just back from his wanderings. He met here a young Oxford man, and their convictions on *all* subjects were almost entirely the same. One formed them in Oxford, the other on the Hudson. My generation determined to band themselves together in a club, called The Rhymers' Club, and nearly all of them held in theory this idea of making our poetry personal. One or two did not hold it in theory but carried it out in practice, driven to it by their lives or in unconscious imitation of the rest of us.

One thing I had not forseen in Ireland. If you are going to make yourself personal you will have some kind of a troubled life. Goethe says, "No man ever learned to know himself by contemplation. We learn to know ourselves by action only." It meant for us a troubled life. It meant for *me* patriotic societies, and an endless amount of heterogeneous activity, the perpetual desire to measure oneself against other men. It meant *to others* dissipation. Addington Symonds says that dissipation is the only form of activity that remains to the modern man of letters, the sedentary man. They were a strange, doomed generation. Two went mad; one committed suicide; two died of drink. Various misfortunes overtook others amongst them. But I think they were entirely a sincere generation, the generation of the Rhymers' Club. A friend wrote to me after the last lecture, "Please don't praise the poets of the Rhymers' Club. Surely it was a pose!"[23] I do not think it was. There was one among us and a lady invited him to read a romance in her drawing room. He went and started to read the romance. Well, it was not quite the sort of thing to be read out, and gradually as he went on the audience melted away, till there was no one left except the artist, the old lady and one ardent moralist (laughter). Then the artist, feeling a little discouraged, went home, and the old lady said to the ardent moralist, "You must not think the young man is affected. I assure he is not at all affected. It's merely bad he is" (laughter).

We had among us Lionel Johnson, *Arthur* Symons,[24] Ernest Dowson, John Davidson, and others. Ten of us made up the Club, but many more gathered in the "Cheshire Cheese" at that time, and

23. The stenographer first wrote "hoax," but this she has deleted and has substituted "pose."
24. The stenographer wrote "Addington Symons," but Yeats deleted "Addington" and substituted "Arthur."

what had brought them to the same mind as myself, by a different path, was largely French influences. Just as Tennyson and Swinburne in England, so Victor Hugo had filled his work with heterogeneous interests. Verlaine led the revolt. One of his pages we used to quote contained these words: "Take rhetoric and wring its neck!" (laughter). If you are not going to have great causes, rhetoric, sounding ideas, you are driven back on your own life *to personal utterance* to get something of equal power, something to compete[25] against the loud-tongued rhetoricians.

The man among all the Rhymers who became most my friend was Lionel Johnson. The first time I ever met him he wrote out a poem on Absinthe. I remember still the impression he made on me—the delicate, distinguished face, very small, very beautifully made. He read poetry in the most marvellous way. Even poor verses sounded magnificent from his mouth. He asked me to go and see him. He lived in those days with a group of artists and critics, with a man-servant in common. When I went, the man-servant opened the door: it was about 5 o'clock. I said, "Can I see him?" He said, "Well, sir, he's not yet up" (laughter). Then he shifted about on his feet and said, "But, sir, he's always up for dinner at 7"—as if he feared he might have put his master in a bad light (laughter). I found the form of life Johnson had made for himself was not made from the necessity of knowing life if you are to make personal poetry. He had inverted existence. He got up when it was dark and he could write. I said, "Don't you want to see life and *people*?"[26] He said, "I have my life in my books."

It is part of the principles of the whole art of our generation that we have no sympathy with that idea of Tennyson that the life of the poet does not belong to the people. The poet is what he is. If a good poet, because he lives sincerely, he makes an experiment in life, good or bad, but a sincere experiment. He may *not* live his life out of acquiescence, *out of* routine.[27] If you said to Johnson, "Do you know so-and-so?" or if you mentioned any distinguished man or any

25. The phrase read in the transcript before Yeats altered it: "you are driven back on your own life to get something of equal power, to get this personal utterance, something to compete. . . ."
26. "people" replaces "go about" in the transcript.
27. The sentence in the transcript gives the opposite meaning to what Yeats intended. The sentence, before Yeats altered it, reads: "He may live his life out of acquiescence in routine."

noted woman of fashion in his presence, he always said, "I know
him"—or "her"—"intimately" (laughter). Then would follow a
marvellous imaginary conversation which I think he believed perfectly true, in which this person was characterised, in which there
was all kinds of wisdom, *yet never*[28] too wise to have really happened; and years might pass but he would never vary in that conversation. He had created for himself an imaginary world, in which
he lived, and I think he made a kind of happiness out of it. His
poetry seems to me on the whole happy poetry. He founded this
imaginary world in ecstasy. The first poem of his that excited me
very much was called "To Morfydd." He told me he had been on a
walking-tour in *Wales*,[29] and that he heard a woman singing in
Welsh, and two of the lines delighted him, and he wrote this poem:

> A voice on the winds,
> A voice by the waters,
>   Wanders and cries:
> Oh! what are the winds?
> And what are the waters?
>   Mine are your eyes!
>
> Western the winds are,
> And western the waters,
>   Where the light lies:
> Oh! what are the winds?
> And what are the waters?
>   Mine are your eyes!
>
> Cold, cold, grow the winds,
> And wild grow the waters,
>   Where the sun dies:
> Oh! what are the winds?
> And what are the waters?
>   Mine are your eyes!
>
> And down the night winds,
> And down the night waters,
>   The music flies:
> Oh! what are the winds?
> And what are the waters?
> Cold be the winds,

28. These two words replace "only" in the transcript, as the meaning conveyed by the word "only" is the opposite of what Yeats intended.
29. The stenographer wrote "the wilds," but Yeats has deleted this and substituted "Wales."

And wild be the waters,
  So mine be your eyes!   (applause)

   Religion to him made up for the loss of a great deal of life. He
had written a story, I remember. It has never been published, and I
do not know what has happened to it. The hero kills himself because
of his thirst for the other world, in which he imagined everything of
beauty and magnificence: and I think that thirst for the other world
was very deep in his own soul. He was a devout Catholic, as you all
know, but I often wonder whether if Catholicism had been a more
popular religion in the country in which he lived he would not have
cared for it so much—whether it was not for him, to some extent, a
flight from life into a dream world. He wrote this poem, "The
Church of a Dream":

> Sadly the dead leaves rustle in the whistling wind,
> Around the weather-worn, grey church, low down the vale:
> The Saints in golden vesture shake before the gale;
> The glorious windows shake, where still they dwell enshrined;
> Old Saints, by long dead, shrivelled hands, long since designed:
> There still, although the world autumnal be, and pale,
> Still in their golden vesture the old saints prevail;
> Alone with Christ, desolate else, left by mankind.
> Only one ancient Priest offers the Sacrifice,
> Murmuring holy Latin immemorial:
> Swaying with tremulous hands the old censer full of spice,
> In grey, sweet incense clouds; blue, sweet clouds mystical:
> To him, in place of men, for he is old, suffice
> Melancholy remembrances and vesperal.   (applause)

   Gradually, however, the darkness gathered about him. I think I
need not speak to you of the infirmity that in the end brought him
to his death. The poet makes his genius out of the struggle in his
soul. If you could find a perfectly sweet nature you would certainly
find a perfectly silent one so far as poetry and the arts are concerned.
All the great things of life are the result of victory. When you know
a poet has lived a strange, disorderly, melancholy life it does not
follow he has given you in his poetry his morbidity. Johnson wrote
probably the most ecstatic religious poem of his time:

> Ah, see the fair chivalry come, the companions of Christ!
> White Horsemen, who ride on white horses, the Knights of God!
> They, for their Lord and their Lover who sacrificed
> All, save the sweetness of treading where He first trod!

These through the darkness of death, the dominion of night,
Slept, and they woke in white places at morning tide:
They saw with their eyes, and sang for joy at the sight,
They saw with their eyes the Eyes of the Crucified.

Now, whithersoever He goeth, with Him they go:
White Horsemen, who ride on white horses, oh fair to see!
They ride, where the Rivers of Paradise flash and flow,
White Horsemen, with Christ their Captain: for ever He!

Johnson fled from life; he had always fled from it, seeking this interior life and ecstasy, making a joy of it.

Then there was Ernest Dowson. I never knew him as well as I knew Johnson: there was always the bond of Irish blood with Johnson. I met Dowson a great many times. He sat in the club shy and silent; we knew[30] of the wild life he lived after the club meetings were over. He was turned out of a cabmen's shelter because he was considered too disreputable for the cabmen (laughter). His poetry is full of delicate little rhythms. When a man is approaching a truth or a notion for himself he approaches it timidly, shyly. The thoughts that are loud-tongued in us are really the thoughts of other people. I think it was Sir Isaac Newton who said he never believed in his own discovery till he got ten other men to believe in it. You preach truth, full of hesitation, *of doubt* of the discovery. So these very sincere men you often find *speak with* faintness and weakness. When you get to Dowson you have got a long way from that academic morality! He simply puts into his poetry what he lived and what he felt. He does not ask himself, "Are these quite worthy thoughts for poetry?" He would not at all have understood the saying of Wordsworth, that he had not written any love poetry because if he did it would be "so very, very warm" (laughter). He gives you all himself, and only aimed that it should be well-written. There is something of Dowson's life in this:

> Wine and woman and song,
>   Three things garnish our way:
> Yet is day over long.

30. The phrase in the transcript is "but we know"; Yeats deleted the "but" and added "nothing" after "know," but then deleted the "nothing," indicating his uncertainty about whether he did or did not know of Dowson's wild activities after the Rhymers' Club meetings.

> Lest we do our youth wrong,
>   Gather them while we may:
> Wine and woman and song.
>
> Three things render us strong,
>   Vine leaves, kisses and bay:
> Yet is day over long.
>
> Unto us they belong,
>   Us the bitter and gay,
> Wine and woman and song.
>
> We, as we pass along,
>   Are sad that they will not stay;
> Yet is day over long.
>
> Fruits and flowers among,
>   What is better than they:
> Wine and woman and song?
>   Yet is day over long.   (applause)

Arthur Symons has put on record Dowson's life-story.[31] There was a girl in a London restaurant whom he was in love with, and who finally married the waiter. No doubt it was out of that that he made his greatest poem, perhaps the greatest poem of that decade, the famous "Cynara":

> Last night, ah, yesternight, betwixt her lips and mine
> There fell thy shadow, Cynara! thy breath was shed
> Upon my soul between the kisses and the wine;
> And I was desolate and sick of an old passion,
>   Yea, I was desolate and bowed my head:
> I have been faithful to thee, Cynara! in my fashion.
>
> All night upon mine heart I felt her warm heart beat,
> Night-long within mine arms in love and sleep she lay;
> Surely the kisses of her bought red mouth were sweet;
> But I was desolate and sick of an old passion,
>   When I awoke and found the dawn was grey:
> I have been faithful to thee, Cynara! in my fashion.
>
> I have forgot much, Cynara! gone with the wind,
> Flung roses, roses riotously with the throng,
> Dancing, to put thy pale, lost lilies out of mind;

---

31. Yeats is referring to the "Memoir" Symons published in his edition of Dowson's *Poems* (London 1905), and from which Yeats was undoubtedly quoting.

But I was desolate and sick of an old passion,
   Yea, all the time, because the dance was long:
I have been faithful to thee, Cynara! in my fashion.

I cried for madder music and for stronger wine,
But when the feast is finished and the lamps expire,
Then falls thy shadow, Cynara! the night is thine;
And I am desolate and sick of an old passion,
   Yea, hungry for the lips of my desire:
I have been faithful to thee, Cynara! in my fashion.

(applause)

I *had been defending the work of* Aubrey Beardsley on the ground *that it was* inspired by wrath against inequality *and told him so.*[32] He said, "If it were inspired by that, the work would be no different." Life can do no more than be conscious of itself. The simple statement of a piece of experience implies *law and wisdom if it gives the joy* or *sorrow* the artist has *endured;*[33] he has done all he could in giving it to you. And so in these poems of Dowson one does not know when one reads them always whether it is a sinner or a saint who speaks.

      The fire is out, and spent the warmth thereof,
      (This is the end of every song man sings!)
      The golden wine is drunk, the dregs remain,
      Bitter as wormwood, and as salt as pain;
      And health and hope have gone the way of love
      Into the drear oblivion of lost things.
      Ghosts go along with us until the end;
      This was a mistress, this, perhaps, a friend.
      With pale, indifferent eyes, we sit and wait
      For the dropt curtain and the closing gate:
      This is the end of all the songs man sings.

    At the end of the book there is this poem, which might serve as the epitaph of Beardsley and all the doomed generation:[34]

32. Yeats has altered the following sentence in the transcript: "I was defending, to Aubrey Beardsley, the work of poets inspired by wrath against inequality."
33. Yeats has altered the following phrase in the transcript: "implies all the hopes the artist has had."
34. The stenographer has transcribed Dowson's "O Mors!" but since Yeats has a note on the top of the page, "wrong poem," and since this poem is not near the end of the volume, I have substituted the poem which does conclude the volume and which seems to be a truer epitaph of Beardsley and the "doomed generation."

Let us go hence: the night is now at hand;
  The day is overworn, the birds all flown;
  And we have reaped the crops the gods have sown;
Despair and death; deep darkness o'er the land,
Broods like an owl; we cannot understand
    Laughter or tears, for we have only known
    Surpassing vanity: vain things alone
Have driven our perverse and aimless band.

Let us go hence, somewhither strange and cold,
  To Hollow Lands where just men and unjust
  Find end of labour, where's rest for the old,
Freedom to all from love and fear and lust.
Twine our torn hands! O pray the earth unfold
Our life-sick hearts and turn them into dust.

To bring back the arts of personality, the personality of the
lyrical[35] poet or the dramatic personalities of plays—that was our
thought, consciously or unconsciously. But a great deal follows
from it. It involves a change from contemplative thought to active,
from an impersonal[36] contemplative culture to a culture that could
only be attempted in action. That is all involved in one's definition
of the art of personality. Personality is not character. Character is
made up of habits retained, all kinds of things. We have character
under control in the normal moments of life. But everyone has not
the same personality, which means a certain kind of charm and
emotional quality. If we want to speak of an artist who is really good
we say he has personality.[37]

Personality is greater and finer than character. It differs from
character in this, that it [i.e. character][38] is always to some extent
under the control of our will. It is mixed up in style. When a man

35. Yeats has substituted this word for "allegorical" in the transcript.
36. Yeats has substituted this word for "positive" in the transcript.
37. There are vertical strokes in the typescript indicating that the passage
    from "Character is made up of" to the end of the paragraph was at one
    time to be deleted, but since Yeats has written "stet" in the left margin
    I have preserved the passage.
38. Yeats must mean that character, and not personality, is under the control
    of the will. See the lecture on "The Theatre" where Yeats said: "But all
    our ways of life, everything, above all our system of education, are
    producing more and more will and less personality." Later in the same
    lecture Yeats said: "In this world, where will has succeeded to personality,
    words, the most intimate expression of the soul, are getting less and less
    important."

cultivates a style in literature he is shaping his personality. William Morris had a robust, active cheerful character, but in all the first half of his life his poetry is idyllic, sad, utterly unlike his character. His poetry came from a certain *gift*[39] of passion and desire, which is higher than character. I feel often that present culture is shaped, *the culture of* Pater *let us say*,[40] under an influence that makes us passive men. The end of *our* culture is a feminine nature, a passive nature, a nature which seeks to protect itself with codes of all kinds. But the culture of the Renaissance *was* based *not* on self-realization, *on* a knowledge[41] of things, *on things* reflecting themselves *in the soul*, but upon the deliberate creation of a great mask. What else was the *imitator*[42] of Alcibiades? Do you not always feel that mask consciously created when at the death scenes of Plutarch's people? If a man is to use his own character, his own being, he necessarily does so consciously and deliberately. Wordsworth was dull as compared with Shelley and Byron, because these men had the theatrical quality which enabled them to project an image of themselves. The image of one who has lived passionately and sincerely is always more important than his thought.

The movement of the time towards personal poetry died down and we got a movement of impersonal poetry, and there is one man of genius, very little known, a man of the most exquisite talent, of whom I wish to speak to you. His work is quite pure. There is no intermixture of moral maxims, there are no anecdotes, there is no form of moral code. He is interested, not in men but in nature. I speak of Sturge Moore. I do not suppose many of you know his poetry. Any man with a reasonable command of language *can* get an immense popularity by writing a poem about the East End of London or the British flag (laughter). You can be popular by writing on any popular theme, or by telling people to do right in the most obvious way—by appealing to the "Egregious Spectator." But the pure artist has to wait, because he has nothing to offer people but a portion of his own soul. Sturge Moore is somewhat difficult to read out because he does not make his feeling so plain as some others to

39. Yeats has substituted "gift" for "bit" in the transcript.
40. Yeats has altered the phrase, "as Pater says," in the transcript.
41. Yeats has altered the following phrase in the transcript: "But the culture of the Renaissance based nature on self-realization as a mature knowledge. . . ."
42. Yeats has substituted this word for "motive" in the transcript.

the listener. You want to read him for yourselves. Here is his
Semele:

> Semele lay in bliss all night,
> Loved and loving without light,
> Blind but tingling like a string
> Struck by dying poet when
> Glorified he ceases sing
> Listened to by gods and men.
>
> Semele dared a wish,—to see;
> That her eyes might equals be
> With her heart and lips and ears:
> Night on perfect night she pled.
> Sudden lightning drank her tears,
> Life and sweetness: she lay dead.
>
> Semele dying thus yet bare
> Fiery rapid Bacchus fair
> Who, nursed by goddesses and in
> High heaven reared, hath since progressed
> Throughout all Asia with the din
> Of cymbal, drum and voice possessed.   (applause)

You get almost the same thought in his "Dying Swan." As one
reads it one feels as if one almost gets an insight into the animal
nature.

> Oh silver-throated Swan
> Struck, struck! a golden dart
> Clean through thy breast has gone
> Home to thy heart.
> Thrill, thrill! O silver throat,
> O silver trumpet, pour
> Love for defiance back
> On him who smote;
> And brim—brim o'er
> With love; and ruby-dye thy track
> Down thy last living reach
> Of river, sail the golden light—
> Enter the sun's heart—even teach,
> O wondrous-gifted pain, teach thou
> The god to love, let him learn how.   (applause)

I had also meant to speak of Mr. Binyon's poetry.[43] (The Chairman: "You can't"; and laughter.) I see there are advantages and
disadvantages in having a very firm Chairman (laughter). There

43. Yeats and Sturge Moore had met through Laurence Binyon.

was his Tristram and Isoult—a wonderfully live poem, a most exquisite and astonishing thing. But it requires to be read as a whole. It is very delicate in style and entirely vocal: all beautiful speech. In some of his works he is affected by the academic attitude, but in that one poem I think he has done a beautiful thing (applause).

MR. EDMUND GOSSE: I will not insult the subtle thoughts of Mr. Yeats by inviting you to discuss them, nor will I have the impertinence to say anything about them myself. As we disperse I hope the beauty of thought will rest in our minds and that we shall approach modern literature with a keener sensitiveness and a greater intelligence than we have ever shown before.

CONTEMPORARY IRISH THEATRE[1]

Friday, 11 March 1910. Mr. George Bernard Shaw presiding.

MR. YEATS: Some years ago—three or four years ago—I remember watching a play by a great friend of mine with very excited and very variable feelings. I went expecting to be delighted, and in the end I was. It was by my friend John Masefield—a wonderful dialect play.[2] I said at the end *of act one*, "He hates that woman"—one of his characters—and then a terrible thought came to me: "he is really not moved by aesthetic emotions but by humanitarianism," and I got more and more gloomy as the *second*[3] Act went on. I began to see myself going all over London denouncing him, trying to keep silent because he was a dear friend but gradually finding it impossible to keep silent, and this finally leading to a quarrel. And I sat there serious and *miserable*.[4] The third Act began, and a wonderful old man came on talking *beautiful*[5] tragic things, and I was delighted and I said, "He has aesthetic inspiration, not humanitarian." I was quite happy.

1. Yeats has inserted this title at a later date. At an even later date he has scrawled in pencil "(Synge and the Ireland of his Time)," indicating that he was using some of the material in this lecture in his published essay with that title.
2. *The Tragedy of Nan*, first produced in London on 24 May 1908, under the direction of Granville Barker.
3. Yeats has substituted "second" for "third" in the transcript.
4. Yeats has altered the phrase in the transcript: "quite serious and profound."
5. Yeats has altered "beautifully" in the transcript.

That is always the doubt about a writer now. More *and more*[6] writers are ruined by humanitarian feeling than anything else. The artist lives a lonely life; he is understood only by a few fellow artists. The moment he displays humanitarian feeling the world is his friend. The artist has only one subject, human life; he has to keep his thoughts always upon that. He is always expressing that *human life for its own sake.*[7] Of course, he may use argument in his work: he may use every means provided it is an exposition of that one thing. I was delighted yesterday by a character of Mr. Bernard Shaw's—his girl acrobat who read her Bible while tossing her balls in the air. I remember some student of Eastern magic, I think an Oriental, who said, "Imagine in front of you a flame, and if you can keep your thoughts for two minutes fixed entirely on that flame you will obtain Nirvana." But no one can do so. It would be, *the train you lost*[8] yesterday? or Will it be a fine day tomorrow? The mind wanders off in endless irrelevancies. The arts are like that. Keep your thoughts fixed on what is entirely human. That is the great difficulty, and all *passing interests* are a temptation to draw you away.[9] I remember Lionel Johnson saying one day to somebody, "God asks nothing of even the highest soul except attention;" and the problems of sanctity are all there in the arts. I have said that merely, as it were, to state my subject.

If you go down low enough—below the newspapers, politics, science[10]—down to the mass of the people, if you *can* find *them* living in a culture more or less created by themselves, you always come to people, I think, who are interested in life for the sake of life —in other words, who are quite natural. I remember in Ireland, not very long ago, seeing two old men sitting on the hill-side, and I went over to them and began talking to them about the past that they remembered or that their fathers had told them of. They told me a

6. This phrase replaces "artist" in the transcript.
7. Yeats has altered the following phrase in the transcript: "human life for the sake of human life."
8. Yeats has altered the following phrase in the original: "Did you miss a friend yesterday?"
9. The phrase in the transcript, before Yeats altered it, reads: "and all mechanical incidents are a temptation to draw you away from the desirable thing."
10. The phrase reads in the transcript: "below the fact of newspapers, the fact of politics, the fact of science," but some deletions have been made.

story, and I will tell it [to] you because it is a type of all great stories. It had been remembered for *three* generations merely because the human life in it was interesting. I believe that eleven grand jurors in the county of Galway got their death by famine fever—attending fever cases in the cottages. They are forgotten, but *men who served less are remembered for ever because of what they were in themselves.*[11] It told how a certain Colonel Martin, in their grandfathers' day, travelled all over Europe, and had got to know all the languages, the Russ, Pruss, and Span. When he came back his wife had taken up with a rich man near the town of Galway. Colonel Martin wanted to get rid of her but had no evidence. One day in the road he saw a pedlar. He changed clothes with the pedlar, and in a shop in Galway bought the grandest jewellery in the world. He put it in his pack and went to the back door of the rich man's house and showed it to the kitchen maid. She said, "Pity, *my mistress* isn't up. She would like some of that jewellery." He said, "Take it and show her and let her have any she cares for." The maid took it and he followed her, though she did not know it. He wore slippers: he was a very clever man (laughter). She went *through* door *after*[12] door. Upstairs she came to the door of the room where the rich man was, and the wife, and Colonel Martin heard his wife say, "That's the step of Colonel Martin on the stair;" and he rushed in past the kitchen maid; and there were two revolvers on the table at the foot of the bed, and he took them up and pointed one to the rich man and said, "I don't like to kill a man who can't defend himself." But he had his evidence, and he got "two kegs of gold *in* damages" (laughter). He then said to his man Tom—"Put the kegs of gold on the ass-cart and go through the town of Galway and scatter the gold through the streets." And the rich man had a man at every corner to shoot Colonel Martin, but when they saw the gold being scattered they would not shoot a man who was doing all that *for the poor*. During the day Colonel Martin said to Tom, "Tom, did you keep any of the gold for yourself?" and Tom said, "*Indeed*,[13] no," and Colonel Martin said, "You'll want it

11. This phrase replaces the following phrase in the transcript: "but the story will be long remembered because it is interesting in human life."
12. Yeats has altered the phrase in the transcript: "from door to door."
13. The stenographer, obviously following Yeats's imitation of Tom's pronunciation, has written "Indade" in the transcript, but this Yeats has altered.

before you die" (laughter). "And he did," said one of the old men; "My old father saw him getting a living by collecting sea-weed on the shore."[14]

There you have the kind of thing that created the Odyssey—the delight in human nature because it is a[15] strange, passionate thing. It was because of stories of that kind that I heard in my childhood that I believed it would be possible to make in Ireland a movement which would be a movement of real literature, to base on the imaginations of the people an imaginative theatre. The Elizabethan, the old theatre, was imaginative. I felt that the old theatre was so simple because it dealt with only one subject, human nature.

My conviction grew *stronger*[16] when I went about with Lady Gregory visiting the people in the cottages in Galway. There was a story told among them of *a peasant beauty who died many years ago*[17]—they spoke of her as the old men of Troy spoke of Helen. One said, "I tremble all over when I think of her." Another, an old woman in the hills, said, "The sun and the moon never shone upon anything so beautiful." It was a strange thing to find in these rough peasants this passion for physical beauty, like the passion of the Greeks. It was here that Lady Gregory began translating the old Irish heroic tales into the speech of the people, taking what is really their daily speech, full of imagination and style, and not, of course, exactly reproducing it, but using no word that they could not use, and making this an instrument for a reconstruction of the old Irish epics which I believe will take its place with Sir Thomas Malory. It was the creation in modern English of a new style: and nothing can be of the same literary importance as the discovery of a new style, for a new style is a new mood of the soul—a thing more profound and searching than a new thought, for every mood employs many thoughts, and creates them. She has in this book translated for the first time in simple speech stories which are traditional in all the Western cottages. There is no Western Irish-speaking countryman who does not know something of the story of Oisin and Patrick, and

14. Yeats was fond of incorporating the story of Colonel Martin into his lectures (see *Theatre and Nationalism in Twentieth-Century Ireland*, ed. Robert O'Driscoll (Toronto and London 1971), pp. 72–73).
15. Yeats has deleted the word "striking" after "it is a."
16. This word replaces "very intense some years ago" in the transcript.
17. Yeats has altered the following phrase in the transcript: "an old lady who died and was put into a coffin."

it is from that I am going to give you some quotations. Oisin was a great poet of ancient Ireland, and in the story he meets friends and companions of the Fianna, and Finn and the others were all defeated in a battle fought on the edge of the sea. The battle is over and the remnant remaining hunts a hornless deer, and it was turned into a beautiful girl. She invites Oisin to go with her to fairyland. He is there three hundred years, and the longing to see his friends comes to him. She gives him leave to go, but says he will never return to her. He goes back to Ireland and rides the country, and finds everywhere a degenerate people and instead of the tramping of horses and the sounds of arms he hears everywhere the bells of the priests. At last he sees two men stooping under a great stone which they cannot lift. He stoops from his horse to help them, the saddlegirth breaks, and he comes to the ground. He becomes an old man. St Patrick converts him to Christianity—*or to a grumbling half-belief in it.*[18] It is a dialogue between him and St. Patrick that I am going to read to you. He is perpetually regretting his youth.[19]

> It would be a great shame for God not to take the locks of pain off Finn; if God Himself were in bonds, my King would fight for his sake.
> Finn left no one in pain or in danger without freeing him by silver or gold, or by fighting till he got the victory.
> For the strength of your love, Patrick, do not forsake the great men; bring in the Fianna unknown to the King of Heaven.
> It is a good claim I have on your God, to be among his clerks the way I am; without food, without clothing, without music, without giving rewards to poets.

He says:

> *I saw the household of Finn. It was not the household of a soft race; I had a vision of that man yesterday. I saw the household, the High King, he with the brown sweet-voiced son; I never saw a better man.*[20]

18. Yeats has altered the phrase in the transcript: "a sort of grumbling Christian."
19. After "youth" the following phrase has been deleted in pencil in the transcript, "but is converted by the sight of the household of Finn."
20. Yeats is of course quoting from Lady Gregory's *Gods and Fighting Men* (London 1904), pp. 456–60. The passage in italics, which Yeats has inserted at a later date, replaces the following passage in the transcript:

> *I saw the household of Finn; no one saw it as I saw it; I saw Finn with the sword, Mac an Luin. Och! it was sorrowful to see it.*

A King of heavy blows; my law, my advisor, my sense and my wisdom, prince and poet, braver than kings, King of the Fianna; brave in all countries; golden salmon of the sea, clean hawk of the air, rightly taught, avoiding lies; strong in his doings, a right judge, ready in courage, high messenger in bravery and in music.

Then he laments his own fallen state:

It is long the clouds are over me tonight! it is long last night was; although this day is long, yesterday was longer again to me; every day that comes is long to me!

That is not the way I used to be, without fighting, without battles, without learning feats, without young girls, without music, without harps, without bruising bones, without great deeds; without increase of learning, without generosity, without drinking at feasts, without courting. . . . .[21]

(applause)

Our thought was—my own thought for many years was—that we could take this heroic literature, bring it back to the towns, and make them receive it there, partly because it was beautiful in itself, partly because it was of their own country. In Sicily such stories, or marionette shows, are known to everybody. Could we not take these wonderful stories from the West, *from* the Gaelic-speaking peasants, and bring them to the towns? And could we not also take the life of the peasant, so rich in form and fancy, and make that the foundation of another art? Could we not create the dialect drama?

We knew we had one great difficulty. Humanitarianism is not in Ireland the enemy of the arts. There is a deep distaste of the

---

I cannot tell you every harm that is on my head; free us from our trouble forever; I have seen the household of Finn.

It is a week from yesterday I last saw Finn; I never saw a braver man.

21. Those words conclude page 8 of the transcript. The next page is numbered p. 10 but since the first words on p. 10 continue the quotation on the previous page the stenographer obviously misnumbered the pages. The conclusion of the quotation, which has been cancelled by Yeats, reads:

. . . generous women; for all that I have suffered by the want of food, I forgive the King of Heaven in my will.

My story is sorrowful. The sound of your voice is not pleasant to me. I will cry my fill, but not for God, but because Finn and the Fianna are not living.

philanthropist through all the population. The enemy of the arts in Ireland is a re-statement *of Art* for the purpose of politics. In Ireland in 1848 there was a wonderful journalistic movement, which created certain images in the popular mind—the artist, the soldier, the ideal peasant—and the young men growing up in Ireland have fixed ideas of all these things. These phantoms haunt all life. If you write a play you must illustrate all these ideas to suit the patriot. A life which is always surprising is never the same thing twice. Wherever young men gather together all over Ireland they are discussing such questions as the virtues of the Irish people, how much they are slandered by England, and so on. Scotland in the eighteenth century got into an attitude of the same kind, which resulted in a condition of gloom. A poet came to destroy that attitude of mind. Instead of celebrating piety and *like*[22] things he celebrated drink, and lust, and everything men thought wicked, and out of that celebration of iniquity he created a celebration of life itself. It became an explosion of human life—human life, which is the one thing always being thrust aside for some specialism. We artists are all for human life.

It was in Paris in 1897, I think, that I met the man who is to be for Ireland what Burns was for Scotland. I was staying in a students' hotel, and I heard there was a young Irishman *who loved literature* in the hotel even poorer than myself—living higher up (laughter). They said, "He has come from Trinity College, Dublin." I said, "Impossible. *He loves literature.* Such a man never came from Trinity College, Dublin" (laughter). I got to know him—a strange, silent man—John M. Synge. He had wandered all over Europe. He had a fiddle which he brought everywhere with him. This fiddle opened all hearts to him. Before he left Ireland he had learned Irish. He was full of curious, intense ideas of life. He said to me, "There are three things, any two of which have come together in the past, but never all three—asceticism, ecstasy, stoicism. I desire that we may bring together all three." He showed me his writings. They were not very good at that time. They were melancholy. They were haunted with the thought of death and with the whole tragedy of the world. We are told how he was to meet his sweetheart at the corner of a street. Instead of her coming two funerals pass and he shudders. He produced little whimpering *gloomy impressions*[23] sometimes in

22. Yeats has substituted "like" for "connected" in the transcript.
23. Yeats has altered the phrase in the transcript: "whimpering bits of gloom."

prose, sometimes in verse. I urged him to go to Ireland. I said, "To
create a great art you must find a life that has never been expressed."
He went to the Aran Islands, where he learned the pure Gaelic. He
studied these people and their heroic *dreams*.[24]

For a long time his work was simply the creation of a personal[25]
style and above all, of course, the moulding of *a* dramatic style. He
was not the first to use this dialect for dramatic purposes; Lady
Gregory had also used it. But Synge transformed it into a strange
thing of his own, as strange as the poetical style of Edgar Allen Poe,
and in his style as he finally created it you see very clearly something
which is in all style, a double attitude of the mind: the hand, as it
were, and the eye. The vision looks out at all the great things that
have been said to all the traditional images. It is so in all poetic arts,
and in the hands there is shaping joy, *mastery*, exultation,[26] a
complete contradiction between the melancholy submissive dreaming
soul—between what comes in at the visionary eye—and what is in
the hand. When you find in a man's *hand* this fantastic *power*,[27]
this whimsical strength, you feel that man is a strong nature, a strong
man. I read you some exquisite poems by Dowson on Wednesday
(applause). But they do not give you an impression of a strong
nature. He was only a delicate nature. You got the seeing, submissive
eye, and you did not get the joy. One of Synge's poems I am anxious
to read. I read the poems rather than the plays because you have
seen these; but the poems you never will see, probably, for people
go to see plays when they do not read books. This is a poem which I
think is a sympathetic mockery of myself. It is my style, but there is
a grotesque salt in it which is not of my style.

> Seven dog-days we let pass
> Naming Queens in Glenmacnass,
> All the rare and royal names
> Wormy sheepskin yet retains,
> Etain, Helen, Maeve, and Fand,
> Golden Deirdre's tender hand,

24. Yeats has altered "dramas" to "dreams."
25. The stenographer first wrote "heroic," but this she has deleted and has
    substituted "personal."
26. The phrase in the transcript, before Yeats altered it, reads: "It is so in
    all tragic poetic arts, and in the hands, there is shaping joy, mystery,
    exultation. . . ."
27. The phrase in the original, before Yeats altered it, reads: "when you find
    in a man's soul this fantastic shape."

Bert, the big-foot, sung by Villon,
Cassandra, Ronsard found in Lyon,
Queens of Sheba, Meath, and Connaught,
Coifed with crown, or gaudy bonnet,
Queens whose finger once did stir men,
Queens were eaten of fleas and vermin,
Queens men drew like Monna Lisa,
Or slew with drugs in Rome and Pisa,
We named Lucrezia Crivelli,
And Titian's Lady with amber belly,
Queens acquainted in learned sin,
Jane of Jewry's slender shin,
Queens who cut the bogs of Glanna,
Judith of Scripture, and Gloriana,
Queens who wasted the East by proxy,
Or drove the ass-cart, a tinker's doxy,
Yet these are rotten—I ask their pardon—
And we've the sun on rock and garden,
These are rotten, so you're the Queen
Of all are living, or have been.

And always throughout his plays you will find this, the grotesque reality beside the vision. Every one of his plays comes down to that when you analyse it. You have two old blind people, for instance, who are awakened, brought back to sight by a saint, and what they see with their eyes is merely the grotesque reality compared with their vision, and they go back into their blindness, and when the saint wishes to cure them again they refuse with indignation. Then you have "The Shadow of the Glen," where you have a passionate woman with desire, *of* every kind of splendour life has to give, who spends her life between a young milksop, a man who goes mad on the mountains, and a half-drunken dirty tramp! In "The Playboy" you have such a thirsting for something out of the common that you find they glorify a young man who believes he has killed his father. This strange whimsical thing, this touch of salt, this condiment, has inverted everything that is conventional in Ireland. And Synge *could* do this, which I think was his real work, *because he was* incapable[28] of a political idea. He was the only man I ever met who could not form a political idea. I do not know what his ideas were on any political question whatever. One *sentence*[29] of philosophy was the

28. Yeats has altered the following phrase in the transcript: "Synge might do this, which I think was his real work. He is incapable . . ."
29. Yeats has altered "question" in the transcript.

only philosophical sentence I ever heard from him. I have never met a man who was more entirely absorbed in his own thought. He had beautiful manners, selfless manners; he came of a family with a fine tradition. I do not know at all whether he liked my work; I have not the faintest idea whether he liked it or not. I do not think he read any modern books or liked any, and this solitariness made him, by an extraordinary intervention of Providence, just what we required in a gregarious Ireland like ours. I am speaking of Catholic Ireland, in which we had to do our work. Here every man has a social and political end in view. A young man comes to you: he does not want to become an interesting, cultivated man, but what he wants is to be a good Irishman and to hold right opinions.[30] We go about terrorising each other into the right opinions (laughter). And into this country came this brooding man, who came flying from organised life. He lived in Aran as a peasant, and afterwards, when others went there to learn Gaelic, he moved on to the Blasket Islands, an out-of-the-way spot where they had never paid a tax, and where the people were [so] proud of the fact that when a tax-gatherer was sent to them forty years ago they drowned him (laughter). He got a letter from the Returned Letter Office when he arrived, with the Government mark on it, *and because of its official look felt himself in danger for a while* (laughter).[31]

When he joined us in Dublin we had got our players—from our revolutionary clubs, the only place where they could be got! They were all fervid patriots (laughter). I asked Synge to write a play on '98, and he spent a fortnight writing the scenario. Whether it was mischief or whether it was but the overflowing of a simple soul I can't say, but it created a sensation. There are two women in the rebellion of '98 who have taken refuge in a cave, one a Catholic, one a Protestant. The Protestant has taken refuge in the cave because she is afraid of the amorous attentions of the rebels, and the Catholic because she is equally afraid of the soldiers. They start a violent quarrel about their respective religions. They quarrel about Henry the Eighth—(laughter) and other things in a low voice. At last the quarrel gets so fierce that one of them says any fate would be better

30. The stenographer first wrote "ideas," but this she has deleted and has substituted "opinions."
31. Yeats has altered the following passage in the transcript: "and he had to write many letters to the Post Office before he could feel that he was out of danger."

than to remain in such heretical and abominable company, and she walks out (laughter). It was never produced at the theatre, I tried to get him to write *it* for years, but never succeeded. I think later on he came to know more of Irish public opinion.

Then came "The Playboy." It was like the coming of Burns into Scotland. In a country where everybody is a biased Catholic or Protestant we do not approach anything simply: we want, rather, to "think rightly" about things. Into this country came "The Playboy," which was set before an audience who in their heart of hearts thought that the Boucicault peasant was really the peasant of Ireland. Into that came this character *and creation of a* man[32] who was made a hero of because he believes he has killed his father! Synge had an incident in real life to base it on. I went to Aran three years before Synge went there. I went in a fishing boat. There was a heavy mist on the sea, and I must have looked rather mysterious getting out of the boat. A little group of people met us on the shore. They said, "We'll bring you, sir, to the oldest man on the Island." He said to me, speaking very slowly—he was very old—"If any gentleman has done a crime we'll hide him. There was a gentleman that killed his father, and I hid him in my own house nine months till he got away to Ameriky!" (laughter).

I need not tell you much about "The Playboy." On the second night of the performance about forty men turned up with tin trumpets and other means of annoyance. We had to call in the police, which for Irish Nationalists was a thing unheard of. Before the end of the week we were victorious, but we had seventy police in the pit (laughter). One paper said there were 500 police engaged altogether. It was said we had absorbed all the available police, and we could not go on (laughter). I said, "We must go on. We must conquer the crowd." They replied, "Then we will arrest you all." I said, "Go on, then, but we must win the battle, because the whole freedom of intellect is involved." People used to stand up in the middle of an Act and make speeches (laughter). I always said, "Come down next Monday and we will debate the whole question." That meeting on Monday began at 8 and went on in tumult till 12. They shook their fists. We were prepared at any moment to have the platform stormed, the chairman and I having decided that the platform being high we could defend it with chairs (laughter). Well, we

32. Yeats has altered the phrase in the transcript: "character of a man."

have won the battle. "The Playboy" is now a popular play. The last time we revived it it got a great reception from a Saturday evening audience, and I want to say that the people who made the row have not deserted us. They swore, some of them in public, on that platform, that they would never enter the theatre again. But, as they said afterwards, there was no other theatre to go to (laughter). The people who never came back were the people in the stalls. They looked upon it as a rowdy theatre and they never came back.

I thought, at the time of Synge's illness, that it was due to the trouble of "The Playboy." But it was explained to me that it was nothing to do with that, and that for a year he was dying. He told no one except his sweetheart, and in all that time he was writing "Deirdre of the Sorrows," the last play we have performed in Dublin. You will see in that play how he had made up his mind for death. It is all a reverie over death.

He was entirely personal as a writer—as personal as the writers of the Rhymers' Club whom I talked about on Wednesday. In these poems of his he justifies himself by saying a man must express his whole nature in his work, and *there must be*[33] a certain brutality in it. He says that poetry in which there is no touch of brutality or of the grotesque seems the more strong because there is beside it a poetry of the other kind. He tried to create in Ireland this sincere, brutal poetry, in which a man could express his own nature. In those little lyrics which he wrote, most of them in his last year when dying, you get these wild outbreaks. There was one I was reminded of at his funeral. It was a very accurate description of the funeral. A funeral is a public thing in Ireland. *Some of the* disturbers who had done their best by their writings to stir up a riot were present *too*.[34] He foresaw that.

> I asked if I got sick and died, would you
> With my black funeral go walking too,
> If you'd stand close to hear them talk or pray
> While I'm let down in that steep bank of clay.
>
> And, No, you said, for if you saw a crew
> Of living idiots, pressing round that new
> Oak Coffin—they alive, I dead beneath
> That board,—you'd rave and rend them with your teeth.

33. Yeats has altered the following phrase in the transcript: "he must justify."
34. Yeats has altered the following in the transcript: "public thing in Ireland, and his family were there. The disturbers who had done their best by their writings to stir up a riot, with entire success, were not present."

The play of "Deirdre of the Sorrows" is the most beautiful thing he did. He wrote it when he knew he was dying, and it was unfinished, so that it was not so strong as it might have been. In this play he has *shown* his mastery of sentiment, of beauty; and following his practice he would have woven across it a grotesque element. He would have put in the salt, the pepper. He interpreted the story in a way of his own. The story is that Deirdre is loved by the King of Ulster, Conchubor, an old man who keeps her hidden away in a mountainous place till she shall be old enough to be his wife. But she loves Naisi, a young man, and marries him, and they go away. She is enticed back with her husband by King Conchubor. But the husband is killed by Conchubor, and she kills herself on his body. Synge interprets Deirdre's motives in going back to the King, in a way that differs from the usual interpretation. When she shrank from Conchubor it was not merely from him but from old age. When the false promises come she chooses to go back and make her husband Naisi go with her. She is not sure, but she thinks it probably means death; but she feels that that is better than for her love for Naisi gradually to dwindle away with age.

> I've dread going or staying, Lavarcham. It's lonesome this place having happiness like ours till I'm asking each day will this day match yesterday, and will tomorrow take a good place beside the same day in the year that's gone, and wondering all times is it a game worth playing, living on until you're dried and old, and our joy is gone for ever.

The fool, Owen, comes, and Owen says to her:

> It's Naisi, Naisi, is it? Then I tell you, you'll have great sport one day seeing Naisi getting harshness in his two sheep's eyes and he looking on yourself. Would you credit it, my father used to be in the broom and heather kissing Lavarcham, with a little bird chirping out above their heads, and now she'd scare a raven from a carcass on a hill. Queens get old, Deirdre, with their white and long arms going from them, and their backs hooping. I tell you it's a poor thing to see a queens' nose reaching down to scrape her chin.
> (laughter and applause)

These speeches of the fool are the things that sent her back. Then the love of life comes back to her and she says:

> Woods of Cuan, woods of Cuan, dear country of the east! It's seven years we've had a life was joy only, and this day we're going west, this day we're facing death maybe, and death should be a poor untidy thing, though it's a queen that dies.

Then when they go back they are brought to Conchubor's guest-house, and there they find at the back of the guest-house an open grave dug to receive Naisi. And there at the edge of the grave they quarrel. They have come back that their love may be perfect, and at the very edge of the grave it loses its perfectness. They have come back too late. Then there is a cry from her, one of the most poignant things in all literature. Then Naisi is killed, and Conchubor comes to take Deirdre; and Fergus, friendly to her, comes to avenge her. Then there is this dialogue, first between Deirdre and Conchubor and then between Deirdre and Fergus:

DEIRDRE: It's yourself has made a crazy story, and let you go back to your arms, Conchubor, and to councils where your name is great, for in this place you are an old man and a fool only.

CONCHUBOR: If I've folly I've sense left not to lose the thing I've bought with sorrow and the deaths of many. [*He moves towards her.*]

DEIRDRE: Do not raise a hand to touch me.

CONCHUBOR: There are other hands to touch you. My fighters are set round in among the trees.

DEIRDRE: Who'll fight the grave, Conchubor, and it opened on a dark night?

LAVARCHAM: There are steps in the wood. . . . I hear the call of Fergus and his men.

CONCHUBOR: Fergus cannot stop me . . . I am more powerful than he is though I am defeated and old.

FERGUS: I have destroyed Emain, and now I'll guard you all times, Deirdre, though it was I, without knowledge, brought Naisi to his grave.

CONCHUBOR: It's not you'll guard her, for my whole armies are gathering. Rise up, Deirdre, for you are mine surely.

FERGUS: I am come between you.

CONCHUBOR: When I've killed Naisi and his brothers, is there any man that I will spare? . . . and it is you will stand against me, Fergus, when it's seven years you've seen me getting my death with rage in Emain?

FERGUS: It's I, surely, will stand against a thief and traitor.

DEIRDRE: [*stands up and sees the light from Emain*]: Draw a little back with the squabbling of fools when I am broken up with misery. . . . I see the flames of Emain starting upward in the dark night, and because of me there will be weazels and wild cats crying on a lonely wall where there were queens and armies, and red gold, the way there will be a story told of a ruined city and a raving king and a woman will be young forever—I see the trees naked and bare, and the moon shining— Little moon, little moon of Alban, it's lonesome you'll be this night, and tomorrow night, and long nights after, and you pacing the woods beyond Glen Laid, looking every place for Deirdre and Naisi, the two lovers who slept so sweetly with each other!

(applause)

And then soon after that her death comes, and her last words are:

It's a pitiful thing to be talking out when your ears are shut to me. It's a pitiful thing, Conchubor, you have done this night in Emain. Yet a thing will be a joy and triumph to the ends of life and time.

Out of this thing he made, as I have said, a new mode for the world and for literature. There is one other thing I wanted to read. When he was studying this thing of his he made a wonderful translation of one of Villon's poems. He calls it "An Old Woman's Lamentation:"

The man I had a love for—a great rascal would kick me in the gutter—is dead thirty years and over it, and it is I am left behind, grey and aged. When I do be minding the good days I had, minding what I was one time, and what it is I'm come to, and when I do look on my own self, poor and dry, and pinched together, it wouldn't be much would set me raging in the streets.

Where is the round forehead I had, and the fine hair, and the two eyebrows, and the eyes with a big gay look out of them would bring folly from a great scholar? Where is my straight shapely nose, and two ears, and my chin with a valley in it, and my lips were red and open?

Where are the pointed shoulders were on me, and the long arms and nice hands to them? Where is my bosom was as white as any, or my straight rounded sides?

It's the way I am this day—my forehead is gone away into furrows, the hair of my head is grey and whitish, my eyebrows are tumbled from me, and my two eyes have died out within my head,—those eyes that would be laughing to the men,—my nose has a hook in it, my ears are hanging down, and my lips are sharp and skinny.

That's what's left over from the beauty of a right woman—a bag of bones, and legs the like of two shrivelled sausages— (laughter)—going beneath it.

It's of the like of that we old hags do be thinking, of the good times are gone away from us, and we crouching on our hunkers by a little fire of twigs, soon kindled and soon spent, we that were the pick of many.

I feel often in that last poem that strange tragic ecstasy. I said on Monday that the old work was joyous, and some misunderstood me and thought I said it had no tragedy. But in all good work there must be tragic joy. It may be the ecstasy of a great emotion before the sorrow of the world, or the ecstasy of Deirdre's feeling that her death, for all its sorrow, will be a tale to be told to the world. In fact, no tragedy is a legitimate tragedy, in the right sense of the word, unless it is a triumph for the one who dies.

Life is the only theme of the arts, and it is on that we have to keep our thoughts. The old writers thought about life—Chaucer, Sophocles, Homer, Shakespeare—the character of their friends, the destiny of their children, the beautifulness of life, and that is why they have done good literature. We think of other things, the things in the newspapers—the hurry of mechanical things. For a man to do great literature he must be a solitary, unsocial creature, like some beast wandering away into the woods. And even when a saint goes into the wilderness I believe he goes, not flying from life but seeking for life, seeking for life separated from everything else, the life of his own soul. And, after all, is it not eternal life he hopes for? Is not that his reward? Even from the wilderness I think life says to him, as it says in the great poets,—"Come to me, my beloved, for you have given up everything for me."   (applause)

MR. GEORGE BERNARD SHAW: I have very little to say; in fact, nothing. All I have to say on this subject has been said with great exactitude by Mr. Yeats. What he has been saying is really, to every person who understands true poetry, a commonplace—which is the highest compliment I can pay to the lecturer. That is why he often makes a statement of great extravagance and great remoteness. But it would be a very disastrous thing if you in this audience imagined that, because Mr. Yeats is pronouncedly an Irishman, and because this lecture would not be delivered by Mr. Gosse—if you went away with the impression that Synge was a different sort of person from an Englishman, and the problem he endeavoured to solve, to bring art into Existence—for poetry is only an attempt to try and get at the profoundest object of your life—it would be a mistake if you were to suppose it was at all a thing peculiar to our country.

It is a very significant thing that Synge began his career by wandering all over the world, and I think it probable that he did not become acutely conscious of Ireland till he got out of Ireland (laughter). I was asked where this movement began, and I said I thought, to the best of my knowledge, it began in Bedford Park (laughter). That may not be strictly true, but what I meant was that it really exists everywhere. If you want to get an idea of the art that comes from an intense interest in life you have nothing to do but look at a great artist—as Rembrandt. That was what made him a great artist. He was not an artist of wonderful beauty. He was a man extraordinarily interested in life and all its manifestations. You will find that Bouguereau[35] has an extreme interest in beautiful women. He tries to make their flesh look like ivory (laughter). But if you study the paintings of Rembrandt you will find he took as much interest in old women as in young. That is always the sign of a great man (laughter). I have always been interested in old women myself (loud laughter). The difficulty in Ireland is that they do not want an ugly, mean, cowardly, dirty Irishman; they want an ideal Irishman just as Bouguereau wants his pretty women with skin like a visiting-card (laughter).

In Ireland we still have a strong sense of religion and a strong sense of honour, things you don't meet with in England (laughter). When I speak of religion I speak of it in a large sense. Once get a man who wants to develop life and make more of life and you have got hold of an extremely dangerous man, who will sacrifice himself, and if necessary sacrifice you. For the last 150 years England has been thoroughly commercialized. Perhaps it can't be helped. But since the object of commerce is to buy cheap and sell dear, and to try to "get on," and since that is entirely incompatible with religion and incompatible with honour—(laughter)—and since you can't live without something to look for, you have got to get something from which you can get some respect for yourselves, and you get

35. Adolphe William Bouguereau (1825–1905), immensely popular during the mid-nineteenth century, but whose subjects and treatments were severely criticized after the general acceptance of impressionist techniques.

Morality! (laughter) That means, you do what everybody else does. It is different in Ireland. We have not had to supersede religion and honour by morality. I believe in this country it will some day be no longer necessary for you to do that. I believe such remnants of religion and honour as remain among you are with those who have nothing to do with morality—who do not buy and do not sell (laughter). As far as you have got a little corner of society in which you have this—you who are living for your country and don't want to be paid so much per cent for doing it—you have common ground of understanding with Irishmen. We may in Ireland have to go through the same process. Then perhaps you will have religion and honour in England and we in Ireland shall have morality.

If you will do what none of you in this room have ever done, take up your Bible and read it from one end to the other (laughter), you will be surprised to find that morality is not alluded to from the first page to the last, and where it is indirectly referred to it is with every opprobrium and contempt. If you will turn to the works of the tinker, Bunyan, you will find when he wants to express what is most utterly damnable he describes a place called Morality, and introduces two of its leading citizens as Mr. Legality and Mr. Worldly-Wiseman. He didn't see that by the Nineteenth Century you would all be in the town of Morality (laughter). And that is why some of you quarrel with my play (laughter).

I do not believe the wonderful genius referred to by Mr. Yeats is confined to Ireland. If you meet an artist you always find he is a monomaniac. He is born with it and must go through with it. I believe the greatest artists are the men who respond to a demand. They must have talent, if you like, but after all the really great man is always a utilitarian. I say that because I am a utilitarian myself (laughter). I did not begin to write plays because I was inspired to do it; I began to write a play because one was asked for. I always set down myself and Lady Gregory, if she will allow me, as being persons in comparatively advanced life who found we could do something that people wanted, and we did it (laughter and applause). I am so anxious that the peculiar impression Mr. Yeats makes in coming from a strange land and a strange people should not discourage you. Perhaps it fills you with contempt! (laughter) I would like people to understand that there is just as much artistic genius in England as there is in Ireland. Now, do not, for Heaven's sake, let the moral of this evening be for you an interest in Ireland

(Mr. Yeats: hear, hear; and laughter). Ireland can take care of herself. What you have got to do is to seek your own salvation (laughter and applause).*

Yeats's Lecture Notes for "Friends of My Youth"

Joseph Ronsley

INTRODUCTION

Yeats's lecture, entitled "Friends of My Youth," was delivered on 9 March 1910, in London, probably at the home of Sir Arthur Birch, and with Edmund Gosse presiding. The lecture itself was recorded, as spoken, by a stenographer, but Yeats spoke from notes dictated beforehand in Dublin. His habit when lecturing was not to read but to speak semi-extemporaneously, with casual references to his notes. Thus the notes do not present a record of the lecture he gave, but provide a record of the genesis of it, and, more important, at times a clearer statement than the recorded lecture itself. Although in the lecture hall the effect Yeats made was enhanced by his oratorical eloquence and his imposing personal presence, the notes he used so casually had been more deeply considered than the variations that came to him spontaneously while speaking, with the result that they tend to present his subject more lucidly and even, sometimes, more eloquently for the reader. Yeats returned to the lecture as late as 1936, when he reworked some of the material—which he had not used in the interim—into his essay, "Modern Poetry."

"Friends of My Youth" is an important document, because it is one of the more direct statements about the influence on Yeats of his father and the basic harmony of their ideas, about Yeats's friends in the nineties, and how his father's influence had prepared him to share the artistic attitudes of these friends. Furthermore, it contains such hints as the possibility that Lionel Johnson—who read poetry with a clear, "crystal line of monotone in which every consonant had its full weight without taking from the music of the whole"—may have strongly influenced the development of Yeats's own chanting monotone style of reading, and that Yeats's poem, "There," may have taken its rhetorical form from a poem by Columcille, quoted by Johnson while "speaking of Paradise": "There music is not born for music is continual there." It is important also because it is perhaps the earliest version of much of the material in *The Trembling of the Veil*, antedating considerably the "Memoirs" of 1916–17. When I was working on the autobiographies, I had available to me rather extensive passages from these lecture notes, and I quoted from them in order to support certain arguments. It is only now, with the complete notes before me, that I can see clearly the extent to which they are notes, or even a first rough draft, for much of "Four Years" and "The Tragic Generation."

In his preface to *The Trembling of the Veil* Yeats says that his friends "were artists and writers and certain among them men of genius, and the life of a man of genius because of his greater sincerity, is often an experiment that needs analysis and record." Although written more than twelve years later, this sentence reflects an attitude that pervades "Friends of My Youth." In fact, the lecture notes contain what is certainly the original expression of the thought: "A poet is by the very nature of things a man who lives with entire sincerity, or rather the better his poetry the more sincere his life; his life is an experiment in living and those that come after have a right to know it." Sincerity of the artist, and personal candour, are themes that recur throughout the lecture. Many aspects of that tragic generation, examined and explored fully in the later work, are first raised in the earlier one. It was not until 1922, however, with the help of the system evolved in *A Vision*, that certain enigmas, arising out of the "experiment" conducted during the 1890s, and explored in 1910, were finally resolved.

The Trembling of the Veil, of course, portrays many of Yeats's friends, each of whom functions within the cosmic pattern that he had formulated and is part of his complete philosophical and aesthetic design, whereas the 1910 lecture focuses on Lionel Johnson and Ernest Dowson. Johnson and Dowson are central figures in *The Trembling of the Veil* as well, representing, despite the contrast of their natures, the intellectual tone of the Rhymers' Club. In both works the conflicts of opposing impulses, the split and fragmented personalities of his friends, are emphasized. Johnson, Yeats says in the notes, "was I think a great religious poet and he made his poetry out of the struggle with his own soul which the sword of Fate had as it were divided in two. All the great things of Life seem to me to have come from battle, and the battle of poetry is the battle of a man with himself." Seen from the perspective of *A Vision*, the "sword of Fate" is still operative, but the metaphor changes and the "struggle" of Johnson with his soul is explained as the struggle of subjective and objective impulses, characteristic of a certain lunar-classified type of personality. Vague and inconclusive hypotheses in 1910—that, for instance, the generation was "under a curse"—are replaced in 1922 with philosophical conclusions. The struggle of the generation against society is seen as the inevitable consequence of phase 22 of the historical lunar cycle, but Yeats in 1910 is still reluctant to accept the explanation proposed by a friend—although it anticipates his own metaphorical system—, "that in every generation the life of an artist is harder to endure, is welcome less and the world about him less gracious and less beautiful." That tragedy to be exalted later in *The Trembling of the Veil* as an heroic stand against an increasingly objective and mechanical world, is adumbrated in 1910 when Yeats observes that "somewhere at the end of the nineties, the tide changed and our brief movement was over," that a new kind of poetry, exemplified in the impersonal work of Sturge Moore and Laurence Binyon, had replaced that of his own generation of young poets; and when he celebrates the passionate lives of his friends, wondering in spite of all "whether we have been right or wrong." In 1922 he is less unsure, and points to 1897 as the date when he narrowly escaped, plunging into the objective life of Irish nationalist literature and politics as a corrective to the narcissistic romanticism destroying his friends. Moreover, the tragic joy with which he endows his friends in *The Autobiography*, and himself in "Last Poems," can be foreseen in Yeats's reminiscence—using the famous image of Pater who was their mentor—of that group of artists: "We cared for nothing but passion, the point of fire, the end of a spear, the blue heart of the flame." The tragic joy of later years was built upon a much vaster philosophical, and emotional, foundation.

The lecture notes exist in three typescript drafts, each expanding on the previous one. Draft #3 is divided into seven sections according to the general topics of the lecture, each marked by an uppercase letter and beginning a new page. Section G, however, while following F in the pagination, is not marked with a letter, and its precise sequential location is not certain, since it does not follow in substance Section F but covers the whole ground of the preceding sections in capsule form. It may be either another early draft, or a summary with a new dramatic conclusion.

I have silently corrected spelling and punctuation, but indicated by brackets where I have filled in missing words. The typescript occasionally rambles so as to make punctuation and syntax uncertain. Yeats's sometimes eccentric capitalization has been retained because he appears to have used it, at least at times, as a kind of emphasis, giving special value to certain words. Passages which he crossed out have also been retained, and these are clearly indicated.

[DRAFT #1]

I am going to be very personal in what I say, writing of other things by writing about my own mind, and I would defend myself with the words of Montaigne (quote). I first began to think much about poetry when I was going to school in Dublin. My father used to read [to] me when we were at breakfast in his studio—we lived some miles from Dublin and I always used to take my breakfast at his studio on my way to school. He used to read me passages from Shakespeare and Victor Hugo, from Shelley, from Swinburne, never long poems, nothing but passages, selecting always the most passionate moment, the most passionate line. I shall always return in imagination that I may renew my values, my standards, to my first hearing, to the talk of Coriolanus with the servants of the house of Aufidius, the child playing with the distaff of the Fates in "Atalanta in Calydon," Manfred's description of the spirits that have spoken to him with such great scorn as sweet and [melancholy] voices as though they could not even in anger put off their immortal sweetness, my first hearing of "Rose Aylmer." We talked of poetry a great deal; certain poets were to us not only bad poets but very bad men, the epidemic moralists, those who carried on the moral tradition of Wordsworth. ~~In after years I came to understand that the moralizing of the poets has become as unreal as the epidermis form of the painter.~~ . . . I remember an old clergyman who sat to my father for his portrait and whose long and blameless life did not keep my father from suspecting him of every kind of wickedness and for no other reason than because he interpreted the shape of his head by the light of the old clergyman's devotion to Wordsworth. Academic form in painting was no more to be respected, and once my father described to me his convictions as to the wickedness of the private life of Raphael. Nothing was worthy of respect but passion in its moment of splendour and nobility in its hour of pride or of sweetness. Perhaps there is a philosophy that came out of Blake at some time or other during the pre-Raphaelite movement and was past and came to me from a painter that was once of that movement. Rossetti may have taught these things, scorning as a hypocrisy and seeming belief what men imagine or hold to without transforming passion.

~~When I came to London and began to meet the poets of my generation I found that we had all something of the same thought. There are seasons in the mind as in the earth and all over the land the same leaves come out and the same flowers month after month.~~

I brought to London with me for a philosophy of life that thought —a thought that was perhaps natural in a country like Ireland where there is so much tumult and so little law. One day a young Welsh poet[1] whom I got to know through some work done for a publisher came to see me. I proposed that we should gather together all the poets of our generation of our own age that we liked, whether for their poetry or for themselves. He said, "I have come to propose to you exactly the same thing." I said, "We will be all friends then and," quoting Blake, "get rid of the artist's jealousy that is the honey bee." We used to meet, this club of poets—the Rhymers' Club we used to call it—, in the Cheshire Cheese in the Strand, an eating house in the Strand. Ernest Dowson, Arthur Symons, John Davidson, Le Gallienne, Horne—now best known as an art critic—, Victor Plarr, Ernest Rhys, and others less known were of the company. William Watson was promised once but never came, Francis Thompson came once or twice and somebody read his poems to us before anything had been published. There was a beautiful young Hindu with long hair which made me think of Absolom in some pictorial Bible. He wrote fine poetry and took opium and lived in London as it were Bagdad and told stories of his adventures in it in much the same voice with which he told his fairy tales. He would speak of Soho or Bloomsbury with an awe struck voice as when he said "There was a Princess of Delhi that had a purple parrot." Most of them are dead

1. Ernest Rhys, who commissioned him to edit *Fairy and Folk Tales of the Irish Peasantry* in 1888.

now or wrecked in some way: one died of drink, one died of drink and starvation, one committed suicide, two have been mad. Their friends are dead too, dead in early manhood for the most part. Conder and Beardsley were their friends and nearer to their souls than any other. I wonder why that generation was accursed. I ask myself that again and again. I wonder was our philosophy of life to blame. Sometimes I blame it, more often I commend my fellows and rejoice in them and comfort myself with certain old sayings: "the further from Jupiter the further from the lightning," or that Jewish saying, "He who sees Jehovah dies." At other times I say to myself, "the noblest art is always a forlorn hope, a dangerous attempt." I found amongst them much the same philosophy that I had learnt in Dublin. The old generation had filled its thought with many things; above all it had filled its thought with impersonal and academic morals, with scientific speculations, with theology, with multifarious circumstance. It had produced an "In Memoriam," "The Ring and the Book," "Songs before Sunrise." We must quarrel with it; we would have no ideas, no arguments, nothing but what was impersonal [sic] and impassioned; we would put into poetry our absolute impressions. Some of us would have said all, all that we feel whether it is good or bad, we have only to express ourselves, to give our absolute feelings, what we have done, what we have felt. What have we to do with good and evil?

Begin by narrative quite unphilosophical, conversations in my father's studio as before. We suspected the academic moralists, we suspected the academic painter, we could not be sure that anything so passionate did not hide some wickedness. Then decribe coming to London, formation of Rhymers' Club, membership as before, they too sought passion, the technical perfection that gives it expression. Describe their poetry, quote, only at the end mention their fate and discuss the reason of it and elaborate the philosophy; then pass on to describe the new movement, Sturge Moore and Binyon, a poetry once more rich and voluminous, elaborate and impersonal. Hold to it that we were right, our path the more dangerous.

[DRAFT #2]

The generation of poets to whom [sic] I belong—the generation that began to write in the late eighties and early nineties—was for some strange reason under a curse. Those were my companions in

those days, who met together in the "Cheshire Cheese" in the Strand
to read poems and discuss their art. I am almost the only one that
is left; two have gone mad, one has committed suicide, one died of
drink and starvation, one died from the result of a fall when drunk.
We were only a dozen and for the most part the more genius a man
had the worse his destiny, nor did their friends or rivals prosper
better than themselves. Francis Thompson was still, I think, when
we began to write, sleeping under some arch and selling matches.
Nor were the painters we admired any happier. The names perhaps
we spoke oftenest were Beardsley and Conder. Since then I have
often and often wondered over it and tried to find some reason for
it, but all that is uncertain; the only thing I am sure of is that it was
the strongest and richest natures that came soonest to their bad end.
Still one cannot help guessing at the riddle. I came from Ireland in
'87 and wishing to know my generation and having in me an Irish
organizing instinct I looked out a certain Welsh poet, and finding
him with some thought of the same kind we gathered together all
the poets whose work we cared for or thought to be bad merely in
some harmless way. We used to meet every week or every two
weeks—I am not now certain which—in an upstairs room at the
"Cheshire Cheese." At first there was a general desire to call ourselves the Rhymesters' Club that no one might say we took ourselves
seriously, but I being Irish and quite serious carried "Rhymers."
Our meetings were very dull but we learnt a great deal and we quite
killed "the poison of the honey-bee that is the artist's jealousy." We
were dull because any kind of general idea, anything that could be
disputed over, was a kind of bad form. One evening I explained an
elaborate theory of the development of literature that I still hold and
when I had finished no one spoke; there was a troubled silence until
somebody said "What do you think of So-and-so's last book" and
we began to discuss his last book and his first book without philosophy and without ideas. It had come to us from Oxford, that stupid
or distinguished reticence, and I had been talking like a professor
or a journalist. Presently I was conquered and like the others was
content to spend my evening discussing little technical points, reading or listening to little poems which shook the earth from their
wings as a sparrow does when it rises up from the dust. But now
after all these years I will venture general ideas. I put away that
distinguished reticence that I may understand it. I can see that the
great generation of Tennyson and Browning had filled their verse

with reasoning, with science, with geology, with the topics of their day, and that with us a new way had come. We cared for nothing but passion, the point of fire, the end of a spear, the blue heart of the flame. That generation to which I myself only imperfectly belong, for I am a provincial—I belong to a country still lost in mere rough energies—, that generation expressed itself perfectly in two lyric poets especially on whom the curse lay very heavily, Lionel Johnson and Ernest Dowson. Their work, full of intensity and monotony, for nothing interested them but one or two moods of lofty emotion attained to by noble [blank]. Of the two Johnson was my friend. He was very small with a delicacy like that of ivory or porcelain, with more personal dignity than I have met in any man. He banished from his thoughts not merely all ideas that one can argue over, but everything that was merely action, merely life. When I went to see him for the first time the door was opened by a man servant whom he and certain artists possessed in common.[2] I said, "Is Mr. Johnson in," [and] he replied, "yes Sir, but he is not yet up." It was five in the afternoon. And then [he] added, evidently feeling that he was not showing his master in a good light, he added very effusively, "he is always up for dinner at 7." When the sun went down Lionel Johnson began to live, and nothing but early confession, for which he had to wait up all night, ever brought him out of his dim library. Caring nothing for life he found the silent hours when there was no sound of wheels most fitting for conversation and for work. But life, that is to say of the imperfect, the unchanging, had to come to him in some form or other. It came to him in allusions [illusions?]; he believed or pretended to believe that he had met all the great men of his time. You could speak of no one, Gladstone, Cardinal Manning, hardly even of some reigning beauty, that he would not begin to tell you some imaginary conversation which you would believe for years. When he wrote he verified every reference. He would not leave out a comma from a quotation, but these conversations, they were his life. When one knows one has written well, when that which is to live after one is in order, may one not play a little in one's life? Of his own feelings he never spoke, but his puppets moved him to elo- quence. I think that in the depth of his own nature he struggled hourly with gloom and his form of temptation, and that he made out of that struggle his noble verse—the most stoical magnanous

2. Herbert Horne, Selwyn Image, and an architect named MacMurdo.

[*sic*] of our time. If I could but read it to you as he himself would have read it with that clear, that crystal line montone in which every consonant had its full weight without taking from the music of the whole. (Quote "The Companions of Christ"[3]) Certain words were perpetually upon his lips: "life should be a ritual," "everything that had interested men at any age is worthy of study," a phrase which he attributed to Pater in some imaginary conversation, and he would no more admit to the book he had not read than he would admit there was a person he had not spoken to. And certainly his learning was very great. His reveries were full of courtly figure, and sometimes [when] we tried, driven perhaps by some fear of taking sides, of seeming to form an opinion, to celebrate some rough person, his heart was not in it. His Cromwell[4] is an oratorical nothing, his Charles the First is magnificent (quote "Charles the First"[5]). The Masons have, I believe, in their ceremonies a black and white pillar, two opposing powers between which their candidate is placed, and between too much life and too little my generation lost itself. Ernest Dowson, Johnson's very intimate friend, loved a girl in some restaurant in a back street and celebrated her or lamented her his life long, or tried to drown her memory. He has more fame than Johnson I think today. There was something in the mood of his time, I think, that welcomed him. French lyric poetry helped his contemporaries to an understanding of his. Johnson was a traditionalist whose words seemed proudly to display their ancient descent, but Dowson speaks out of broken nerves and tumultuous emotions (quote "Cynara"[6]). It was my desire to possess his work before he had published any volume of it that led to the publication of the books at the Rhymers' Club, and I still think of his work in those books. His form has not disengaged itself in my memory. I read him with the surprise and delight I first felt at that melancholy in which the soul itself seems to speak. After the will and the heart which had cried out so abundantly in Swinburne and Rossetti had fallen silent, may not there be renunciation in excess, in madness itself, in reject-

3. "Te Martyrum Candidatus" which begins, "Ah, see the fair chivalry come, the companions of Christ! / White horsemen, who ride on white horses, the Knights of God!" Lionel Johnson, *Poetical Works* (London 1917), p. 252.
4. In the poem, "Cromwell," *ibid.*, p. 210.
5. "By the Statue of King Charles at Charing Cross," *ibid.*, p. 14.
6. "Non Sum Qualis Eram Bonae Sub Regno Cynarae," Ernest Dowson, *The Poems of Ernest Dowson* (London 1911), p. 27.

ing all from life except its moments of excitement, in renouncing even that sanity which fills so many tills and turns so many wheels to no good purpose? (quote Dowson's poem about the madman[7]). The same mood was through us all that day. If I read you an epitaph by Victor Plowers [Plarr?] or some little poem by Symons you will find a meloncholy not so unlike that of sanctity though the excitement of the flash [flesh] had made it (quote) to renounce perplexities, interests, everything contemporaneous, journalistic, all that moral zeal which never fails to buy popularity. To give up everything but the inmost life of thought and passion, that was what my generation sought, that is why they were accursed. They had gone into the wilderness and they had found there what St. John at the Cross [sic] has called the "obscure night of the soul," but the saint too finds that wilderness—and to find it is the beginning of sanctity— [but] can more easily than the poet pass safely through the gloom. The wilderness is full of wild beasts, the passions become infinite and powerful energy because they are no longer controlled and limited by circumstance and habit but must be faced in the depth of the mind. To enter into the mind, to renounce all but the mind or what excites it to its highest intensity, that is the toil of the saint and the lyric poet. But all those passions which the saint may at last tame the poets need in their wildness. I can understand that generation, for I was of it. I almost shared its curse without any excess to help the strain of the emotion which was the foundation of our work. The only thing in life that we valued left me at last worn out with a nervous excitement. I renounced a lyrical mood that I might remake myself.

[DRAFT #3]

A

When I was a boy I used to breakfast in my father's studio on my way to school. We lived out in the country and so used to have to start early. My father's studio was in Dublin. Most of the convictions that I have now about poetry and the Arts are rooted I think in the thoughts of that time. My father used to read me passages from the great poets; he cared for nothing but the moments of intensity and so I got to know many masterpieces in fragments. He would tell me the story and then he would read me some passage or other where the

---

7. "To One in Bedlam," *ibid.*, p. 10.

story reached a moment of excitement. Those moments are very vivid to me now: Coriolanus arriving at the house of Aufidius; above all his answer to the servant "that he slept under the canopy" is so vivid to me that when I see *Coriolanus* played I unconsciously listen always for that moment and judge the play by it. No one has ever yet spoken it with the Byronic melancholy that clings to it in my imagination. He read me two bits of Swinburne, "Tristram and Iseult," and "Prometheus [Unbound]"—the opening passages of [it where Prometheus is] bound to the rock—, and one day he read me the curse out of "Manfred." The voices of spirits curse Manfred and when they are silent Manfred calls them "sweet and melancholy voices" and my father explained to me that being spirits they could not put off even in anger their melancholy sweetness. I think that thought became a part of my being, an ideal for life and letter, unattainable and heroic. Then we used to discuss Life and Literature —you must not mind my being so personal for by being personal I will escape perhaps from rhetoric and opinion. In literature nothing was of value but the passionate moment or the circumstances that led to it and created it. ~~Indeed all this circumstance was necessary for the lyric let us say that did not arise out of an action or a personality seemed to us to lack more than half its power. There was one thing we both hated and that was academic morality, as it has come down from Milton in whom it was a noble passion through Wordsworth who helped it to grow cold and formal till in our own day it had become the mask and the apology for many hollow men. I do not know if I am reflecting into the past any ideas of the present but I think not. I know that in those days I always suspected of some hidden wickedness any one who seemed more influenced by this tradition than by Life itself. I remember an old clergyman against whom I had nothing but a taste of the dull parts of Wordsworth in the shape of whose head—he was sitting to my father for a portrait —I believed myself to have discovered dreadful propensities. Sincere life, that is to say passionate life, must I thought take always some new shape, have something strange and startling about it. These academic morals had they not some correspondence with the academic form of the popular painter against which the new painters were beginning to protest. That academic form which now covered our chocolate boxes had also come down from the Renaissance and had its root in classical learning. I don't think I saw the parallel in those days for I loved the conventions of romantic painting, but I~~

know that my father did, for I remember an attack on the private character of Raphael who he believed to be no better than the clergyman. A little later on I came to go once a week to a patriotic society[8] which used to meet near to us in a rather shabby street and there one day in a twinkling of an eye I learnt something that seemed to complete all my thoughts. I was reading a patriotic poem in a newspaper that someone had given me, an emigrant returning home, a political exile I think he had been, [who] described his first glimpse of the Irish mountains. My eyes filled with tears and yet I said to myself that it was badly written, without style, without technical accomplishment, without originality of thought or feeling, [but] it had moved me by its personal sincerity. One felt that one was listening to the very thoughts of a man, that nothing had been thought out for the sake of writing, that every thought came to him for life's sake and that the writing was an afterthought. Probably at that moment a vision presented itself to me that I have never since lost. Lyric poetry also could be made personal, it would reach a new poignance or rather it would recover its old poignance again if we could speak once more simply and naturally as Velong [Villon?] spoke, expressing the emotions that came to us in life, thinking nothing for the sake of literature, everything for the sake of life, writing our poems as if they were letters to some dear and intimate friend.

B

We neither of us cared in those days for impersonal lyricism for there must be a life to take fire as it were. My father did not read me the last wonderful act of ["Prometheus Unbound"] and I don't think I should have cared for it if he had, the picture of Prometheus bound to the rock, oh, that vast personality was necessary to the imagination before I could care for the poetry he spoke or listened to. I was content that my father should for the most part tell me the circumstance that led up to the great moment, but without that circumstance the great moment was nothing. In this way I got to care alone for the forms of art which display personality through some vast action, above all for dramatic poetry. I began to delight in the Elizabethan lyrics, but only when I found them in some play where I knew the man or woman that sang them as it were and the mood

8. The Young Ireland Society. See the recorded lecture.

they arose out of. The moment of great poetry was always the justification; one mighty line might be sufficient for a whole play but it was nothing if the play was not behind it. I cannot tell with this distance of time how far these things came to me philosophically, but I know that we more or less conciously opposed to this profoundly, [not] art, but traditional impersonal substance of poetry, all that rich impersonal poetic diction which has grown to be so unmeaning, above all for that formal lofty moral attitude which was a passion in Milton, a noble shadow in Wordsworth, and is today no more than nothing in many hollow souls. I remember spending a whole breakfast speculating as to the supposed immoral propensities of a no doubt innocent old clergyman against whom we knew nothing but a taste for the dull parts of Wordsworth and Tennyson in his Victorian moods. The old clergyman was sitting to my father for his portrait and we discovered evidences in the shape of his head. I see today analogies between this traditional morality and the academic form of the popular painter. That too was once an enthusiasm, a discovery. It came from the Greek statues, it was reduced to measurements by the Renaissance, and at last it became a lifeless code and painters had to rebel against it often with a reckless extravagance perhaps. I think my father must have seen the analogy consciously for I remember he took precisely the same view of Raphael as of that clergyman. Sincere life moulds itself always into some new shape; it is always strange, always a little startling. When in any matter of supreme moment a man paints or speaks thoughts that have become formal and traditional, and if he speaks those thoughts with great confidence, we have I think a right to suspect his sincerity, to believe that his life belies his thought, that he is not really dignified, not really noble, not really calm, that somewhere under all that dignity and calm there is a stealthy beast of prey.

C

Then I went to London and there I discovered a very strange thing: I became one of a group of poets all of whom, and by the most different paths, had come either to the practice or to the theory of the same truth. All wished to make their lyrics personal, drama did not interest them, indeed, but they wished to make their own poems as personal as if they themselves were characters in a drama, or, if they had no theory, they were living a life of so much drama that they could not help themselves. The mysterious bonds that bind a generation together filled me with wonder. I remember once a young writer who had discovered his talent while shoving a truck at an American factory met a young Oxford Poet at my rooms. He was quite new to London but they shared the same convictions; they loved and hated the same poets. Some mysterious invisible influence had found the one in Oxford, the other on the banks of the Hudson. One thing I had not foreseen when I accepted so joyfully the doctrine of personal utterance, was that it involved the man that lived it [in] a tumultuous life, for as G[oethe] says, "a man only learns to know himself by action, by contemplation never." To me it meant a life spent in Irish society, a life of organizations of all kinds, for every thought that has come to me has come first for life or it would have had no personal quality. To the poets who became my friends in London and founded with me the "Rhymers' Club" it meant an act of life of a more tragic sort. There was no poetical cause to claim their service and so they lived in the words of Ernest Dowson "for wine, and women and song" or at any rate for two out of the three. They were a strange doomed generation, or rather the most talented amongst them were. I do not think it was always the life they lived that brought destruction upon them. They were like men under a curse, they and their friends. One committed suicide, and not from any folly of living so far as one could see, two died of drink, two went mad. Nor were the painters with whom they felt themselves most in kin, Conder and Beardsley, more happy. I have often wondered over it, sometimes I account for it in one way, sometimes in another way. I feel no certainty about it, but one thing I do see, that whether as poets they were great or small, they were in their lives very like Wordsworth's "in their misery dead." Whether they fled from life or whether they sought life, they seemed to be equally under the curse. Perhaps the too passionate heart is always granted but one gift, its mastery over beauty, and that this very gift unfits it for common life. Johnson fled from life, Dowson sought it, and the same doom overtook them. I remember the first time I ever saw Johnson, one night at the Rhymers' Club. It was his first visit to it. He read, and read it with extraordinary expressiveness, the poem to Absynthe. He was very small with very small but beautiful delicate features and a great dignity of manner. He asked me to go and see him. He and a group of artists and architects shared a house together and had a man servant in common. When the man servant opened the door I said, "is Mr. Johnson in," and he said, "he was," but when I asked if I could see him he replied (this was 5 in the afternoon), "he is not yet up," and then, feeling that he had put his master in a bad light, he added, "but he is always up for dinner at 7." Whenever I spoke to Johnson of Life, of the importance of living, he would reply, "I have all the life I need in my books," and point to his room where all the walls were covered with books. He got up at sunset and began his work in the small hours of the morning when all the streets were quiet and visitors impossible. No man ever did so completely try to exclude life, and life came to him in a multitude of shadows and myths. If you spoke to him of some eminent man of the day or even of some famous fashionable lady he would say, "I know her intimately," and then he would tell one with entire seriousness some conversation he professed to have had with her or him, full of human nature, full of wisdom, never too epigrammatic to seem true and always full of admirable delicate grammar. When he wrote he was more scrupulous about his facts, about his quotations, than any one among us and one could always rely upon any statement that he made which came to him from his vast learning. It was only when this strange spectral life which had substituted itself for the natural world came upon him that one could not believe everything. The first poem of his that I ever liked greatly was "To Morfydd." He had been on a walking tour of Wales and had heard an old woman sing in Welsh some poem with the two lines "What are the winds and the waters so mine be your eyes."[9] I never knew whether he ever went [on] that walking tour but the poem is to me to-day as beautiful as when I first heard it (quote). I am speaking of him very candidly. Probably he would not [wish] to be spoken of in this way but I would wish to be spoken of with just such candour when I am dead. I have no sympathy with the mid-Victorian thought to which Tennyson gave his support, that a poet's life concerns nobody but himself. A poet is by the very nature of things a man who lives with entire sincerity, or rather the better his poetry the more sincere his life; his life is an experiment in living and those that come after have a right to know it. Above all it is necessary that the lyric poet's life should be known that we should understand that his poetry is no rootless flower but the speech of a man. To achieve anything in any art, to stand alone perhaps for many years, to go a path no other

9. The refrain of "To Morfydd" reads: "Oh! What are the winds? / And what are the waters? / Mine are your eyes!" Johnson, op. cit., p. 6.

man has gone, to accept one's own thought when the thought of
others has the authority of the world behind it, that it should seem
but a little thing to give one's life as well as one's words which are
so much nearer to one's soul, to the criticism of the world.

D

I suppose his most celebrated poem is the King Charles.[10] I don't
suppose it can ever have for anyone a particular kind of personal
meaning it has for me. I heard it first at the Rhymers' Club and I am
never able to read it quite naturally, for a very vivid recollection of
his curious impressive reading always comes to me. He read with
great expression and yet with very slight variation of note. The
thoughts of the poem, too, express the Johnson that I knew. In
that imaginary world in which he lived every one was full of stately
courtesy and he had continually upon his mouth certain phrases
which expressed this ideal, such as, "that Life should be a ritual, an
art," and so on (quote). As the infirmity which ultimately brought
him to his death—an infirmity too well known for me to speak about
—deepened the darkness of his life, I think his religion increased
his intensity. Latterly he had a perpetual device for conversation:
"I am writing," he would say, "three great books, Catholic Ethics,
Catholic Aesthetics, Catholic Politics." Sometimes he would add a
fourth great book, "I am writing," he would say, "a book on the
vices of men of genius." Not one of these books had he ever written
a line of, but their thoughts filled his conversation with matter and
helped him to bring his art to its point of fire in a few little lyrics
(quote "[The] Age of a Dream"[11]). (Possibly it would be better
not to quote "King Charles" but give a few lines of "The Dark
Angel" and then to pass on from "The Age of a Dream" to the following.) But religion with him was not all sorrowful regret for a
past age. He found ecstasy, health, wisdom, all that he had lost when
he contemplated the things beyond the grave. I remember an unpublished story of his in which the principal character kills himself
that he may reach quickly the world of ecstasy, and once he quoted
to me, speaking of Paradise, a poem of Columcille's which says,
"There music is not born for music is continual there." One has, one

10. Johnson, *op. cit.*, p. 14.
11. Evidently he has in mind "The Church of a Dream." See the recorded
    lecture.

finds, this ecstasy in certain poems, perhaps most of all in "the white chivalry"[12] (quote "White Chivalry" and "daughters of Jerusalem"[13]). He was I think a great religious poet and he made his poetry out of the struggle with his own soul which the sword of Fate had as it were divided in two. All the great things of Life seem to me to have come from battle, and the battle of poetry is the battle of a man with himself. I do not think any nature comes to the self-knowledge that is genius without the original evil which gives the antagonist in that battle whose spoil and monument is knowledge. He emits to evil in gathering darkness a genius which was in its heart of hearts essentially joyous. The genius of Dowson, on the other hand, is always sorrowful. I met him also for the first time at the Rhymers' Club. He read out a love poem. . . .

E

I never knew Dowson as intimately as I knew Johnson; he was more Johnson's and Symons's friend than mine, but I constantly heard of him from both. When I saw him at the Rhymers' he was generally rather shy and silent I thought, but they knew his other life, and how at last he was turned out of a cabman's shelter as too disorderly a character for the society of cabmen. He sought for life as Johnson fled from it. A disappointment in love of which Arthur Symons had told the story [had] given the last shock to a temperament full of morbidity. I find that his poetry grows upon me every year. It is I think profound and simple, there is none of the unearthly joy that Johnson seems to have found in moments of his flight from life. No man of our time has written poetry so sorrowful; it is full of a despair that is half wisdom, half dissipation. His most famous poem celebrates the girl in the Italian Restaurant who seems to have broken his heart (quote). Even in his despair he is never a solitary man—he wishes to sing of a lost community. It is as if it were not Dowson but a generation under a curse that spoke (quote Villanelle[14]). At all times he knows he's doomed; he makes no struggle against it; he has not found Life at the best worth very much—certainly not worth the boredom of taking care of it—and one often does not know whether this sorrow of his comes from satiety or

12. Johnson, *op. cit.*, p. 252.
13. "Christmas," which begins, "Sing *Bethlehem!* Sing *Bethlehem!* / You daughters of Jerusalem!" Johnson, *op. cit.*, p. 189.
14. "Villanelle of the Poet's Road," Dowson, *op. cit.*, p. 129.

from the disillusionment of wisdom. It is often as if he rejoiced in his gloom, as though he were glad to be rising up from the table of Life (quote "Dregs"). I will read one more poem of his, "[A] Last Word" as he calls it, a poem in which he avowedly speaks not for himself alone but for Beardsley, Conder, for Johnson, for all his friends (quote). Both Dowson and Johnson, like Francis Thompson, like others of their generation, seem to me to have paid for personality with all else in the world. I had a dissipation as overpowering, as lasting as theirs, one that seizes every literary man of my country sooner or later. That dissipation is Ireland that draws me away from my work, distracts it, makes the amount of it but little, as they were drawn away from their work by wine or women. I often and often go over it in my mind and I wonder whether we have been right or wrong, and I wonder if my dissipation is better or worse than theirs, but of one thing I am certain: our form of poetry could only be made by men living some kind of active, passionate life. Man knows himself by action only, by contemplation, never; and this mysterious thing, personality, the mask, is created half consciously, half unconsciously, out of the passions, the circumstance of life. It is not the same as character, for all that we mean by character would only mar the expression of men like Dowson and Johnson. It is a certain attitude towards life rather than character, perhaps it is almost a habitual mood. Character is perhaps most strong when most passionate because it is then most normal. Mr. Lowell, the American novelist,[15] in justifying the novel of character against the romantic novel, says that all characters are the same as houses on fire. But personality seems to me to only exist as we are using the word in a house that is perpetually on fire. We recognize it at once in men of passionate, temperate character; we do not find it in studios and contemplative men. I read the other day in some French newspaper that it was the business of a poet—the paper was not speaking mockingly—to invent a new pose, and perhaps that word "pose," if we take it in its original sense, describes best this mysterious thing which is as I think the result of some passionate victory over circumstance. When we read Dowson, when we read Byron, though our characters are utterly different, we take for a moment unconsciously their pose, as we might take the pose of a statue with our body. Is it not a mask laboured at all life long? But

15. Perhaps Robert Traill Spence Lowell (1816–91).

the soul which is bodiless and impalpable will find eyes to look through and lips to speak with. Did not the men of old days find it when they tried to be like Alexander the Great, Christ, or Alcibiades. These men had made their gestures from antiquity and they would copy it and be good actors. Is it not that this mask is half unconsciously created, that there is so often something theatrical in the men of the vastest energy, that Napoleon will invade the east not for State craft only, but that he may copy the career of Alexander? In poets who conspicuously lack it, in Wordsworth for instance as contrasted with Shelley, there is something dull that we all feel. One thing alone would make it conscious, an element that has belonged to all great kings as well as to poets. The moment a man begins to speak to a large multitude of people, and not to two or three people who will know him intimately, and to speak not of facts and figures, but of Life, and the wisdom of Life and the sorrow of Life, he becomes an actor, simplifying and enlarging that he may reach their eyes and ears. He may do it well or ill, but his sincerity consists of making this enlarged and simplified being a fitting form for the utterance of his soul and not for his ambition that is vanity. "I lay upon the ground and eat dung," said Ezekiel to Blake in vision, "that I might prove to men there was an Infinite in all things."

F

Perhaps even when that enlarged and simplified being is built up in all intensity, we come at last always to a form of wisdom and follow it, at last it may be beyond literature, beyond Life itself till it is with us as when of old the stone was rolled back and the linen cloths folded up.

Dowson, Johnson, all that group of poets, were religious men. That too is natural, for if you found your art upon your personal desires those desires grow strong, and being unsatisfied, soon fix their thought beyond the world.

In the generation that came after us, and somewhere at the end of the nineties, the tide changed and our brief movement was over. The young poets, or at any rate the poets younger than myself and my friends, are impersonal, and if their lives are active, or dissipated or vehement they do not sing them. They seem to be tranquil people and the best of them write a beautiful, but entirely impersonal poetry. The one that moves me most is I think Mr. Sturge Moore, and his poetry is so impersonal that it is like some beautiful water plant sowing and re-sowing itself in the stillness of his mind. He does not utter one man's thoughts, whether they have come to him in active life in Ireland or in some French cafe, but rather the whole poetic tradition—centaurs, fauns, nymphs, amazons—, nor do these images and myths become solid enough and complex enough to have strong dramatic personality. One feels that his mind is moved by thoughts and instincts and metaphors that think in him and not he in them. He delights me by a strange instinctive innocence. Individual life with its knowledge of good and evil, its speculation, its weariness, has neither blighted the perpetual happiness of these half-spiritual, half-animal lives (read "Summer Lightning"). It is typical of him that the only tragedies his art seems to know of are the loss of natural and sensuous pleasure through death or through some strange ecstasy that is at once the consummation and end of desire; it is not the attainment of any personal life, but the passing away of a fire or a cloud. The swan sings at its death and singing passes into the sun, that the sun too may learn to love (quote "Dying Swan").

It is hard to find good examples to read out, for his work, if not vocal as our work was vocal, it involved labyrinthine [sic]. It has to be read over slowly to oneself. It is as though some elaborate golden age spoke to us through a multitude of confused voices, whereas with us there was always the simplicity of one man speaking. He is the reverse of everything I have sought and there are moments when he fills me with doubt; would it not have been better, I think, to have welcomed every thought, to have given daily meals to all the children that passed by instead of looking always for one's own. Perhaps, though, there is beauty found upon both journeys, perhaps the greatest beauty is found in this effacement of oneself, or is it that there must always be this antithesis and that the two paths will in the end prove themselves to be the way of nature upon the one hand, the way of the soul upon the other. But [of] the other poets of Mr. Sturge Moore's generation, I think I have found most pleasure in Mr. Binyon. I remember carrying his "Tristram and Isoult" about with me for some weeks, reading it to every one I could get to listen, but I feel in his work some coldness which I do not feel in Mr. Sturge Moore's, some chilling of the fires from that academic tradition which is the enemy of his impersonal art, being its shadow, as it is of my personal art, being its opposite. There are other poets younger still (give names), but for one reason or other they have not entered into my life so I will not speak of them. Tomorrow I may take fire from one or other and be full of speech, but today I can only speak of these few men who are part of my experience of the world.

[G]

Of that group of poets there are few living or writing now. They were a strangely accursed generation: two went mad, two died of drink, one committed suicide. Nor were their friends much more fortunate than themselves. Towards the end we spoke no names more constantly amongst ourselves than those of Conder and of Beardsley. And since then I have continually asked myself, why that generation followed more than any other I know of in the way of the mighty poets in their miserable end. Were [sic] it their temperaments that made that work possible that brought it among them? They were a poor generation and the strain of poverty accounted for something, but not for all, nor is it as a friend of mine is fond of saying, that in every generation the life of an artist is harder to endure, is welcome less and the world about him less gracious and less beautiful. I sometimes think that one or other of these things explains it, but in other moods I find the cause in work itself. They were lyric poets, that only. Life existed for them in a few intense moments that when they were gone left darkness behind them. They had no causes, no general interests to fill up the common day, and then, look back through all the lyric poets of the world, how few of them have been happy or fortunate, Keats, Shelley, Villon, Burns, the peasant poets of my own country, all who have put into lyric poetry an exceedingly personal expression. Is not that perhaps the explanation of all? A Villon, a Verlaine, a Dowson expresses more than all others his own passion; it is from that he gets his poignant charm. He separates himself from all else, for like the Saint he has his wilderness, he knows that there is nothing that sings but passion and that the greatest passions are one's own. He would give nothing but pure flame. Dante, Homer, Shakespeare come only every now and then after hundreds of lines of circumstance, of mild or broken radiance, to the supreme moment of passion, but the lyric poet who sings his own passions must be always in the blue heart of the flame. He cannot amuse himself upon the way with a L[auncelot] Gobbo or a Northern farmer. He will not write many poems no matter how passionate his life—and if his life were not passionate and troubled

how should he write at all? Melancholy desire, strange hatreds, these
will gather about him always and he will often hear about him
before the darkness has fallen terrifying voices. The saint whose
renunciation is not greater though it is different in his obscure night
of the soul, in that time of bitterness and gloom of which all saintly
[*blank*] have spoken, has a much simpler labour. He has but to
conquer and renounce his passions, he has but to kill or drive away
the wild beasts; the Lyric Poet needs them to draw his chariot and
he needs them in their wildness.

To-day there is another school of poetry. The new poets whom I
admire are not personal. Mr. Binyon, Mr. Sturge Moore—and I
think Mr. Sturge Moore a really great poet—do not project themselves. I feel when I read Mr. Sturge Moore that he is so full of
careless abundance because he welcomes every beautiful thought.
It is enough if he believes in it for a moment, that it is part of the
procession that passes his door. He has not to say as Ernest Dowson
said, "did I think that in my life, before I came to speak of it in
verse." He makes no selection amongst the beautiful things; and so
there is through him a certain kindness and evenness, he is well
content with his world, he has no personal tragedy, no personal
delight. And so once more the great impersonal things, many landscapes, many ancient imaginings, Centaurs' forms, hurry about him.
He creates myths and writes plays, and how well he sings of traditional virtues. He is so frank and simple in his pleasure that all is
new and joyous where another found but platitude (quote his poem
called "Kindness"). Mr. Binyon I cannot so easily quote to you for
he is finest in his long "Tristram and Isoult" to whose celebration he
gives himself up as my friends gave themselves to that hidden
meditation wherein they lost or saved their souls and certainly lost
the world. When I first came upon this poem it excited me for days,
I could not read it without tears and now it is still beautiful to me
though it does not mean to me all it once did (quote). Ah, you will
say, after those decadents of the nineties, we have once more wholesome poetry. But if you say that you are forgetting all that the saints
remembered. Tragedy is perhaps the greatest of all things, a gift that
is given to elect and chosen souls and none others. Why should we
honour those that die upon the field of battle, a man may show as
reckless a courage in entering into the abyss of himself.

W. B. Yeats,
Gordon Craig
and the Visual Arts
of the Theatre

James W. Flannery

Yeats's difficulties with actors throughout his long theatrical career are notorious, but he faced even more difficult problems in attempting to develop an appropriate visual style for his own and other plays staged during the early years of the Irish dramatic movement. The spectacular staging methods of the nineteenth-century actor-managers were abhorrent to Yeats, chiefly because they subordinated dramatic values which appeal to the ear to coarse theatrical values appealing solely to the eye.[1] It was therefore necessary for him not only to create the aesthetic of a new art of the theatre but to find the practical means of bringing his ideals to life upon the stage.

Two conceptions—those of ritual movement and patterned scenic decor—dominated Yeats's theory and practice throughout the 1890s.[2] The negative reaction of audiences and critics to *The Countess Cathleen*, when it was produced by the Irish Literary Theatre in May 1899, taught Yeats that in order to survive in the contemporary theatre it was necessary for him to imitate more directly the common actions of life. This led him to a dramaturgical form that laid increasing emphasis upon more realistically portrayed and individualized characters.[3]

1. W. B. Yeats, "The Theatre" (1900), *Essays and Introductions* (New York 1961), pp. 168–69.
2. See James W. Flannery, "Yeats and the Visual Arts of the Theatre," ch. IX, *W. B. Yeats and the Idea of a Theatre* (Ph.D. diss., Trinity College, Dublin 1971), pp. 194–203.
3. See Flannery, pp. 103–8, 280–82.

By 1902 Yeats had determined to perfect his craft as a dramatist and man of the theatre by practical experimentation in the laboratory provided by Willie and Frank Fay's Irish National Theatre Society. In visual terms, during the next few years, Yeats was predominantly concerned with space—specifically the relationship of the three-dimensional actor to his two-dimensional background. The most vital impulse and direction to his research were provided by the innovations of that extraordinary theatrical revolutionist, Gordon Craig.

GORDON CRAIG AND DECORATIVE DESIGN

There are few more controversial figures in the modern theatre than Gordon Craig (1872–1966). Depending on which critic one reads, Craig appears as either the Messiah of a new theatre or a romantic impractical dilettante.[4]

Craig was the son of Ellen Terry and Edward Godwin. He began his theatrical career as an actor, playing minor roles for Henry Irving intermittently between 1889 and 1897. Torn between an intense admiration for Irving himself and a growing dissatisfaction with the grandiose style of theatre embodied in Irving's productions, Craig gave up acting at the end of the 1897 season in order to devote himself to artistic enquiry and scene design.

As with Yeats, Craig's basic aim was to restore theatre to its former dignity. Like Wagner and the French Symbolists, he was trying to create out of a combination of all the arts, an entirely new "Art of the Theatre." His ideal was a visionary art based not upon "man or nature or anything else on the boards of a theatre," but upon the personal response of the designer-producer (director) to a particular play or series of plays.[5]

Craig was a product of the aesthetic movement and an enemy of the naturalists: he insisted that the function of the theatre was to evoke a sense of Beauty divorced from any other end. "Once let the meaning of this word 'Beauty' begin to be thoroughly felt once more

---

4. Cf. Lee Simonson, "Day Dreams: The Case of Gordon Craig," and Robert Edmund Jones, "Towards a New Stage," in John Gassner and Ralph Allen, eds., *Theatre and Drama in the Making* (Boston 1964), pp. 707, 715–16, 724.
5. See Edward Gordon Craig, *On the Art of the Theatre* (London 1966), pp. 11–27.

in the theatre," he said, "and we may say that the awakening day of the theatre is near."[6]

Where Wagner placed the ultimate authority in the musician, Craig viewed the stage director as the most important figure in the theatrical hierarchy. He displayed the bias of the visual artist, however, in claiming that the pre-eminence of the poet had kept the theatre from becoming a popular art:

> The theatre was for the people, and always should be for the people. The poets would make the theatre for a select company of dilettanti. They would put difficult psychological thoughts before the public, expressed in difficult words, and would make for this public something which is impossible for them to understand and unnecessary for them to know; whereas the theatre must show them sights, show them life, show them beauty, and not speak in difficult sentences.[7]

It would seem that in many ways the aims of Yeats and Craig were diametrically opposed. Yet they deeply admired each other's art and ideas. Craig considered Yeats to be "a great play-writer, and without question the greatest of the Irish play-writers."[8] When he founded his famous School of the Theatre at Florence in 1912, he distinguished between his intentions and those appropriate to "literary drama." At the same time, he declared that "we shall in our way and with our material hope to do what Yeats and Synge have done with their material."[9] When Yeats himself considered attending the School, Craig wrote to him:

> My school is not for the likes of you, I fear. You could learn nothing there. What you've learnt already—and what you have of the theatre is positively appalling. Now we shall learn from you about fairies and red dogs.[10]

Yeats, in turn, was one of the earliest and staunchest champions of Craig's theatrical reforms. This may be attributed to Yeats's

6. Craig, "The Artists of the Theatre of the Future," *The Mask*, I (1908), p. 66.
7. Craig, *On the Art of the Theatre*, pp. 11–12.
8. Craig, "Plays for an Irish Theatre with Designs by Gordon Craig," *The Mask*, IV (1911–12), p. 342.
9. Craig, "Is Poetic Drama Born Again?" *The Mask*, V (1912–13), p. 291.
10. Craig to Yeats, 11 May 1911. Unpublished letter in the possession of Michael Yeats.

persistent desire to realize his dramatic ideals in terms of the living theatre. Here Craig offered not only an example but practical help.

Craig's new ideas for the stage were first seen in a production of Purcell's *Dido and Aeneas*, presented in London in May 1900. Two elements—colour and light—were of primary importance in the production. The backdrop, a great purple-blue cloth, bore no resemblance to the traditional perspective views in which the nineteenth century scene-painters took such pride. Against this backdrop, costumes which consisted chiefly of draped robes and veils stood out, coloured in broad strokes of green, purple, blue, and scarlet. In the last act, Craig created a particularly beautiful picture by projecting a yellowish light on to the stage which turned the backdrop into a deep shimmering blue, and brought the greens and blues into rich harmony.[11]

In January 1901 the production was revived in a program which included another theatre piece called by Craig *The Masque of Love* and based upon music by Purcell. Yeats saw this production and sent Craig a warmly appreciative letter in which he described the setting as "the only good scenery I ever saw."[12]

In *The Speaker* for 11 May 1901, Yeats wrote:

> Naturalistic scene-painting is not an art but a trade, because it is, at best, an attempt to copy the obvious effects of Nature by the methods of the ordinary landscape-painter, and by his methods made coarse and summary. It is but flashy landscape painting and lowers the taste it appeals to, for the taste it appeals to has been formed by a more delicate art. . . . Decorative scene-painting would be, on the other hand, as inseparable from the movements as from the robes of the players and from the falling of the light; and being in itself a grave and quiet thing it would mingle with the tones of the voices and with the sentiment of the play, without overwhelming them under an alien interest . . . Mr. Gordon Craig used scenery of this kind at the Purcell Society performance the other day, and . . . . it was the first beautiful scenery our stage has seen. He created an ideal country where everything is possible, even speaking in verse, or speaking to music, or the expression of the whole life in a dance.[13]

A year later, when *The Saturday Review* gave its readers to understand that productions such as Craig's were not worth seeing,

11. Denis Bablet, *Edward Gordon Craig* (London 1966), pp. 41–42.
12. Quoted by Edward Craig in *Gordon Craig* (London 1968), p. 135.
13. Quoted in Bablet, *op. cit.*, pp. 44–45.

Yeats promptly sent a letter to that journal in which he declared that the staging of *Dido and Aeneas* and *The Masque of Love* had given him "more perfect pleasure than I have met in any theatre these ten years." By discovering how to "decorate a play with severe, beautiful, simple effects of colour, that leave the imagination free to follow all the suggestions of the play," Craig had created "a new and distinct art," an art that "can only exist in the theatre." "The staging of *Dido and Aeneas*," he concluded, "will someday, I am persuaded, be remembered among the important events of our time."[14]

Yeats did more than simply offer Craig praise. Shortly after the break-up of the Irish Literary Theatre, he tried to persuade Edward Martyn to employ Craig in an Irish touring company led by the English actor-manager, Frank Benson.[15] He also hoped, for a time, to raise enough money to enable Craig to give *The Countess Cathleen* the staging that it required.[16] Most important, he made Craig's personal acquaintance and set out to learn as much as he could about Craig's "little stage dodges," particularly lighting and costumes.[17]

By the time of the first performance of *Cathleen ni Houlihan* in April 1902, Yeats knew enough about Craig's methods to declare to Frank Fay: "Two years ago I was in the same state about scenery that I now am in about acting. I knew the right principles but I did not know the right practice because I had never seen it. I have now learnt a great deal from Gordon Craig."[18]

Craig's influence is evident in the criticism that Yeats made of the scenery and costumes designed by George Russell for the production of Russell's *Deirdre*, performed on the same bill as *Cathleen ni Houlihan*. Writing in *Samhain* Number Two (October 1902), Yeats stated that Russell's decor was "not simple enough. I should like to see poetic drama staged with but two or three colours," he declared. "The background, especially in small theatres, where its form is broken up and lost when the stage is at all crowded should, I think, be thought out as one thinks out the background of a portrait. One

14. *Ibid.*, p. 47.
15. W. B. Yeats, *Autobiographies* (London 1961), pp. 446–47.
16. Yeats to Lady Gregory, 6 January 1903, *The Letters of W. B. Yeats*, ed. Allan Wade (London 1954), p. 394.
17. Yeats to Lady Gregory, 26 September, 4 December 1902, *ibid.*, pp. 380, 384.
18. 21 April 1902, *ibid.*, p. 371.

often needs nothing more than a few shadowy forms to suggest wood or mountain."[19]

Intricate pattern was now replaced by the focused compositional technique of portrait painting. But the principal new visual element is colour. It was by employing vivid colour relationships and contrasts that Yeats sought either to harmonize or to contrast the actor with this scenic background and lift the play as a whole out of time and place to the realm of "fairyland."[20]

Yeats's first experiment with this new style of decor was made with *The Hour-Glass*, when it was first produced at the Molesworth Hall on 14 March 1903. Staged with costumes designed by Robert Gregory [pl. 1] according to an overall design created by T. Sturge Moore, the colour scheme was striking and effective. The action, as Yeats describes it, took place in front of an olive-green curtain, with the Wise Man and his Pupils dressed in various shades of purple. A third colour, subordinate to the other two, was added by dressing the Fool in a red-brown costume with touches of green to harmonize with the curtain. Because Yeats found himself "annoyed . . . beyond words" by the brown back of the Wise Man's chair during the performance, it was painted for later performances to match the red-brown of the Fool's costume.[21]

Yeats took an active role in supervising every aspect of the production, from approving the material, colour, and patterns of the costumes, to personally designing the Botticellian costume of the Angel.[22] During the intermission between the plays (Lady Gregory's comedy *Twenty-Five* was given its first performance as the second play on the bill), he lectured, with the aid of a model made for him by Craig, on the new art of "decorative" stage design.[23]

The success of *The Hour-Glass* production confirmed Yeats's

19. *Samhain* Number One, p. 5.
20. "Notes to 'The Golden Helmet,'" *Collected Works of W. B. Yeats* (Stratford-on-Avon 1908), IV, p. 243.
21. Yeats to T. Sturge Moore, March 1903, *W. B. Yeats and T. Sturge Moore: Their Correspondence*, Ursula Bridges ed. (London 1953), pp. 5–7. Cf. "Note to 'The Hour-Glass,'" *Collected Works* (1908), IV, pp. 238–39.
22. See Yeats to Lady Gregory, 9 December 1902, Wade, *op. cit.*, p. 388; W. G. Fay and Catherine Carswell, *The Fays of the Abbey Theatre* (London 1935), p. 130.
23. W. G. Fay, "The Poet and the Actor," in *Scattering Branches*, Stephen Gwynn ed. (London 1940), p. 133.

belief in the practical effectiveness of "decorative" design. This is evident in his criticism of a sketch submitted a short time afterwards by T. Sturge Moore for a production of *The Shadowy Waters*:

> I don't like the colour scheme at all. . . . The white sail will throw the hounds into such distinctness that they will become an irritation. . . . Further, the black, brown and white effect is just one of those effects we like in London because we have begun to grow weary with the more obvious and beautiful effects. But it is precisely those obvious and beautiful effects that we want here. . . . Your scheme would upset all my criticism here. I have been explaining on these principles:
> 1. A background which does not insist on itself and which is so homogeneous in colour that it is always a good background to an actor wherever he stand. Your background is the contrary of all this.
> 2. Two predominant colours in remote fanciful plays. One colour predominant in actors, one in backcloth. This principle for the present at any rate until we have got our people to understand simplicity. *The Hour-Glass* as you remember was staged in this way and it delighted everybody.[24]

Yeats went on to make the use of contrasting and vivid colour one of the continuing principles of stage design at the early Abbey Theatre. Decorative design was employed not only for his own plays but for those of Lady Gregory and Synge, and even for cottage sets of naturalistic peasant plays.[25]

Some idea of Yeats's efforts to employ colour to express the emotional mood of particular plays may be seen by comparing his colour scheme for *The Shadowy Waters* with that of *The Green Helmet*. For *The Shadowy Waters*, which was given its first production on 14 January 1904, Yeats asked T. Sturge Moore for a design which would be as "dreamy and dim" as the play itself: "A blue-green sail against an indigo-blue backcloth, and the mast and bulwark indigo-blue. The persons in blue and green with some copper ornaments."[26]

The Green Helmet, "An Heroic Farce," was first performed at the Abbey Theatre on 19 March 1908, under the title *The Golden Helmet*. Intended as a grotesque satire on the bitter quarrels which had by this time destroyed many of Yeats's plans for the Irish

24. Yeats to Moore, March 1903, Bridges, *op. cit.*, pp. 5–7.
25. See Lady Gregory, *Our Irish Theatre* (London 1913), p. 107; Fay and Carswell, *op. cit.*, p. 170; "Preface to the first edition of 'The Well of the Saints' (January 27, 1905)," *Essays and Introductions*, p. 305.
26. Yeats to Moore, March 1903, Bridges, *op. cit.*, p. 7.

National Theatre, the play called for a colour scheme "intentionally violent and startling." The set consisted of a house made of logs, painted in orange-red, with a door showing low rocks and a "green and luminous" sea beyond. Properties, consisting of a table, cups, and a flagon of ale, were painted black with a slight purple tinge. All the characters except the Red Man and the Black Man were dressed in various shades of green, one or two with touches of purple which looked nearly black. The Black Men all wore dark purple, with "eared caps," and at the end of the play Yeats suggested that "their eyes should look green from the reflected light of the sea."[27]

The title change is itself significant, possibly being made because the Golden Helmet of the Red Man did not show up against an orange background. For the later version of the play Yeats called for him to be dressed all in red, "his height increased by horns on the Green Helmet."[28]

Even after Yeats's active influence in the theatre had waned, some attempt was made, partially as a result of deficient resources, to carry on the tradition of simplified decorative settings at the Abbey Theatre—patterned curtains, vivid colour contrasts, and a minimum use of properties. Writing in 1926 of the setting for Lady Gregory's play based on *Don Quixote, Sancho's Master,* Lennox Robinson declared:

> In the Abbey Theatre production the walls were a dull red arras, the furniture a long blue table and two blue chairs, the decoration a pair of crossed swords and two heroic portraits. . . . In the second act, it will be right to consider the well as the only essential thing and to convey the idea of wood as best one can with curtains or set pieces—it all depends on the size of the stage and the size of the producer's purse. The third act should be in strong contrast to the simplicity of Don Quixote's room in the first act. At the Abbey Theatre we used hangings with figures painted in dull curtains and a coloured floor-cloth, but something more gorgeous might be used so long as it does not take away from the colour of the bright dresses of the Duchess and her ladies. . . . In plays like this and in *The Would-Be Gentleman* (Lady Gregory's adaptation of Moliere's *Le Bourgeois Gentilhomme*) it seems a safe rule to have nothing on the stage which is not essential to the action of the play . . . and no ornament which does not comment on the play—the crossed swords, the portraits. And the less ornament the better.[29]

27. W. B. Yeats, *The Green Helmet and Other Poems* (Dublin 1910), p. 13.
28. *Ibid.,* p. 10.
29. Lady Gregory, *Three Last Plays,* App. B (London 1928), pp. 119–20.

LIGHTING THE STAGE

One recurring criticism of Gordon Craig's early experimental work in England is that his extraordinary theatrical effects were created at the expense of the actors: the proportions of his huge sculpturesque settings dwarfed the human figures onstage; his use of light and shade often left the actors' faces in shadow; his coloured lighting effects competed with the actors in expressing mood variation.[30]

Yeats was aware of these flaws. In April 1903, he attended a London production of Ibsen's *The Vikings of Helgeland*, staged by Craig. His reaction was in some ways similar to his response to Wagner's music: he found the scenery "amazing," but felt that it "distract[ed] one's thoughts from the words."[31] Writing in *Samhain* in December 1904, when the Abbey Theatre opened, Yeats stated firmly:

> I have been the advocate of the poetry as against the actor, but I am the advocate of the actor as against the scenery. . . . The actor and the words put into his mouth are always the one thing that matters, and the scene should never be complete of itself, should never mean anything to the imagination until the actor is in front of it.

Yeats goes on to draw a distinction between Craig's conception of the theatre and his own, especially in terms of Craig's use of lighting as it affected the actor:

> If we remember that the movement of the actor, and the graduation and the colour of the lighting, are the two elements that distinguish the stage picture from an easel painting, we may not find it difficult to create an art of the stage ranking as a true fine art. Mr. Gordon Craig has done wonderful things with the lighting, but he is not greatly interested in the actor, and his streams of coloured direct light, beautiful as they are, will always seem, apart from certain exceptional moments, a new externality. We should rather desire, for all but exceptional moments, an even, shadowless light, like that of noon.[32]

30. Cf. Lynton Hudson, *The English Stage: 1850–1950* (London 1951), p. 156; Janet Leeper, *Edward Gordon Craig: Designs for the Theatre* (Harmondsworth 1948), especially pls. 9, 17, 20, 21, 25; Simonson, *op. cit.*, pp. 707–15.
31. Yeats to Lady Gregory, April 1903, *Letters*, p. 398.
32. "The Play, The Player and the Scene," *Samhain* (1904), pp. 31–32; *Explorations* (London 1962), pp. 177, 179.

Yeats's theories on stage lighting were put into practice for the production of *On Baile's Strand* with which the Abbey Theatre opened on 27 December 1904. Willie Fay has described some of the effects that were achieved. The setting itself was made of curtains of unpainted jute, which, when flooded with amber light, "looked like cloths of gold." Upstage centre was a pair of doors, nine feet in height, on which were hung six round shields designed by Robert Gregory: "when the doors were opened to Aoife's son he stood silhouetted against a background of topaz blue, giving an effect of sea and sky, with an atmosphere that could be obtained by paint."[33]

Craig's ideas were obviously used, but only for "exceptional moments" in the production; the main focus of attention was never taken from the actor.

Yet as Yeats's knowledge of the theatre developed, he called for more and more complex lighting effects. Sometimes he sought to employ light as an ironic commentary on action: this is evident from his description of the effect he desired for the final scene in *Deirdre*, when the two fated lovers sit, playing chess, awaiting their doom:

> The sky outside is still bright so that the room is dim in the midst of a wood full of evening light, but gradually during what follows the light fades out of the sky; and except during a short time before the lighting of the torches, and at the end of all, the room is either dark amid light or light amid darkness. The lighting and the character of the scenery, the straight trees, and the spaces of mountain between them suggest isolations and silence.[34]

Like Craig, Yeats experimented with light and shade as an active agent in the dramatic action. He toyed, for instance, with the idea of having the "barbarous dark-faced men" who pass outside Deirdre and Naoise's room appear only as shadows in front of a "blood-red" sunset.[35] This idea, as so many others, was never realized at the Abbey Theatre because of the shallowness of the stage.

Lighting was also employed with great dramatic effect in staging the plays of Lady Gregory and Synge at the early Abbey. One is struck, for instance, by the image of the Sergeant and the Rebel sitting back to back on a barrel, isolated in the moonlight in *The*

33. Fay, *op. cit.*, "Poet and Actor," p. 134.
34. "Notes to 'Deirdre'" (1907), *The Variorum Edition of the Plays of W. B. Yeats*, Russell K. Alspach, ed. (New York 1957), p. xv. This stage direction is omitted from the Macmillan edition of the *Collected Plays*.
35. "Note to 'Deirdre,'" *Plays for an Irish Theatre* (London 1911), p. 215.

Rising of the Moon—an idea apparently suggested to Lady Gregory by Yeats.[36] The great American designer, Robert Edmund Jones, himself a disciple of Craig, has left a vivid recollection of the impression made on him by the scenery and lighting in Synge's *Riders to the Sea*, which he saw on the Abbey Theatre's first American tour:

> The setting was very very simple. . . . Neutral-tinted walls, a fireplace, a door, a window, a table, a few chairs. The red home-spun skirts and bare feet of the peasant girls. A fisher's net perhaps, nothing more. But through the window at the back, one saw a sky of enchantment. All the poetry of Ireland shone in that little square of light, moody, haunting, full of dreams, calling us to follow on. . . . By this one gesture of excelling simplicity, the setting was enlarged into the region of great theatre art.[37]

But none of the other Abbey plays called for the special lighting effects demanded by Yeats's work. In *The Shadowy Waters* Forgael quells a threatened mutiny by the sheer theatrical impact of his magical glowing harp. Perhaps feeling it necessary to justify such an effect after his attacks on the spectacular stage trickery employed by the nineteenth-century actor-managers, Yeats declared:

> There is no reason for objecting to a mechanical effect when it represents some material thing, becomes a symbol, a player, as it were. One permits it in obedience to the same impulse that has made religious man decorate with jewels and embroidery the robes of priests and hierophants, even until the robe, stiffened and weighted, seems more important than the man who carries it. He has become a symbol, and his robe has become a symbol of something incapable of direct expression, something that is super-human.

In conformity with his philosophy of the theatre as essentially the art of the actor, Yeats added: "If the harp cannot suggest some power that no actor could represent by sheer acting, for the more acting the more human life, the enchanting of so many people by it will seem impossible."[38]

36. Frank O'Connor, *The Backward Look* (London 1964), p. 168.
37. "To A Young Designer," in *The Context and Craft of Drama*, Robert Corrigan and James L. Rosenberg, eds. (San Francisco 1964), p. 392.
38. "Notes for 'The Shadowy Waters'" (1906), *The Variorum Edition of the Poems of W. B. Yeats*, Peter Allt and Russell Alspach eds. (New York 1957), p. 816.

By 1908 Yeats was again experimenting with a form of "total theatre." The particular importance that Yeats gave to stage lighting is evident in his notes to *The Green Helmet*:

> No breadth of treatment gives monotony when there is movement and change of lighting. It concentrates attention on every new effect and makes every change of outline or of light and shadow surprising and delightful. Because of this one can use contrasts of colour, between clothes and background or in the background itself, the complementary colours for instance, which would be too obvious to keep the attention in a painting.[39]

Without careful lighting the vivid decorative colour scheme of *The Green Helmet* would have been garish, the action of the play monotonous. Now, however, Yeats built lighting changes into the very stage action. The play climaxes in a fight which produces a "deafening noise." The stage directions read:

> Suddenly three black hands come through the windows and put out the torches. It is now pitch dark, but for a faint light outside the house which merely shows that there are moving forms, but not who or what they are, and in the darkness one can hear low terrified voices.

Three frightened cries pierce the darkness. Then the stage directions continue:

> A light gradually comes into the house from the sea, on which the moon begins to show once more. There is no light within the house, and the great beams of the walls are dark and full of shadows, and the persons of the play dark too against the light. The Red Man is seen standing in the midst of the house.[40]

Even if the symbolism of the black hands or of the Red Man is not understood, the sheer theatrical impact of the scene is as impressive as that of the climax of *The Countess Cathleen*. Unfortunately, it was no more possible to achieve many of these effects at the Abbey Theatre than it was on the makeshift stage where *The Countess Cathleen* was first performed.

39. "Note on 'The Golden Helmet' " (1908), *Collected Works*, IV, p. 243.
40. *The Green Helmet and Other Poems*, p. 31.

Little wonder that by 1908 Yeats had begun to search for another more simplified means of staging his plays. Once again Gordon Craig appeared to have some of the answers to his quest.

THE CRAIG SCREENS, THE ÜBERMARIONETTE, AND THE MASK

In 1905 Gordon Craig published *On the Art of the Theatre*, in which he laid down his principles for the ideal theatre of the future. From 1904 to 1906 he attempted, with varying degrees of success, to realize his ideals in productions on the Continent for such noted theatrical figures as Otto Brahm, Max Reinhardt, and Eleanora Duse. In Germany he was excited by technical innovations such as hydraulic lifts in operation at many theatres. In Italy he renewed his interest in the spectacular Renaissance scenic artist and theoretician Sebastian Serlio. Most of all, he was inspired by the improvised movements of the dancer Isadora Duncan. He began dreaming of a new theatre art that, like her dancing, would express ideas in time and space. No longer would scenery be a mere background to the stage action. By becoming three-dimensional, as flexible, and as interesting in itself as the body of a trained dancer, and by changing shape before the eyes of the audience, it would provide a new kind of theatrical experience.[41]

Craig believed that his visionary theatre of the future would also demand an entirely new concept of acting. No longer would the actor be allowed to exhibit his "incomplete" art, expressed through the accidental whims of personality, emotions, body, and voice. Nor would the actor be allowed to indulge his ego in the forefront of the stage, hypnotizing the spectators with superficial representations of the world of appearances and causing them to lose their sense of the totality of the dramatic work.

Craig began implementing such ideas in Florence in February 1907. He built a model stage using a set of screens that he learnt by experimentation to manipulate almost imperceptibly during the action of a play [pl. 2]. To give scale to his screens, he made tiny wooden mannequins which were also capable of being manipulated so as to produce slight movements, such as the slow rising of a hand or head. Most of them were draped like ancient Greeks, for at that time the Greek tragedies interested him, and it was the scenic back-

41. See Bablet, "Scene and the 'Screens,'" *Edward Gordon Craig*, Ch. VII; Edward Craig, *Gordon Craig*, pp. 234–35.

ground for these plays that most challenged his theatrical imagination.[42]

Craig's experiments with mannequins led him, as it had the French Symbolists,[43] to a concept of acting based upon puppet movements. Craig postulated the creation of what he termed the *übermarionette*—a supremely beautiful creature, something like a Greek statue, that could be made to move, but would not suffer from or be affected by personal emotions. In histrionic terms, this creature would be an actor who had acquired some of the virtues of the marionette, and thus released himself from the servitude of his own human weakness. Acting, therefore, would consist for the main part in "symbolic gesture."[44] By covering his face with a mask, the fleeting and variable expression of the actor would be formed into an everlasting image of the "Poetic spirit."[45] The ideal of the *über-marionette* would, he said, not be "the flesh and blood but rather the body in trance—it [would] aim to clothe itself with a death-like beauty while exhaling a living spirit."[46]

By February 1908, Craig was ready to publish some of his findings. In that month he succeeded in achieving one of his earliest ambitions, which was the creation of the theatrical journal *The Mask*. Five hundred copies of the first issue, which included his celebrated essay, "The Actor and the Übermarionette," were printed in Florence and distributed to leading theatrical figures throughout the world. A copy of *The Mask* reached Constantin Stanislavsky at a critical juncture in the development of the Moscow Art Theatre. It was a time when Stanislavsky had begun to see that further work in the naturalistic genre could only lead to an artistic *cul de sac*. Stanislavsky was so much impressed by Craig's ideas that he invited him to Moscow to produce a play. At the same time he received invitations from Beerbohm Tree in London and Reinhardt in Berlin.[47]

For Yeats also, the period from 1907 to 1908 was a time of great personal and artistic soul-searching. He had staked his own hopes

42. Edward Craig, *Gordon Craig*, pp. 234, 239–40.
43. See Jacques Robichez, *Le Symbolisme au Théâtre* (Paris 1955), pp. 75–76.
44. "The Actor and the Über-marionette," *The Mask*, I (1908), p. 4.
45. Note by Craig, quoted by Leeper, *op. cit.*, p. 18.
46. "The Actor and the Über-marionette," *On the Art of the Theatre*, pp. 84–85.
47. Edward Craig, *op. cit.*, pp. 244–45.

as a dramatist on the development of a company of actors trained
to speak verse by a skilled man of the theatre. These hopes collapsed
with the departure in June 1907—under the concerted pressure of
Lady Gregory, Synge, the Fay brothers, and the unruly Abbey actors
—of Ben Iden Payne, a young English director who had been im-
ported by Yeats for this purpose.[48] The failure of the Abbey Theatre
to win and educate an audience from the followers of the nationalistic
movement was a second grave disappointment to Yeats.[49] Once
again he spoke in *Samhain* (November 1908) of returning to his
own "proper work without ceaseless distraction of theatrical details."[50] It was considered an event when, during the summer of
1908 at Coole, he began to write lyric verse again.[51] Now, however,
it was a blistering satiric verse that mocked the very time he had
wasted:

> On the day's war with every knave and dolt,
> Theatre business, management of men.[52]

For Yeats then the impact of Gordon Craig's theoretical and
practical innovations in the theatre were of profound importance.
What they did was to revive his interest in the theatre at a time when
it seemed that as a dramatist he was about to retire to the study.

Yeats renewed his acquaintance with Craig when Craig visited

48. James W. Flannery, *Miss Horniman and the Abbey Theatre* (Dublin
1970).
49. See James W. Flannery, "Yeats the Theatre Manager in Search of an
Audience," Ch. XI, *W. B. Yeats and the Idea of a Theatre*, pp. 287, 298.
50. A passage from a letter to Synge written in the midst of the controversy
over engaging Payne reveals in graphic detail Yeats's frustration with the
details of theatre management:

> *None of us are fit to manage a theatre of this kind and do our
> work as well. Lady Gregory's work this autumn would have
> been twice as good if she had not the practical matters of the
> theatre on her mind. Several times in the last two or three years
> the enormous theatrical correspondence has been the chief event
> of both her day and mine. Many and many a time we have to
> go to the typewriter the first thing after breakfast with result
> that our imaginations were exhausted before we got to our play-
> writing. Every little question has often to be debated in corres-
> pondence when we are away.*

Yeats to Synge, December 1906, Synge Papers, National Library of
Ireland Ms. P 5380.
51. Joseph Hone, *W. B. Yeats* (London 1965), p. 225.
52. W. B. Yeats, *Collected Poems* (London 1965), p. 104.

London in December 1909 to present Beerbohm Tree with his designs for a production of *Macbeth*. Yeats displayed such enthusiasm and so deep an understanding of his work that Craig offered to make him a set of his model screens, as well as to design costumes and masks for a production of one of his plays at the Abbey Theatre.[53]

Yeats had first to convince Lady Gregory of the feasibility of utilizing the Craig screens at the Abbey. Writing to her in January 1910, he suggested that through Craig's invention it might be possible to solve "all our scenic difficulties." "It would not prevent Robert Gregory designing," he added carefully, "but would give us all the mechanism [*sic*]—a mountain to put our mountain on." A few days later he wrote that he had "gladly" promised that he would use Craig's screens in all his poetical work. Not only would the invention be appropriate for "open air scene[s]," but he had hopes that through them a new method for staging even naturalistic plays might be developed.[54]

Yeats had the model screens in his hands by early February.[55] The first public reference to them occurs in a program note to Lady Gregory's translation of Goldoni's *Mirandolina*, which was performed at the Abbey Theatre on 24 February 1910. Yeats declared: "The rather unsatisfactory scenic arrangements have been made necessary by the numerous little scenes and the necessity of making the intervals between them as short as possible. We hope before very long to have a better convention for plays of the kind."[56]

During the summer of 1910 Yeats experimented with Craig's models. His excitement with their theatrical possibilities is expressed in the preface to *Plays for an Irish Theatre*, which contained three designs by Craig [pl. 3]. Yeats declared that he had now "a scene capable of endless transformation, of the expression of every mood that does not require a photographic realism." "Henceforth," he enthusiastically proclaimed:

> I shall be able, by means so simple that one laughs, to lay the events of my plays amid a grandeur like that of Babylon; and where there is neither complexity nor compromise nothing need

53. Edward Craig, *op. cit.*, pp. 254–55, 263.
54. Yeats to Lady Gregory, 5, 8 January 1910, *Letters*, pp. 545–46.
55. This is indicated in an unpublished letter from Craig to Yeats written in late February 1910, in the possession of Michael Yeats.
56. Preserved in Joseph Holloway, "Impressions of a Dublin Playgoer," 24 February 1910, p. 268, National Library of Ireland Ms. 1809.

go wrong, no lamps become suddenly unmasked, no ill-painted corner come suddenly into sight. Henceforth I can all but 'produce' my play while I write it, moving hither and thither little figures of cardboard through gay or solemn light and shade, allowing the scene to give the words and the words the scene. I am very grateful for he has banished a whole world that wearied me and was undignified and given me forms and lights upon which I can play as upon some stringed instrument.[57]

Craig's ideas on the *übermarionette* and the mask also came to Yeats's attention at an opportune time. In 1909 and 1910 Yeats became increasingly interested in the multifarious philosophic, religious, and theatrical implications of masks.[58] It was also at this time that he began to formulate his concept of tragedy, which in its subordination of "character" to "passion" is related to Craig's *übermarionette* theory as well as to Yeats's own ideas on the dialectic between self and anti-self (or mask) as a means of personal expression. Yeats's important essay, "The Tragic Theatre," which contains the seeds of these personal dramaturgical and theatrical conceptions, was first published in *The Mask* of October 1910.[59]

Ezra Pound is credited with having introduced Yeats to Japanese Noh drama. Here again, however, Craig may have played a larger role than is generally suspected. As early as 1908 Craig began to relate his theories to Oriental theatre. In 1910 *The Mask* concerned itself with Noh drama. With its emphasis on symbolical gesture and its subordination of accidental traits of "character" to essential passion, Noh drama provided Craig with yet another ancient manifestation of what he had been pursuing through his theory of the *übermarionette*.[60]

It is significant to note how closely Yeats's ideas approximated those of Craig when he came to discuss Noh drama. Writing in 1916, he declared that in the Noh he had discovered an ideal model that would synthesize the "pulse of life" with the "stillness of death." Actors of the Dance Plays were even enjoined to "move a little stiffly and gravely like marionettes."[61]

57. Preface to *Plays for an Irish Theatre*, p. xiii.
58. Norman Jeffares, *W. B. Yeats: Man and Poet* (London 1962), p. 161.
59. III, pp. 77–81.
60. Charles R. Lyons, "Gordon Craig's Concept of the Actor," *Total Theatre*, E. T. Kirby ed. (New York 1969), p. 72.
61. "Note on the first performance of 'At the Hawk's Well,'" *Four Plays for Dancers*, p. vi.

Yeats may have thought of employing masks for the "eagle faces" of some of the characters in the early versions of *The Shadowy Waters*,[62] but it was Craig who offered him the first practical means of bringing masks to the Abbey stage. In 1910, writing to Lady Gregory about a production of *The Hour-Glass* to be designed by Craig, Yeats remarked that he was "much excited by the thought of putting the fool into a mask." If the masks "worked" he also intended to employ them for the fool and the blind man in *On Baile's Strand*. "It would," he declared, "give a wildness and extravagance that would be fine. I should also like the Abbey to be the first modern theatre to use the mask," he added[63] [pl. 4].

Yeats had sound practical reasons for welcoming the use of masks. By 1910 the Abbey actors were losing the first flush of their enthusiasm as well as the charm that youth had previously given them on stage.[64] As Yeats explained it, by utilizing masks he was able to "substitute for the face of some commonplace player, or for that face repainted to suit his own vulgar fancy, the fine invention of a sculptor."[65]

Stimulating as Yeats may have found Craig's *übermarionette* and masks, there is no doubt that what most excited him at the time was the idea of actually staging his plays within the three-dimensional scenic environment provided by Craig's screens. A notebook, containing thirty-five sketches of scenes employing Craig's screens provides tangible evidence of what Yeats hoped to achieve.[66] The sketches include possible scenic arrangements for a wide range of plays: Lady Gregory's *Mirandolina*, *Shanwalla*, *The Canavans*, and *The Deliverer*; Yeats's *Deirdre*, *On Baile's Strand*, *The King's Threshold*, *The Land of Heart's Desire*, *The Hour-Glass*, and *The Countess Cathleen*. The variety of the possible configurations and the meticulous detail of the ground plans, lighting effects, colour schemes, and so forth are impressive [pl. 5, 6, 7, 8].

Again, however, Yeats was to discover that it is one thing to conceive of an ideal technique of theatre, but quite another thing to bring that conception to life on the stage itself.

62. *Our Irish Theatre*, pp. 2–3. Cf. David R. Clark, "Half the Characters had Eagle's Faces," *Irish Renaissance* (Dublin 1965) pp. 26–55.
63. Yeats to Lady Gregory, 21 October 1910, *Letters*, p. 554.
64. See *Letters*, pp. 455–60.
65. *Essays and Introductions*, p. 226.
66. Notebook in the possession of Michael Yeats.

The letters from Craig to Yeats about the installation and practical use of his screens at the Abbey Theatre must be one of the most fascinating studies in twentieth-century theatre history. Unfortunately Yeats's side of the correspondence has not been made available to the writer. But from the evidence at our disposal Yeats emerges as by far the more practical of the two.

Yeats's first practical question arose out of the odd shape of the proscenium-opening of the Abbey Theatre, which would, he thought, have marred the perspective of Craig's designs. Craig responded by designing a separate proscenium opening that could be moved up and down.[67]

A second problem was how to move the screens—which were set on castors—upon the raked stage of the Abbey Theatre. Craig protested that the slope of the stage did not really matter.[68] But Yeats saw to it that by July 1910 the Abbey stage floor was made level, despite much grumbling from Joseph Holloway and Shawn Barlow, who were consulted on the matter.[69]

Another problem was that of lighting the stage. In order to maintain perspective it would be necessary to construct a transparent roof over the entire Abbey stage, which would be manipulated on ropes, as the screens were moved in and out of place.[70]

When Yeats inquired how the surface of the screen was to be finished, he received an all too typical reply:

> As to the surface of the screen I like best the natural surface if it is distinguished enough—
> A *silk* yes—or when the screens are made
> oak—yes—(Bronze we shall reach *in time*)
> But meantime I don't much like the natural canvas surface. I should propose something more frankly artificial than paint (which however you may still find suits you best).
> Now for it—take 3 girls—3 pairs of scissors & innumerable pieces of paper
> cream, white—grey—greyer (even pale colours) (rose)
> For grey paper what better than

---

67. Craig to Yeats, 18 January 1910. All letters cited from Craig to Yeats are in the possession of Michael Yeats.
68. Craig to Yeats, 25 January 1910.
69. *Joseph Holloway's Abbey Theatre*, Robert Hogan and Michael J. O'Neill, eds. (Carbondale 1967), p. 140.
70. Craig to Yeats, 9 February 1910.

the Dublin rags
that attack the Abbey Theatre
let the girls cut up all the shapes and sizes of paper & make sacks
full of what we will call our paper mosaic
Then let the artist loose on it—and two strong & obedient
stickers—poster paint will be the best—& the slime of it will (I
believe) just add that gloss which is needful to relieve it
here & *there*
but not all over gloss
please—
See the value of this

I take it you must repair your screens after some accident in an
hours time—you can do it & guarantee the rise of the curtain.
Suppose on Monday you want more blue at the tragedians feet
than you had on Saturday it can be added—& removed by Tues-
day when you want more yellow. . . .

As a rule let your darker tones fall about the base of the screens
& never harm the top which like the cieling [sic] should be
generally pure cream.
I can no more
The King, the Kings to blame.[71]

[pl. 9]

"The King" is, of course, Hamlet's uncle. And some of the vagueness in this and other letters may be explained by Craig's involvement at the time in his first practical experiments with the screens
for the famous Moscow Art Theatre production of *Hamlet.* Many
of Craig's problems and worries with this production—which is
recognized as one of the landmarks of the modern theatre—spill
over into his correspondence with Yeats. At one point, for instance,
he asked whether Yeats had discovered a way of getting his actors
on and off the stage "without our knowing how they came—keeping
them *quite still* [quite!] & returning them as mysteriously." Again,
he asked Yeats to inform him whether he had devised "some special
method for opening and closing [the screens] rapidly & smoothly &
safely."[72] (Craig had reason to worry about this problem since it
proved difficult for the Moscow Art Theatre technicians to shift the
screens for the many scene changes in *Hamlet.* When the screens

71. Craig to Yeats, n.d.
72. Craig to Yeats, April 1910, 6 September 1910.

fell over an hour before the opening performance, Stanislavsky reluctantly decided to lower the curtain for all changes of scene.)[73]

Despite a final difficulty in fitting the screens through the stage door[74] they were set up on the stage of the Abbey Theatre for the first time in November 1910. Apparently Craig's ideas on finishing the surfaces proved either impractical or undesirable, for Holloway described them as "a series of square box-like pillars saffron-hued, with saffron background, wings, sky pieces, and everything."[75]

On 12 January 1911 the Craig screens made their debut at the Abbey Theatre, when they were employed for a revival of *The Hour-Glass* and the first production of *The Deliverer*, by Lady Gregory. *The Irish Times* reviewer declared that the new method was "a great improvement on the old staging of *The Hour-Glass*." He went on to illustrate the innovations in some detail:

> There is in the first place a reduction of the stage furniture to its simplest elements, so that the figures of the players stand out more prominently against the primitive background and attention is concentrated on the human and truly expressive elements of the drama. There is next a careful design and adjustment of the simple elements of staging which still further tends to secure that effect. Lastly, there is a similar care in regard to the supplementary elements—lighting arrangements and costuming.

The review closed, however, with a qualification of considerable significance:

> The success of these aims is the result of the genius of an individual producer, who combines with artistic and thoughtful ideas on the principles of staging, an unusual ability to deal with the mechanical problems involved in giving effect to those principles.[76]

The production of *The Deliverer* proved this last point. While *The Hour-Glass*, with costumes and other effects carefully designed by Craig [pl. 10] and using the Craig screens, was a success, *The*

73. Constantin Stanislavsky, *My Life in Art*, trans. J. J. Robbins (New York 1948), p. 521. Cf. Kauro osanai, "Gordon Craig's Production of *Hamlet* at the Moscow Art Theatre," trans. Andrew T. Tsanhaki, *Educational Theatre Journal* 20, no. 4 (December 1968), pp. 586–93.
74. Undated letter from Craig to Yeats referring to this problem.
75. Hogan and O'Neill, *op. cit.*, p. 146.
76. *The Irish Times*, 13 January 1911, W. H. Henderson Press Clippings, National Library of Ireland, Ms. 1734, p. 6.

Deliverer was an unmitigated failure. Yeats himself in a curtain speech attributed this failure to the haphazard costumes. Holloway declared that there was "nothing about the dress or scenery to suggest Egypt," the locale of the play.[77]

To realize the full potential of the screens, it was evident, as Craig himself insisted, that a skilled stage director was needed to produce an aesthetically harmonious and theatrically effective whole. In the autumn of 1911, accordingly, Nugent Monck was engaged by Yeats specifically to experiment with classical and modern works employing the Craig screens.[78]

Nugent Monck's own speciality in the theatre was the staging of medieval plays. With a company of amateur actors at the Maddermarket Theatre in Norwich, England, he achieved a reputation as one of the "first half-dozen producers in England," especially for his skilful handling of crowd scenes.[79]

When he arrived at the Abbey Theatre Monck's first innovation was to extend the stage into the auditorium to create the kind of apron stage that Yeats had longed for since 1904. For the first time Yeats had at his disposal the physical means of staging his plays so as to interweave portrait and pattern throughout the same play.

Full advantage was taken of this flexibility in a series of plays staged by Monck with the Abbey Second Company during the autumn of 1911. On 16 November 1911 a production of *The Interlude of Youth* was staged in which most of the characters came and went from the auditorium up a set of stairs leading to the apron. In a production of *The Second Shepherd's Play* incense was burned in the foyer, followed by a procession and hymn to put the audience into a proper frame of mind. Subsequently Douglas Hyde's *Nativity Play* was produced with the set and actors dressed in an appropriate medieval style (Monck himself apparently brought over some of his own costumes from Norwich for these productions).[80]

All of this was a prelude to an impressive production of a revised version of *The Countess Cathleen* on 14 December 1911. With

77. Holloway, *op. cit.*, 12 January 1911, National Library of Ireland, Ms. 1811, p. 68.
78. Memorandum concerning the establishment of the Abbey Theatre Second Company, probably composed in the summer of 1911, National Library of Ireland, Ms. 13068.
79. Norman Marshall, *The Other Theatre* (London 1948), pp. 94–95.
80. Holloway, *op. cit.*, 16, 23, 30 November 1911, National Library of Ireland, Ms. 1812, pp. 783–87, 820, 867.

Yeats sitting near the operator of a limelight in the balcony, calling the cues for lighting changes, the play was staged as a medieval pageant, one scene rapidly merging into another, actors entering through the audience and by the wings.[81] Lyrics were written for the processions, including one in which the spirits dance and sing as they steal the Countess's money away. Upstage centre was a curtained recess with a great grey curtain coloured with rich tints of amber from the arc lights. Gauzes were hung from two arches for the third scene in the Hall of the Countess, behind which one dimly saw the trees of a garden.[82]

The spectacular but impossible effects of the last scene in the original version—the thunder and lightning, and the elaborate vision of armed angels on the mountain, ending with the distant note of a horn—were cut. Instead, in this revised version "suitable for performances at the Abbey Theatre," Aleel (who was played by Monck with Maire O'Neill playing the Countess) briefly described the clash of the angels and devils "in the middle air." Then the stage directions called for the entrance of a winged Angel, carrying a torch and sword from stage right. The Angel was stopped by Aleel, and the final dialogue between them and Oona continued as originally written.[83]

Thus, with a skilled and imaginative director, it proved possible to use Craig's screens successfully in a production of a Yeats play. This combination of director and setting was enormously stimulating to Yeats, and the short period during which these factors combined was one of the most creative in his career as a dramatist, especially with regard to the revisions of his earlier work for the Abbey stage. It is significant that Yeats declared that the revised versions of *The Countess Cathleen* and *The Land of Heart's Desire*—the latter also staged by Monck as a kind of morality play[84]—depended "less upon the players and more upon the producer, both having been imagined more for variety of stage picture than variety of mood in the

81. *Ibid.*, pp. 933–936.
82. W. B. Yeats, *The Countess Cathleen* (London 1912), pp. 65–66; stage directions, p. 127.
83. *Ibid.*, pp. 125–27.
84. Holloway, *op. cit.*, 22 February 1912, National Library of Ireland, Ms. 1873, p. 275. Yeats adapted the ending of "The Land of Heart's Desire" so that the curtain fell before the priest's last few lines. The priest remained outside the curtain on the apron and spoke his last lines to the audience.

player."[85] It is equally significant that to many astute critics Monck's productions were, from a visual point of view, far superior to any others staged at the early Abbey.[86]

FROM PUBLIC THEATRE TO DRAWING ROOM

After Monck's departure from the Abbey Craig's screens were rarely used [pl. 11]. In 1913 they were used for only two of sixteen productions: the staging of *The Post-Office*, a one-act play by the Indian dramatist Rabindranath Tagore, and a revival of *The King's Threshold*, the only production of any play by Yeats staged at the Abbey that year.[87]

One of the problems was of course the sheer technical difficulty of setting up and manipulating the screens on the limited Abbey stage. Another was the reluctance of the Abbey technicians and stage directors to accept scenic innovations. Not only did Shawn Barlow (who was often given charge of *designing* as well as building stage scenery) have little use for the Craig screens, but shortly after they were first introduced he had them "cut down a bit in order to fit on to the Abbey stage."[88] To the present day they remain in the Abbey Theatre scene dock, painted a robin's-egg blue by some enterprising technician in the mid-1930s.[89]

Craig was himself also partly to blame for the failure of the Abbey Theatre to make use of his invention. Tours had by 1911 become an essential means of supporting the Theatre, but Craig refused to allow his screens to be used outside Dublin unless he was on hand to supervise every aspect of their operation. Likewise, he insisted on

85. Note to the revised version of "The Countess Cathleen" and "The Land of Heart's Desire," *Variorum Plays*, p. 1291.
86. This was the opinion of H. O. White, late Professor of English Literature, Trinity College, Dublin, Joseph Holloway, and the noted theatre historian, W. J. Lawrence. See Alan Cole, *Stagecraft in the Modern Dublin Theatre* (Ph.D. diss., Trinity College, Dublin), p. 37; tribute by Holloway on Monck's departure from the Abbey Theatre, *Evening Telegraph*, 5 March 1912, in Holloway, *op. cit.*, National Library of Ireland, Ms. 1813, p. 286; and *W. J. Lawrence Press Cuttings*, National Library of Ireland, Ms. 4296, p. 53.
87. Holloway, *op. cit.*, 17 May, 30 October 1913, National Library of Ireland, Ms. 1815, pp. 895–97; Ms. 1816, pp. 744–46.
88. Cole, *op. cit.*, p. 36.
89. Interview with Tanya Moisievitch, 3 October 1965.

making and showing the Abbey actors how to use the masks that he designed for Yeats.[90]

It is clear that Yeats was reluctant to have any more direct collaboration with Craig than by letter. Correspondence between himself and the Irish actress Florence Darragh in 1913 concerning a proposed theatre venture in London with Craig as "producer" and himself as "literary adviser" reveals some of Yeats's qualms about working more closely with Craig. Warning Miss Darragh about Craig's "vagueness," Yeats refused to consider any further commitment to the project until a "written statement . . . signed by all three" had been prepared. Without such an agreement, he explained, "Craig and I might . . . very quickly find ourselves opposed to one another and suspecting each other of things. Craig has a difficult temperament. He is a great genius, but we will need more skill than the others have shown if we are not to disappoint his hopes or our own."[91]

For the Abbey tours of 1913–14, however, Yeats himself designed an extremely flexible scenic arrangement that bore a striking resemblance to Craig's screens. Within the proscenium opening was constructed an "inner proscenium," formed by placing two rectangular pillars shaped like matchboxes on end, with a third laid across the top. In each "matchbox" was a door. The colour of the pillars was grey, and around the stage was hung a grey-blue cyclorama cloth flooded with light.

The chief virtue of the arrangement was the variety of settings it could accommodate. When a big cross was placed in the middle of the stage, for instance, the setting was complete for the first act of *The Well of the Saints*, with the door on stage left leading to the church. When the cross was replaced by a well, a small piece of hillside scenery at the back, and red lights within the stage door left, the scene was transformed to Timmy's forge, the setting of the second act.

By the use of various backdrops and simple stage properties the setting was made appropriate for other plays, including Lady Gregory's *The Canavans* and *The Rising of the Moon*. Of Yeats's plays, however, only *The King's Threshold* appears to have been

90. Craig to Yeats, 25 January, 1 May 1910, 11 May 1911, 20 November 1910.
91. Yeats to Florence Darragh, 28 March 1913, unpublished letter in the possession of Michael Yeats.

performed within this inner proscenium. In its deliberate concentration and framing of the stage action, this arrangement is reminiscent of Yeats's earlier idea of the stage as a tiny jewel-like image. The setting for *The King's Threshold* consisted of a long flight of stairs set between the two pillars, with a patterned backdrop of a mountain range and a waterfall.[92]

It is significant, however, that it was not so much the setting as the costumes designed and made by Charles Ricketts that excited Yeats's imagination when the Abbey presented a revival of *The King's Threshold* in London in June 1914. He wrote to Ricketts:

> I think the costumes the best stage costumes I have ever seen. They are full of dramatic invention, and yet nothing starts out, or seems eccentric. The Company never did the play so well, and such is the effect of costume that whole scenes got a new intensity, and passages or actions that had seemed commonplace became powerful and moving.[93] [frontispiece]

A comment of Lady Gregory in a letter to Ricketts requesting advice in "shuffling costumes" for other plays is still more revealing: "I feel you are giving us a new start in life. Yeats will enjoy seeing his plays, which he hasn't done for years."[94]

Mainly because of a financial crisis which the Abbey Theatre underwent in 1914,[95] it was impossible to think of giving Yeats any further productions of such visual splendour. Within a year, out of sheer frustration at being unable to realize his theatrical ideals, he turned to the austere model offered by Japanese Noh drama: an ancient theatre made simply by "unrolling a carpet or marking out a place with a stick, or setting a screen against a wall;" a stage which, instead of employing light and shade to cast a "veil" between the sound of the actor's voice and his audience, would require only "the light we are most accustomed to;" properties which could all be carried by the actors in a cab; the only "picture" that of the player's

92. Interview with Lennox Robinson, April 1914, in *Holloway Press Cuttings*, National Library of Ireland, Ms. 4418; cf. Holloway, *op. cit.*, 30 October 1913, National Library of Ireland, Ms. 1816, pp. 744–46.
93. 14 June 1914, *Letters*, p. 587.
94. Letter dated June 1914, reproduced in *Self-Portrait: Letters and Journals of Charles Ricketts*, comp. T. Sturge Moore, Cecil Lewis ed. (London 1939), p. 198.
95. See James W. Flannery, "A Financial Record of the Early Abbey Theatre," App. B, *op. cit.*, p. 338.

mask, itself an image which would make the face of the speaker "as much a work of art as the lines that he speaks or the costume that he wears."[96]

Yeats, the man of letters, became involved with the Irish National Theatre Society in order to explore and master the practical problems of the theatre. Now once again for practical reasons he left the public theatre for the theatre of the drawing room.

96. *Essays and Introductions*, p. 224; "Note on the first performance of 'At the Hawk's Well,'" pp. 86, 87.

Dialogue Into Movement: W. B. Yeats's Theatre Collaboration With Gordon Craig*

Karen Dorn

"I have done nothing but theatre for months," Yeats wrote to his father in 1912.[1] After Synge's death, three years earlier, Yeats's responsibilities at the Abbey Theatre had greatly increased. He had even taken on its financial support, lecturing in England to raise funds for the theatre's maintenance. But in the midst of this business, he renewed an old friendship with Gordon Craig which not only benefitted the Abbey but affected the whole of Yeats's own drama. His decision to revise some early plays (1910–13) was prompted by the chance to restage them in Craig's new scenery, and this new use of stage space anticipated Yeats's adaptations, several years later, of the Japanese Noh drama.

Today Craig's theatre revolution has become as much a matter of course as the Victorian scenery had been in his time. We need to think back from present-day dramatic productions in which actors, amid shifting lights, perch upon scaffolding or movable walls, to the conditions of the Victorian stage. At that time, the actor had little "real" light and shadow to move within. Instead, as the photograph of the old Empire Music Hall, Newcastle [pl. 12], reveals, the actor stood in front of a painted illusion. Light and shadow were painted into the perspective, and much of the street space was obviously

*The author wishes to thank the American Association of University Women for the fellowship held at the time of the completion of this essay.

1. *The Letters of W. B. Yeats*, ed. Allan Wade (London 1954), p. 567.

inaccessible. Yeats wanted a different kind of theatre. Even before
he saw Craig's productions, he often criticized "naturalistic scene-
painting"[2] and "meretricious landscapes."[3] "Illusion," he insisted,
". . . is impossible, and should not be attempted. We should be
content to suggest a scene upon a canvas, whose vertical flatness we
accept and use. . . ."[4]

The important years of Yeats's and Craig's collaboration were
from 1909 to 1912: years of the introduction of Craig's scenery at
the Abbey Theatre, revivals of *The Land of Heart's Desire*, *The
Countess Cathleen*, and *The Hour-Glass*, and early drafts of *The
Player Queen*. The friendship though had begun much earlier, in
the days of the Irish Literary Theatre. Yeats saw Craig's first production in 1901, and he realized immediately that it was a style of
theatre he wanted. As he wrote to Craig, "I thought your scenery to
'Aeneas and Dido' the only good scenery I ever saw. You have
created a new art. I have written to Frank Harris to ask him to let
me do an article on the subject in his new paper 'The Saturday
Review.'"[5] Yeats's interest in Craig's early productions for the
Purcell Operatic Society was partly practical. There was no need
for costly elaborate scenery and, as Yeats confided to Lady Gregory,
a stolen glimpse backstage had given him ideas for inexpensive
staging and costumes at the Abbey.[6] Moreover, Craig's early productions showed him how to alter the stage space. By means of
lighting, draped ribbons could become a tent; tied grey curtains, the
columns of a grand interior. An actor, freed from the blocking
demanded by footlights, could move into new spaces on a stage lit by
back and side lighting. Stage space, then, offered the actor new
possibilities for movement. In Yeats's words:

> The primary value of Mr. Craig's invention is that it enables one
> to use light in a more natural and more beautiful way than ever
> before. We get rid of all the top hamper of the stage, all the hang-

2. *Essays and Introductions*, ed. Mrs. W. B. Yeats (London 1961), p. 100.
3. *Ibid.*, p. 169.
4. *Explorations*, ed. Mrs. W. B. Yeats (London 1962), p. 178. The Victorian
   theatre was the culmination of the type of theatre developed in the late
   fifteenth century in Italy by neo-classical architects, such as Palladio, who
   used the new technique of painted perspective.
5. Gordon Craig, *Index to the Story of My Days: Some Memoirs of Edward
   Gordon Craig, 1872–1907* (London 1957), p. 239. One of Yeats's letters
   to the *Saturday Review* is in *Letters*, pp. 365–66.
6. "I have seen all the costumes too, and hope to get patterns. He costumed
   the whole play—30 or 40 people I should say—for £25." *Letters*, p. 380.

ing ropes and scenes which prevent the free play of light. It is now possible to substitute in the shading of one scene real light and shadow for painted light and shadow. . . . One enters into a world of decorative effect which gives the actor a renewed importance.[7]

This kind of theatre—where form is content, to use Kenneth Burke's phrase—especially caught Yeats's imagination because he thought the Abbey productions would help shape an emerging Irish nationalism. In all his work written during those years he placed emphasis on form. "A beautiful soul," Yeats paraphrased Spenser, "makes for itself a beautiful body,"[8] and he suggested in "Edmund Spenser" (1902) that the original Irishman "spoke a language even in which it was all but impossible to think an abstract thought."[9] For the same reason, he praised Lady Gregory's *Cuchulain of Muirthemne* (1902): "I knew of no language to write about Ireland in but raw modern English; but now Lady Gregory has discovered a speech as beautiful as that of Morris, and a living speech into the bargain."[10] Irish dramatists who write in English, Yeats noted, have "difficult work, for English has been the language in which the Irish cause has been debated; and we have to struggle with traditional phrases and traditional points of view."[11]

Just as Yeats valued Lady Gregory's language, he saw in Craig's scenic art a form inseparable from an actor's language and movement: "Decorative scene-painting would be . . . as inseparable from the movements as from the robes of the players and from the falling of the light; and . . . it would mingle with the tones of the voices and with the sentiment of the play, without overwhelming them under an alien interest."[12] "The truth is," he announced in 1901, "that the Irish people are at that precise stage of their history when imagination, shaped by many stirring events, desires dramatic expression."[13] His fanciful description of Merrie Englishmen reads both as a type for modern Irishmen and as an ideal of a theatre which might teach Ireland a new image of itself: "Men still wept when they were moved, still dressed themselves in joyous colours, and spoke with

7. "Letter" to the *Evening Telegraph* (9 January 1911) quoted in Denis Bablet, *Edward Gordon Craig*, trans. Daphne Woodward (London 1966), p. 130. The book was originally published in Paris in 1962.
8. *Essays and Introductions*, p. 366.
9. *Ibid.*, p. 375.
10. *Explorations*, p. 4.
11. *Ibid.*, p. 104.
12. *Essays and Introductions*, p. 100.
13. *Explorations*, p. 74.

many gestures."[14] He fashioned Spenser into the type of artist who "seemed always to feel through the eyes, imagining everything in pictures,"[15] but he took for his own model the Elizabethan dramatists whose subject "was always the soul, the whimsical, self-awakening, self-exciting, self-appeasing soul. They celebrated its heroical, passionate will going by its own path to immortal and invisible things."[16] Nietzsche's terms begin to appear in this essay, enforcing the argument for a theatre based not on pictures but upon a space inseparable from the actor, a theatre not of the eye but of the body. "In Ireland, where the tide of life is rising, we turn, not to picture-making, but to the imagination of personality—to drama, gesture."[17]

Craig's productions, then, gave direction to Yeats's early work at the Abbey. In 1902, Yeats encouraged the Abbey actor, Frank Fay, to keep at his "acting of verse" because he himself had been "in the same state about scenery that I am now in about acting. I knew the right principles but I did not know the right practice because I had never seen it. I have now however learnt a great deal from Gordon Craig."[18] In his lecture, "The Reform of the Theatre," Yeats illustrated the new stage design on a small model stage Craig had made for him.[19] Edith Craig took Yeats backstage during her brother's production of Housman's *Bethlehem* (1902). As he recounted to Lady Gregory, "I have learned a great deal about the staging of plays from 'the nativity,' indeed I have learned more than Craig

14. *Essays and Introductions*, p. 364.
15. *Ibid.*, p. 383.   16. *Ibid.*, p. 370.
17. *Explorations*, p. 163.   18. *Letters*, p. 371.
19. Yeats wrote to Lady Gregory, "I am also bringing my model theatre and have a plan of giving two lectures in the autumn. One on a simpler theatre, and one on the speaking of verse to notes." *Letters*, p. 375. William Fay has described Yeats's demonstrations with Craig's model theatre: "It was a simple horizon cloth with some rocks and trees in the foreground, painted in monochrome, but lit in three different colours. For the first time it produced a feeling of atmosphere in stage lighting." "The Poet and the Actor," in *Scattering Branches*, ed. Stephen Gwynn (London 1940), p. 133. Fay's description suggests that the model was the set for "Dido and Aeneas," which Yeats saw in 1900 and 1901. The use of a model theatre to illustrate lectures was standard practice, and Craig first saw the combination of electric lights, gauze, side-lighting, music and dance at the theatre in Bushey, when the Bavarian artist Hubert von Herkomer used a model set in 1892 to illustrate his talks. Edward Craig, *Gordon Craig: The Story of His Life* (London 1968), pp. 78–79.

likes. His sister has helped me, bringing me to where I could see the way the lights were worked. He was indignant—there was quite an amusing scene. I have seen all the costumes too. . . .”[20] The three of them—Yeats, Craig, and his sister—planned several joint productions. Edith Craig persuaded the Stage Society to produce Yeats's play, *Where There Is Nothing*, though Craig too wanted "to produce it with elaborate scenery instead of the Maeterlinck which they had asked him to do."[21] Two of their plans for Yeats's plays, as we shall see, would eventually be worked out at the Abbey. One was a production of *The Hour-Glass* which, in scenario form, "greatly delighted" Craig.[22] But the grandest scheme of those early years was a production which would have combined the verse-speaking and stage design Yeats wanted:

> Sturge Moore was round with me last night and he made to Gordon Craig (through a friend of Craig's that was there) an offer on Ricketts' behalf. He proposed that Ricketts should raise nearly £600 which should be used by Craig to stage my *Countess Cathleen*. All the speaking of verse to be left entirely in the hands of Sturge Moore and of course the author.[23]

Yeats thought such a production would "enormously strengthen my position," but he soon realised that Craig's intentions were quite different from his own. Craig wanted a drama composed of movement and light, the kind of drama later developed by Diaghilev's Russian Ballet.[24] Yeats was more concerned with language than movement. Though he often praised Craig for creating "an ideal

20. *Letters*, p. 380.
21. In this letter to John Quinn, Yeats wrote that Craig "is the great innovator here in the matter of scenery and has begun experiments which may perhaps revolutionize the whole art." From the files of The Macmillan Company (New York), *The Variorum Edition of the Plays of W. B. Yeats*, ed. Russell K. Alspach (London 1966), p. 1167. *Where There is Nothing* was produced by Granville Barker at the Royal Court Theatre on 26, 27, and 28 June 1904, with Edith Craig as one of the tinkers. *Letters*, pp. 382–83.
22. *Letters*, p. 375.   23. *Ibid.*, p. 394.
24. Janet Leeper describes Craig's production of *The Vikings*: "Colour was used in combination with the movement of the stage, and we already see here—in 1900–3—the beginning of what was to lead to Diaghilev's Russian Ballet." In 1906–7, Craig planned a ballet, *Psyche*, which Diaghilev refused because he thought it too daring. *Edward Gordon Craig: Designs for the Theatre* (Harmondsworth 1948), pp. 8, 18.

country where everything was possible," his own ideal theatre included "speaking in verse, or speaking to music."[25] Craig's scenery, he wrote to Lady Gregory after a performance of *The Vikings* (1903) "is amazing but rather distracts one's thought from the words."[26] He invited Florence Farr to Dublin to see his own scenery for the 1905 production of *The Shadowy Waters*: "You will I think prefer it to Craig. It is more noble and simple."[27] Though he described this production in Craig's terms—"What I have done is but a form and colour in an elaborate composition"—he really wanted these stage conventions to frame a "speech even more important than gesture upon the stage."[28] Having kept in close touch with Florence Farr's London production of Greek tragedies, Yeats placed his own notion of theatre in that tradition. Ancient Greek acting had been great, he claimed, "because it did all but everything with the voice." The new style of theatre would combine Craig's art and his own: "modern acting may be great when it does everything with voice and movement."[29] Not until his later collaboration with Craig was Yeats able to present on stage that combination of language and movement which had been his early ideal.

"He has altered his verse and his drama to fit the stage. He has done wrong. . . ."[30] This pronouncement was part of Craig's review of Yeats's *Plays for an Irish Theatre* (1911). By the time the review appeared, Yeats was once again altering his dramas to fit a stage. This time, though, Yeats was not working simply with the proscenium stage Craig had dismissed. The tiny Abbey stage had been transformed by Craig's new scenery, and in January 1911, the scenery made its first appearance in Lady Gregory's *The Deliverer* and Yeats's *The Hour-Glass*.[31] Craig's scenery did more than trans-

25. *Essays and Introductions*, pp. 100–1.
26. *Letters*, p. 398. Yeats may have exaggerated the distraction; Wade notes that the musical director, Martin Shaw, "did not use the words supplied by Yeats but returned to William Archer's version of the song as being more like Ibsen; small wonder that Yeats could not distinguish his words during the performance."
27. *Ibid.*, p. 456.
28. *Variorum Plays*, p. 1293; *Explorations*, p. 108.
29. *Ibid.*, p. 110.
30. Unsigned review by Craig, *The Mask*, IV (1911–12), p. 343. Craig had special interest in *Plays for an Irish Theatre* because the volume was illustrated by four of his drawings.
31. In December 1911, Craig's screens appeared for the second time in Stanislavski's production of *Hamlet* at the Moscow Art Theatre.

PLATE 1:
Costume designs by
Robert Gregory for
first production of
The Hour-Glass, 1903.

PLATE 15: (*above*) Gordon Craig working with his model stage in England, 1910.

PLATE 16: (*below*) Mask of the Blind Man for *On Baile's Strand*, 1911, by Gordon Craig.

PLATE 1:
Costume designs by
Robert Gregory for
first production of
The Hour-Glass, 1903.

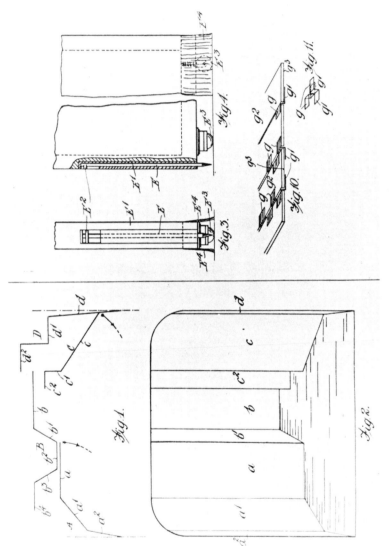

PLATE 2: Detail from patent application for Craig screens.

PLATE 3: Idealized rendering of set design by Gordon Craig for *The Hour-Glass*, 1911.

PLATE 4: (*above*) Design by Gordon Craig for the Fool's mask in *The Hour-Glass*, 1911.

PLATE 5: (*opposite*) Sketches by W. B. Yeats for setting of *The Deliverer* by Lady Gregory and *The Hour-Glass*, utilizing the Craig screens.

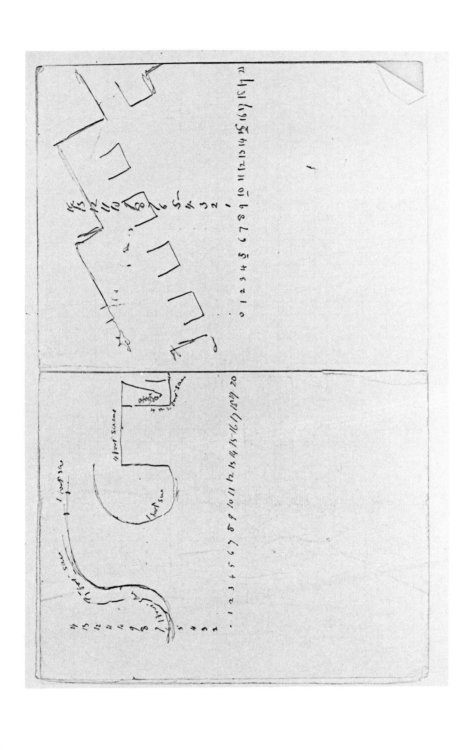

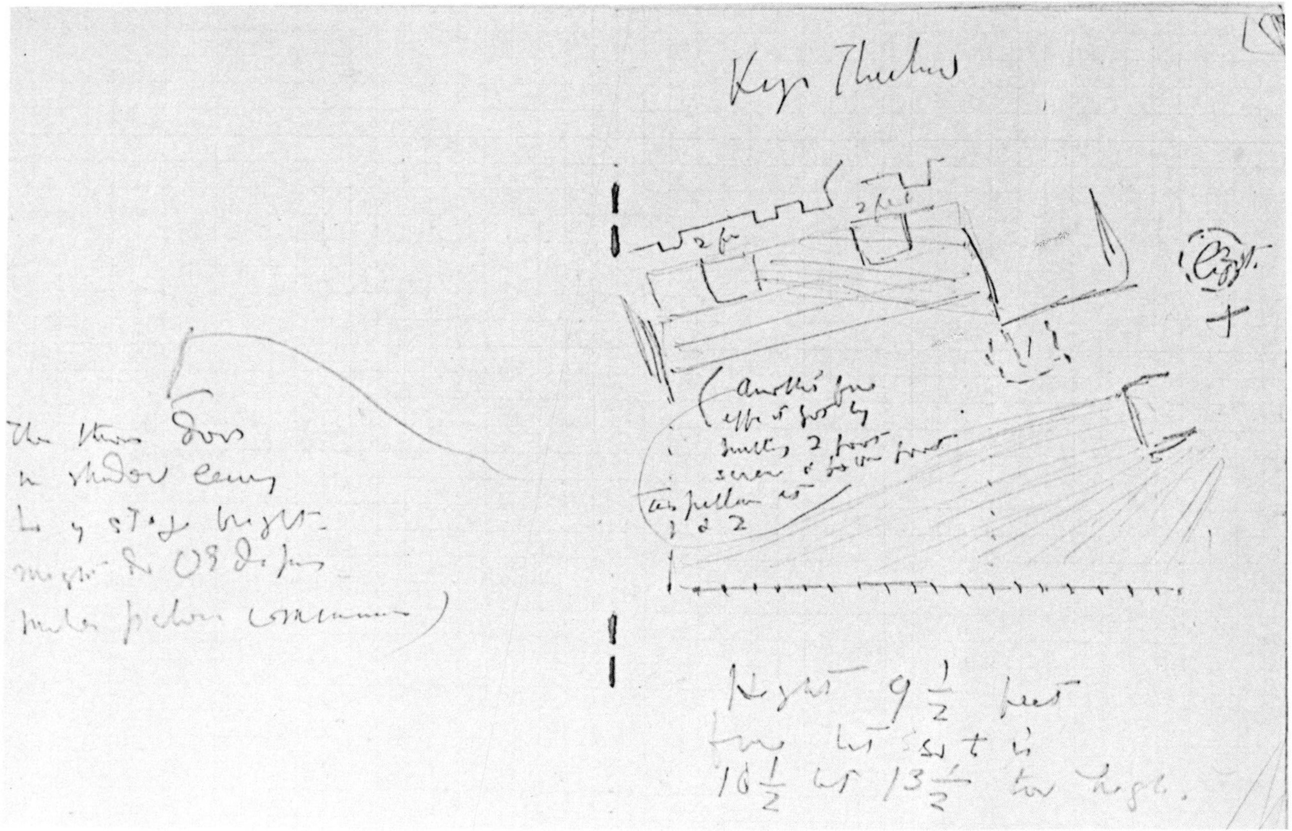

PLATE 6: Sketch by W. B. Yeats for a revival of *The King's Threshold* utilizing the Craig screens.

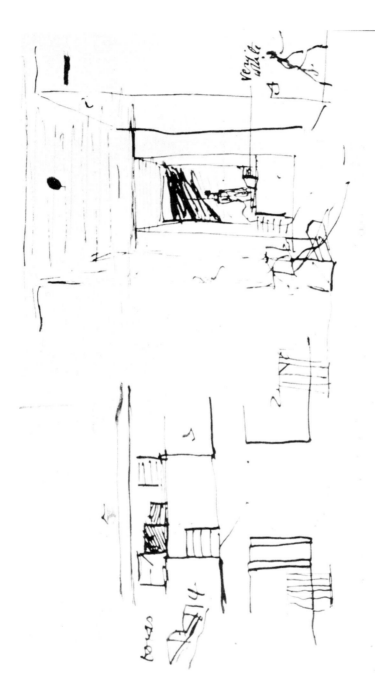

PLATE 7: Sketch of W. B. Yeats for projected revival of *On Baile's Strand*.

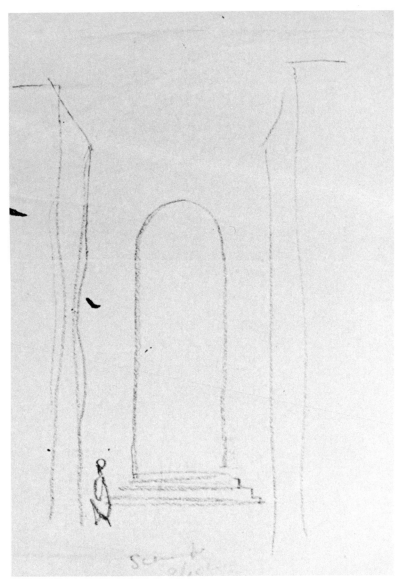

PLATE 8: (*above*) Sketch of W. B. Yeats for arch employed in the revised version of *The Countess Cathleen*, 14 December 1911.

PLATE 9: (*opposite*) Extract from an undated letter from Gordon Craig to W. B. Yeats.

The size of the paper should be according to the size of those screens —

You will not need very large mosaics —

Put 3 inches square or will not be too large.

but only actual experience will tell you this. Mainly let your darker tones fall about the base of the screen & reserve from the top which like the ceiling should be generally pure cream.

I can no more

The king, the king's to blame —

EVC.

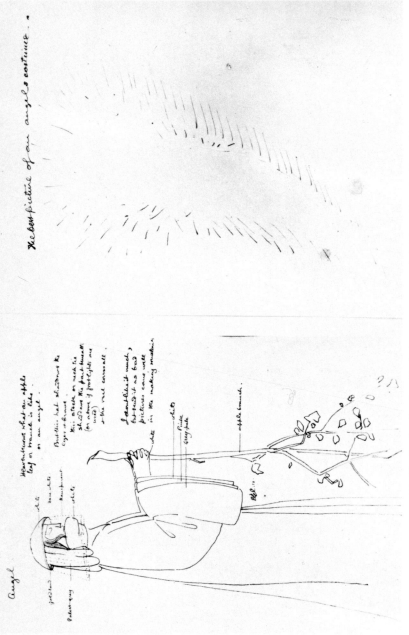

PLATE 10: Design by Gordon Craig for the costume of the Angel in *The Hour-Glass*.

PLATE 11: Photograph of the Craig screens in operation at the Abbey Theatre.

PLATE 12: (*above*) The old Newcastle Empire Music Hall.

PLATE 13: (*below*) Gordon Craig's first drawing for *Scene*, 1906.

PLATE 14: (*opposite*) A moment of arrested motion in Gordon Craig's conception of *Scene*.

PLATE 15: (*above*) Gordon Craig working with his model stage in England, 1910.

PLATE 16: (*below*) Mask of the Blind Man for *On Baile's Strand*, 1911, by Gordon Craig.

PLATE 17: Costume of the Fool for *The Hour-Glass*, 1911, by Gordon Craig.

PLATE 18: Photograph of a dinner given by the Abbey Theatre Company to honour Yeats on his reception of the Nobel Prize, 1922. Head table (*from left to right*): Michael Dolan, Mrs. John Larchet, obscured figure, Mrs. Ernest Blythe, W. B. Yeats, Mrs. Yeats, Ernest Blythe, Maureen Delaney, Dr. John F. Larchet. Left-hand side table (*from left to right*): Johnny Perrin, Ria Mooney, Sean O'Casey, Barry Fitzgerald, Arthur Shields, obscured lady, Gabriel Fallon. Centre side table: Lennox Robinson (*standing*). Arthur Shields, obscured lady, Gabriel Fallon. Centre side table: Lennox Robinson (*standing*). Right-hand side table (*left to right*): Sean Barlow, unknown lady, Dossie Wright, Mrs. Arthur Shields.

form the Abbey, but before we see how it affected Yeats's revision and subsequent work, we need to recall both what Craig intended and what he invented as a practical solution.

Early in 1907, Craig completed the design for his ideal "Scene," as he called it. He wanted "a *'scene'* so mobile, which (within rules) might move in all directions—tempos—in all things under the control of the one who could dream how to move its parts to produce *'movements.'* "³² He designed a "pliable floor" divided into a grid of squares, with cubes rising from each square. There would also be "a roof composed of the same shapes as the floor—suspended cubes, each cube exactly covering (and meeting when lowered) each square on the floor."³³ By means of a remote-control instrument, he would control the lighting and movement of these cubes, composing performances of movement. To illustrate such a performance, he made a series of wood engravings [pls. 13 and 14] showing moments of "arrested motion" during a performance of the Scene.³⁴ After he had designed this ideal scene, he began experimenting in his Florence theatre with a more practical solution for the small theatres not equipped with an hydraulic system. For these theatres, he invented hinged screens which could be folded to form his cubes or expanded into larger shapes. The screens could even be moved about very slowly during a performance of a play.³⁵ He built a model [pl. 15] in order to practise with the lighting and screens.

It was a sketch of this model which reanimated Yeats's interest

32. Craig's note on the end-paper of his famous volume of Serlio. Edward Craig, *Gordon Craig*, p. 235.
33. *Ibid.*
34. This series of wood engravings was not published until 1923 in a volume entitled *Scene*.
35. Craig believed that the Abbey Theatre never understood the principle behind his screens; "hovering, hiding, advancing, retreating," they were to create an impression of timelessness and motion. Craig's letter to Ann Saddlemyer, 27 February 1960, quoted in " 'The Heroic Discipline of the Looking-Glass': W. B. Yeats's Search for Dramatic Design," *The World of W. B. Yeats* (Victoria 1965), p. 96. Craig was also disappointed that Stanislavski chose to keep the screens stationary during the 1911 production of *Hamlet* because several members of the cast and stage crew had been injured by a screen falling over during rehearsal. Edward Craig, *Gordon Craig*, p. 258. Craig's scenery was not often used in these early years because of difficulties he created himself. He took out a patent for the screens, and insisted on giving permission and supervising any productions which used them.

in their early plans for productions. In London during January 1910, Craig dined with Yeats, sketching and explaining his invention. The following day Yeats wrote to Lady Gregory, "I am to see his model. . . . I think I shall, if it seems right, order one for us. . . ."[36] Yeats saw that the invention would radically alter the problems of dramatic construction posed by the Abbey stage. "I now think," the letter continues, ". . . that a certain modification will give us an entirely adequate open air scene. That we shall have a means of staging everything that is not naturalistic, and that out of his invention may grow a completely new method even for our naturalistic plays. I think we could get rid of side scenes even for naturalistic plays."[37] Craig, anxious that his invention be used professionally, was a stern bargainer. Yeats was discouraged from using the scenery for a proposed production of *Oedipus Rex*: "he wants us to play about with his model first and master its effects."[38] But even the firmest part of the bargain was no obstacle for Yeats: "If we accept the invention I must agree, he says, to use it for all my poetical work in the future. I would gladly agree."[39]

And so Craig's screens were adopted by the Abbey Theatre. The next few seasons were filled with experiment and revision, until the war drove Yeats's players into the music halls to make a living.[40] In the meantime, Yeats had committed not only the Abbey to Craig's theatre. On 24 November 1910, he wrote to his father, "I shall get all my plays into the Craig scene. . . ."[41]

---

36. *Letters*, p. 546. Yeats referred to Craig's invention as "his 'place' " and the conversation was remembered by Craig who recalled in *Scene* that a friend had called his model "a nice place," a better name than "scene." *Scene*, p. 1.

37. *Ibid.*   38. *Ibid.*   39. *Ibid.*

40. The screens were still at the Abbey Theatre in the late forties, when Eric Bentley discovered them in the storeroom. Bentley, *In Search of Theatre* (London 1954), p. 228.

41. *Letters*, p. 555. The Abbey architect and constant playgoer, Joseph Holloway, took quite a different view of the new scenery. After a visit in November 1910, he wrote "I called in at the Abbey and saw the stagehands setting Gordon Craig's new idea of scenery—a series of square box-like pillars, saffronhued, with saffron background, wings, sky pieces and everything. The entire setting struck me as like peas, only on a big scale, of the blocks I as a child built houses of. As Yeats never played with blocks in his youth, Gordon Craig's childish ideas give him keen pleasure now." Quoted in Liam Miller, "W. B. Yeats and Stage Design at the Abbey Theatre," *Malahat Review* 16, pp. 59–60.

The plays Yeats first put into Craig's scenery were not new ones. That work came later. Instead he took three old plays, *The Land of Heart's Desire, The Countess Cathleen, The Hour-Glass*, and produced them in the new scenery (1911) before rewriting them. The new versions were then produced the following year.[42] We can only guess at the reasons why Yeats selected these plays. *The Land of Heart's Desire* had long been the most popular of his plays for amateur groups, and he may have wished to bring it closer to contemporary stage techniques.[43] *The Countess Cathleen*, perhaps his favourite play, and *The Hour-Glass* were both plays which he and Craig had once planned to produce. Possibly Yeats wanted to rework these three plays because of his current studies. "I have been lecturing on the Other World," he wrote to his father in 1912, "and am now writing the lecture as an introduction to Lady Gregory's big book of Fairy Belief. I think I have made the first philosophic generalization that has been made from the facts of spiritism and the facts of folk-lore in combination."[44] As Richard Ellmann notes, Yeats considered *The Land of Heart's Desire* and *The Countess Cathleen* as miracle plays "by which he meant plays not necessarily Christian but manifesting in one way or another the existence of an invisible world."[45] *The Hour-Glass*—originally called a morality play—was in Yeats's words "a parable of the conscious and the subconscious life."[46] Yeats made *The Hour-Glass* into one of the best of his early one-act plays, and it deserves close consideration. But we should first look briefly, in the other two plays, at the new

42. The plays were first revived in 1911 (*The Hour-Glass* in January, *The Land of Heart's Desire* in February, *The Countess Cathleen* in December). After revisions and productions during the winter, each was restaged in the 1912 versions (*The Land of Heart's Desire* in February 1912, *The Countess Cathleen* in September, *The Hour-Glass* in November).
43. Yeats wrote in June 1912, "During the last year I have spent much time altering 'The Countess Cathleen' and 'The Land of Heart's Desire' that they might be a part of the repertory of the Abbey Theatre. I had written them before I had any practical experience. . . ." *Variorum Plays*, p. 1291.
44. *Letters*, pp. 567–68.
45. *Yeats: The Man and the Masks* (London 1949), p. 131. The point was made by Yeats himself when he chose to include the two plays with his four dance plays in *Plays and Controversies* (London 1923).
46. The play was originally entitled *The Hour-Glass: A Morality*. Yeats's comment on the play as a parable is quoted in George Brandon Saul, *Prolegomena to the Study of Yeats's Plays* (Philadelphia and London 1958), p. 63.

use of stage space and language which anticipated the changes in *The Hour-Glass*.

The Land of Heart's Desire was the least revised of the plays. Though Yeats was now much more skilled in dialogue construction, the characters remain the embodiment of lyric voices in the early poems, especially "The Stolen Child," "The Ballad of Father Hart," and "The Song of the Old Mother."[47] This little play depicts the choice between the visible and invisible worlds, the daily round of Christian duties or the life of the Faery. The young wife Mary chooses the Faery way, against the persuasions of her husband's parents and a superstitious well-meaning priest. Her dreamy husband, "too full of drowsy love," sighs that he cannot give her both choices:

> Would that the world were mine to give it you,
> And not its quiet hearths alone, but even
> All that bewilderment of light and freedom,
> If you would have it. (62)[48]

The 1912 revision embodies this choice—between Mary's book or the mother's hearth, the world of poetry and the Faery or the weariness of the "four tongues"—in the spaces within the stage set.

The original stage directions called for a kitchen room, with everyone except the Faery child on stage the entire time. All argument about the two choices was in the dialogue. But in the new version, Yeats set the play in the kind of scenery he used for *Deirdre*: a room opening onto trees and beyond, using Craig's lighting, to a "vague, mysterious world."[49] This new stage space gives greater coherence to metaphors in the dialogue. Take, for instance, the love scene between Mary and Shawn which, like the chess scene in *Deirdre*, combines the words with the stage set. In the new scenery, the hearth and family are to the right, Mary's bench

47. In 1904, Yeats complained that this play shared with the early lyrics "an exaggeration of sentiment and sentimental beauty." *Letters*, p. 434. Peter Ure suggests that the play is dependent upon the early poetry, *Yeats the Playwright* (London 1963), p. 4.

48. Quotations from the plays are taken from *The Collected Plays* (London 1952), the page numbers given in parenthesis.

49. Yeats had also used this kind of stage space in earlier Abbey productions of *The Golden Helmet* (1908) and *The Green Helmet* (1910). According to William Fay, Craig's new method of lighting and staging was first tried at the Abbey for its opening play, *On Baile's Strand* (also set in a room with a view beyond).

and book of poetry to the left, and beyond, the mysterious wood with its silver light. These new spaces help to create poetry which, though still slight, is what Yeats called a poetry growing logically from the action.

> MARY: O, you are the great door-post of this house,
>   And I the branch of blessed quicken wood,
>   And if I could I'd hang upon the post
>   Till I had brought good luck into the house. (61–62)

Mary's attentions are fixed on the faery world outside, yet she can still imagine a sort of domesticity. Her speech has more relation to her stage space than the original lines,

> O, you are the great door-post of this house,
> And I the red nasturtium climbing up.[50]

Yeats's revisions create a language which not only acts with the stage space, but grows from movement. Mary's talk of "blessed quicken wood" recalls her previous action, when she placed a bough of quicken wood upon the door post to keep out the Faeries. In the original version, she had strewn primroses before the door. Now, the branch is quickly removed by a Faery Child from the "vague, mysterious world." By using the set together with the words and actions of the players, Yeats has constructed the whole of Mary's choice. In this way, her final words to the Faery Child—"I will go with you"—conclude an action which began in the stage movement.

Yeats's revision of *The Countess Cathleen* was more extensive than that of *The Land of Heart's Desire*. With a much different stage setting, he staged it as it had first appeared—as a series of pictures. Before its first complete production in May 1899, the play had been performed as a sequence of "living pictures," each a different episode in the play.[51] But these *tableaux vivants* and the following production were a disappointment, for Yeats had not yet learned how to make a theatre with "scenery and costumes which will draw little attention to themselves and cost little money."[52] That disappointment, he

50. *Variorum Plays*, p. 192.
51. The *tableaux vivants* were staged in January 1899, as part of the publicity for the play. *Letters*, p. 306n.
52. *Ibid.*, p. 308. Yeats's letter was part of the debate in the *Daily Chronicle*, January 1899, between William Archer, who suggested that the play be staged in an expensive, elaborate set, and George Moore, who hoped it would be staged with neither scenery nor costumes.

recalled after revising the play for Craig's scenery, had led him to another kind of drama: "It was, indeed, the first performance of 'The Countess Cathleen,' when our stage-pictures were made out of poor conventional scenery and hired costumes, that set me writing plays where all would depend upon the player."[53]

Yeats entirely reworked Scene II of *The Countess Cathleen*, the scene of Cathleen's choice, from which the rest of the action develops. As in *The Land of Heart's Desire*, Yeats reconstructed this choice so that language and movement are complementary. In the earlier version, this scene is set in the great hall of Cathleen's home, where she returns for refuge against the famine. The backcloth is a tapestry "representing the loves and wars and huntings of the Fenian and Red Branch warriors."[54] The tapestry is a simple kind of didactic theatre. Its idealized traditional figures dominate the entire scene. Oona, the foster mother, uses the tapestry to comfort Cathleen, suggesting that she

> . . . make a soft cradle of old tales,
> And songs, and music . . .[55]

The world of legend can suffice as a refuge. At the end of the scene, though, Cathleen abandons that refuge and decides to give her own riches to save the peasants, but the tapestry belittles that choice. When Yeats wrote about the two opposite kinds of poetry—the creation of pictures and the imagination of personality—he wrote that "pictures make us sorrowful. We share the poet's separation from what he describes. It is life in the mirror. . . ."[56] For all her choosing, Cathleen in the early version is sorrowful. The tapestry

53. *Variorum Plays*, p. 1291.
54. M. J. Sidnell discusses early changes in the tapestry from "the old heroes" to the appearance of "Oisin and Niamh." In interpreting these changes as parallels to the changing situation between Yeats and Maud Gonne, he is one of the latest critics in the tradition of biographical interpretation of Yeats's works. "Yeats's First Work for the Stage: The Earliest Versions of 'The Countess Cathleen,' " in *W. B. Yeats: Centenary Essays on the Art of W. B. Yeats*, ed. D. E. S. Maxwell and S. B. Bushrui (Ibadan 1965), pp. 182–3. Scenes I and II were rewritten for the 1912 edition. Yeats was reworking the 1895 version, a revision of which had been published up to 1908. Yeats found the story for this play in a collection of Irish folklore. He considered it to be the Irish equivalent of the Greek parable of Alcestis. *Variorum Plays*, p. 170.
55. *Variorum Plays*, p. 53.
56. *Explorations*, p. 163.

remains a reminder not of what she has chosen, but of what she has deserted.

There is no tapestry in the 1912 version. The second scene is now set in a "wood with perhaps distant view of turreted house at one side, but all in flat colour, without light and shade and against a diapered or gold background." The poet and lover Aleel has been added, and together with the foster-mother he represents retreat— Oona offers comforts of the hearth, Aleel, the refuge of legend:

> I thought to have kept her from remembering
> The evil of the times for full ten minutes. ... (19)

The three characters now move within a space, no longer dominated by the tapestry picture, which takes its meaning from their speech and movement. Cathleen enters:

> Surely this leafy corner, where one smells
> The wild bee's honey, has a story too? (17)

Oona tries to catch her attention by pointing out the house, the end of her journey, but Cathleen's thoughts are with Aleel. His words create the first meaning of the space.

>   A man, they say,
> Loved Maeve the Queen of all the invisible host,
> And died of his love nine centuries ago.
> And now, when the moon's riding at the full,
> She leaves her dancers lonely and lies there
> Upon that level place, and for three days
> Stretches and sighs and wets her long pale cheeks. (17)

Cathleen and Aleel take up the story of the two legendary lovers, but Oona's insistence—"There is your own house, lady"—ends the tale. But it is not simply the telling that is interrupted, as though Aleel were reciting an old tale, just as Oona had once pointed to the figures on the tapestry. Cathleen and Aleel had discovered in the story a situation similar to their own. They had spoken to each other through the tale: might the distracted Cathleen, like Queen Maeve, forget her lover:

> But there is nothing that will stop in their heads,
> They've such poor memories, though they weep for it.
> O yes, they weep; that's when the moon is full. (18)

Aleel is angry at Oona's interruption, for the tale might have ended with a more hopeful image for the lovers:

A curse upon it for a meddlesome house!
Had it but stayed away I would have known
What Queen Maeve thinks on when the moon is pinched. . . . (18)

The two following episodes—the arrival of the Steward and then of Teig and Shemus—are greatly compressed from earlier versions. The new set does not require so much explanation for their appearance as the old interior room did. Just as the stage space had become a place where lovers could re-enact ancient legend, it could also become the Steward's approach to the house or, for Teig and Shemus, part of the neighbourhood path. By the end of the scene, the dialogue has given yet another meaning to the stage space. Cathleen makes her choice. No longer is she searching for a private refuge, a house to keep out the troubles:

> Come, follow me, for the earth burns my feet
> Till I have changed my house to such a refuge
> That the old and ailing, and all weak of heart,
> May escape from beak and claw; all, all, shall come
> Till the walls burst and the roof fall on us.
> From this day out I have nothing of my own. (24)

When Yeats finished the 1912 version of *The Land of Heart's Desire* and *The Countess Cathleen*, he explained what had guided his revision: ". . . in their new shape—and each play has been twice played during the winter—they have given me some pleasure, and are, I think, easier to play effectively than my later plays, depending less upon the players and more upon the producer, both having been imagined more for variety of stage-pictures than variety of mood in the player."[57] *The Countess Cathleen* remains, as Professor Ure notes, a construction "devised episode by episode." Yeats's changes in the play and the threading of Aleel's story through the original plot, explain much of its episodic nature. It may also be true that the play's early staging, even the sequence of "living pictures," held the changing plot within a sequence of episodes. In Yeats's early Abbey work—*The King's Threshold*, *Deirdre*, and *The Shadowy Waters*—Professor Ure sees a drama of single episode which Yeats would develop in his later plays.[58] He suggests that ". . . one method

---

57. *Variorum Plays*, p. 1291.
58. *Yeats the Playwright*, pp. 29–30. Frank O'Connor thought Yeats an "absolute master" of the one-act miracle play form, though he could not advise on longer constructions done at the Abbey Theatre, for instance,

of distinguishing his more successful plays from the others is to observe that in them the story is *about* the place, or, to put it another way, that the characters have come to just this place, and no other anywhere in the world, so that this story may happen."[59] The single episode of *The Hour-Glass*, set within Gordon Craig's new scenery, was the most important of Yeats's 1912 revisions.

The new version of *The Hour-Glass* reflects most clearly Yeats's new style of theatre in which the dialogue is enacted in performance. The episode for the play was based on Lady Wilde's story "The Priest's Soul," and Yeats's revisions give it as varied a history as *The Countess Cathleen*.[60] From the time he first read Craig the scenario in 1902, until the play was produced in Craig's scenery and published the following year in *The Mask*, *The Hour-Glass* had changed not only from one style of theatre to another, but from one kind of language to another. There is the early verse, in the Angel's speech:

> You have to die because no soul has passed
> The heavenly threshold since you have opened school,
> But grass grows there, and rust upon the hinge;
> And they are lonely that must keep the watch.[61] (308)

Synge's *Playboy of the Western World*, which, according to O'Connor, ought to have revealed before Christy's bragging scene that his father was not really dead. *The Backward Look: A Survey of Irish Literature* (London 1967), p. 170.

59. "The Plays," in *An Honoured Guest*, ed. Denis Donoghue and J. R. Mulryne (New York 1966), p. 153.

60. Lady Wilde's story, from her *Ancient Legends of Ireland* (1887), is reprinted in *Variorum Plays*, pp. 640–44. The original prose version of Yeats's play, produced at the Abbey in 1903, was reprinted with minor revisions until 1911. The final prose version of 1922 has the new ending developed in the verse versions. After producing the 1911 prose version with Craig's scenery, Yeats made the first verse version for a production the following year (November 1912) with that scenery. This version, printed in 1913 in Craig's theatre journal, *The Mask*, was followed by another verse revision with a new ending (1914). The final verse version (1922) includes the "medieval Latin" passages. S. B. Bushrui discusses some aspects of these revisions in " 'The Hour-Glass': Yeats's Revisions, 1903–1922," in *Centenary Essays*, pp. 189–216.

61. T. R. Henn calls these changes in language the "strata on a cliff face." *The Lonely Tower* (London 1965), p. 281. I use Dr. Henn's two examples of verse.

Here is the Pre-Raphaelite imagery, the poetry of picture-making, which Yeats had come to see as a weakness in his verse. This imagery works in the same way as the prose in the original version. In Yeats's words, as we saw before, "We share the poet's separation from what he describes." Translated into stage movement, this is Oona pointing to the tapestry of heroes. The early prose passages work in the same way. There is no movement of thought enacted in the words. The prose, with its even rhythms and repetitive logic, merely refers:

> WISE MAN: Though they call him Teigue the Fool, he is not more foolish than everybody used to be, with their dreams and their preachings and their three worlds; but I have overthrown their three worlds with the seven sciences. [He touches the books with his hand.] With Philosophy that was made from the lonely star, I have taught them to forget Theology; with Architecture, I have hidden the ramparts of their cloudy Heaven; with Music . . .[62]

"With Music, . . . with Arithmetic . . . Rhetoric and Dialectic . . .": neither the imagery nor the rhythm of such language can embody a moment of changing perception, of dramatic movement.

Despite the early prose, there is the kind of verse which, in Dr. Henn's words, anticipates "the thought of the 'irrational force' of 'The Second Coming,' the dance of agony and frenzy that is the background to 'Byzantium.' "[63] This is imagery of perception:

> Reason is growing dim;
> A moment more, and Frenzy will beat his drum
> And laugh aloud and scream;
> And I must dance in the dream.
> No, no, but it is like a hawk, a hawk of the air,
> It has swooped down—and this swoop makes the third—
> And what can I, but tremble like a bird? (303)

The rhythm is uneven, creating the tight, labouring breath of fear. The images are spatial: "dance," "swoop," "tremble." The language is spatial in another sense too. As Yeats wrote in "Discoveries," the greatest art expresses moods which are a "conflagration of all the energies of active life," the energy of "the whole man."[64] In dramatic art, this is the energy displayed in an actor's voice and movement.

62. *Variorum Plays*, pp. 592, 594.
63. Henn, *The Lonely Tower*, p. 281. Yeats first used this imagery of sudden violent action in *The Unicorn from the Stars*, *Where There is Nothing*, and *The King's Threshold*.
64. *Essays and Introductions*, pp. 277, 279.

When Yeats revised *The Hour-Glass*, he matched his verse to the kind of movement made possible by a new stage space.

Gordon Craig's stage setting was a catalyst for the new revision. When it was first produced in November 1912, Yeats praised Craig's designs. They "helped me wonderfully, and I think I have banished platitude from the 'Hour-Glass.' . . ."[65] Craig's scenery, though designed for the Abbey's proscenium stage, differed radically from the symmetrical set of the original production in 1903. That first set was the Wise Man's study—a room with back and side doors, and adorned with an astronomical globe, a map, and musical instruments. "The master's desk," Yeats was advised, "is to stand bang in the centre of the stage but near the back wall, leaving only room for his stool behind it."[66] Such emphasis on the Wise Man's learning, though, had the same effect as the overpowering tapestry in *The Countess Cathleen*. Yeats later regretted this constant visual focus: "I found that the brown back of a chair during the performance of *The Hour-Glass* annoyed me beyond words."[67]

In Craig's new design [pl. 3], the Wise Man's study is only part of the set. The desk, now in profile, is in an alcove at the right front corner, in shadow. From the study, a corridor of screens curves round to the left, disappearing back centre stage into light. This arrangement suggests that the Wise Man's place is at one point of a circular pathway, that his domain of learning is at the dark end of a path moving towards light. The set anticipates the circling, gyring, and lunar phases of Yeats's later imagery, the kind of movement Yeats already considered symbolic: "Motions are also symbolic. . . . Going and returning are the typical eternal motions, they characterize the visionary forms of eternal life. They belong to *up and down*, to *in and out*."[68]

65. From an interview given to "Hearth and Home" by Yeats, November 1912, quoted by Craig in *The Mask*, VII (1914), p. 141.
66. Ursula Bridge, ed., *W. B. Yeats and T. Sturge Moore: Their Correspondence 1901–1937* (London 1953), p. 5.
67. *Ibid.*, p. 5. By this time Yeats was experimenting with an asymmetrical set for the 1905 production of *The Shadowy Waters*.
68. From the Ellis-Yeats edition of Blake, quoted in Edward Engelberg, *The Vast Design* (Toronto 1964), p. 3. Craig too could talk of movement as if it were symbolic. He wanted the human body to express eternal gestures in movement: ". . . the movement of two and four which is the square, the movement of one and three which is the circle. There is ever that which is masculine in the square and ever that which is feminine in the circle." *On the Art of the Theatre* (London 1957), p. 52.

In addition to a stage set composed of opposites—light, shadow, circle, square—Craig helped shape another pair of opposites in *The Hour-Glass*. Yeats used Craig's mask designs to alter the relationship of the Fool and the Wise Man. During rehearsal for the revival production in January 1911, Yeats wrote to Lady Gregory that he was "very much excited by the thought of putting the fool into a mask and rather amused at the idea of an angel in a golden domino. . . . Craig evidently wants to keep what is superhuman from being inhuman."[69] For several years, Craig had included in his theatre journal, *The Mask*, many drawings and articles on the art of the mask. In Craig's words, masks were "the only right medium of portraying the expressions of the soul as shown through the expressions of the face."[70]

> The advantage of a mask over a face is that it is always repeating unerringly the poetic fancy . . . . Durability was the dominant idea in Egyptian art. The theatre must learn that lesson. . . . Let us again cover the actor's face with a mask in order that his expression—the visualized expression of the Poetic spirit—shall be everlasting.[71]

Yeats hoped the Abbey would be "the first modern theatre to use the mask."[72] He saw in Craig's "visualized Poetic spirit" a way of altering not only *The Hour-Glass*: "If the masks work right I would put the fool and the blind man in *Baile's Strand* into masks."[73] After the 1911 revival he began revising both plays. "If you will read my play *Baile's Strand* in the book I send you," he wrote to Craig, "I'd like to know if you think that the fool and the blind man ought to wear a mask."[74] A month later Craig sent him the designs [pl. 16].

The coincidence of revising and redesigning both plays left its

69. *Letters*, p. 554.
70. "The Artists of the Theatre of the Future" (1907) reprinted in *On the Art of the Theatre*, p. 13. Craig was comparing acting styles: "I should say that the face of Irving was the connecting link between that spasmodic and ridiculous expression of the human face as used by the theatres of the last few centuries, and the masks which will be used in place of the human face in the near future." (pp. 12–13)
71. Quoted in Leeper, *Edward Gordon Craig*, p. 46.
72. *Letters*, p. 554.
73. *Ibid.*
74. Yeats to Craig, 3 November 1911, quoted in the exhibition catalogue "Gordon Craig et la Renouvellement du Théâtre" (Paris, Bibliothèque Nationale 1962), p. 61.

mark on *The Hour-Glass*. In *On Baile's Strand*, Yeats had made the conflict between Cuchulain and Conchubar the same as the one between the Fool and the Blind Man. As he explained, Cuchulain "is the fool—wandering, passive, houseless and almost loveless. Concobhar is reason that is blind because it can only reason because it is cold. Are they not the cold moon and the hot sun?"[75] A similar pattern appears in the verse revision of *The Hour-Glass*. No longer does the Wise Man merely interview the Fool. Now the two characters act out complementary roles, one with words, one with movement. As the Fool remarks at the end, "You and I, we are the two fools, we know everything but we will not speak."

In the explanation of his verse revision, Yeats stressed the new importance of mask and movement. "An action on the stage," he noted in his preface to the version printed in *The Mask* (1913), "is so much stronger than a word that when the Wise Man abused himself before the Fool I was ashamed."[76] He had had special problems with the Wise Man, a kind of character passionate only in argument.[77] "Those learned men who are a terror to children and an ignominious sight in lovers' eyes, all those butts of a traditional humour where there is something of the wisdom of peasants, are mathematicians, theologians, lawyers, men of science of various kinds. They have followed some abstract reverie, which stirs the brain only. . . ."[78] Yeats's revisions of the dialogue were all made to emphasize the limits of the Wise Man's wisdom. In the 1922 verse version, the addition of "medieval Latin" passages isolated more clearly the mode of argument of the Wise Man and his pupils from the rest of the dialogue.[79] But the main revision of the Wise Man lies not in the dialogue alone, but in the relation between his words and the Fool's mimes. "I even doubt," Yeats wrote, "if any play had

75. *Letters*, p. 425.
76. *Variorum Plays*, pp. 646, 577.
77. In "Discoveries," Yeats called argument "almost the only kind of passion that displays itself in our daily life." *Essays and Introductions*, p. 275. Yeats's use of the morality form saved this character from the debates of a drawing room setting, but the difficulty is found in the source story itself. Lady Wilde wrote of the Wise Man that "one of his great triumphs was in argument." The Fool is Yeats's own addition to the story.
78. *Essays and Introductions*, p. 292.
79. Yeats explained that the Latin passages had been added to remove some repetitions in the verse. *Variorum Plays*, p. 646. These additions are usually dismissed as unnecessary and undramatic.

ever a great popularity that did not use, or seem to use, the bodily
energies of its principal actor to the full."[80] In *The Hour-Glass*, the
bodily energies are those of the Fool who mimes the Wise Man's
learning in such a way that the Wise Man's discoveries are presented
as much in movement as in dialogue.

The first of these changes occurs in the opening stage arrangement. No longer is the audience presented with the Wise Man alone.
Instead, his pupils appear before the curtain to choose a subject for
the day's lesson. This revision, in S. B. Bushrui's words, "allows us
to come to know the protagonist, at first, through the remarks and
comments made by his pupils. The confusion and doubt in which the
Pupils find themselves lead to the atmosphere of doubt and spiritual
frustration which has been the achievement of the Wise Man."[81] The
pupils' uncertainty is interrupted by the Fool:

> FOOL: Give me a penny.
> SECOND PUPIL: Let us choose a subject by chance. Here is his big
> book. Let us turn over the pages slowly. Let one of us put down
> his finger without looking. The passage his finger lights on will
> be the subject for the lesson.
> FOOL: Give me a penny. (300)

From his first entrance the Fool mimes the role of others on stage.
The pupils' choice, hardly a considered decision, is left to chance.
Their poking for snippets of a text differs little from collecting the
odd penny. This similarity is expressed in the Fool's mime which
ends the scene:

> FOURTH PUPIL: Down on your knees. Hunch up your back.
> Spread your arms out now, and look like a golden eagle in a
> church. Keep still, keep still.
> FOOL: Give me a penny. (300)

No supporting lectern, no open book, and as the Fool plays at hold-
ing up the book, the pupils play at choosing a lesson from it.

> FIRST PUPIL: There, I have chosen. Fool, keep still—and if what's
> wise is strange and sounds like nonsense, we've made a good
> choice. (300)

The curtain opens, revealing the Wise Man at his corner desk. A
pupil reads him the text:

80. *Essays and Introductions*, p. 266.
81. Bushrui, " 'The Hour-Glass': Yeats's Revisions," pp. 203–4.

'There are two living countries, one visible and one invisible, and when it is summer there, it is winter here, and when it is November with us, it is lambing-time there.' (301)

The Wise Man frantically begins the lesson, recognizing in that passage the same irrationality which had guided the pupils' choosing. That troublesome passage, one student tries to explain, was written by a beggar upon the walls of Babylon, Yeats's city of mathematical abstraction.[82] They ask their own beggar to suggest a meaning for the passage. The Fool does not answer in the Wise Man's terms:

> To be sure—everybody knows, everybody in the world knows, when it is spring with us, the trees are withering there, when it is summer with us, the snow is falling there, and have I not myself heard the lambs that are there all bleating on a cold November day—to be sure, does not everybody with an intellect know that? And maybe when it's night with us, it is day with them, for many a time I have seen the roads lighted before me.[83] (302)

The Fool is also "Teigue," the traditional name for a stage Irishman. In the original production, Yeats had followed that traditional type even in Teigue's costume. "Let the fool's wig," he had written to Frank Fay who was rehearsing the part, ". . . be red and matted."[84] The Fool and the Wise Man, then, are types of the Irishman and the Englishman. The Wise Man translates the Fool's foolishness into the language of an educated scholar—he speaks of human faculties, worldly kingdoms and spiritual kingdoms. But his pupils, not yet having mastered their lessons, change his terms back into the Fool's own imagery:

> If he [the beggar of Babylon] meant all that, I will take an oath that he was spindle-shanked, and cross-eyed, and had a lousy

82. Yeats's meaning for Babylon is discussed by Richard Ellmann: "Yeats gives Babylon the role of ushering in Christianity because the astronomers there, who plotted the stars, helped to reduce man's status in relation to the universe by promulgating the inhuman abstractions of science." *The Identity of Yeats* (London 1954), p. 262.
83. Yeats's early metaphor, the words used by the beggar, first appeared in Yeats's essay "The Queen and the Fool" (1901) in *The Celtic Twilight* (London 1902), p. 194.
84. *Letters*, p. 378. G. C. Duggan quotes Bourgeois's "John Millington Synge and the Irish Theatre" (1913) for his definition of the stage Irishman, always called Pat, Paddy, or Teague, with fiery red hair and a gift for blarney. *The Stage Irishman* (London 1937), pp. 288–9.

itching shoulder, and that his heart was crosser than his eyes, and that he wrote it out of malice.[85] (302)

The Wise Man's critical language soon gives way to the verse quoted earlier, to frantic rhythm and images of violent bodily movement.

> Reason is growing dim;
> A moment more and Frenzy will beat his drum
> And laugh aloud and scream;
> And I must dance in the dream. (303)

His words point beyond the character to the stage space. Reason grows dim; his study remains in shadow, while his pupils disappear down a corridor of light. For the moment, the Wise Man insists that "whole wisdom" is "to see rightly whatever the dream" because "everybody is a fool when he is asleep and dreaming." Yeats makes full use of the stage in this notion of seeing.

This is the classical sense of seeing, as in Sophocles' *Oedipus Rex* which Yeats had hoped to produce in 1910:[86] sight is blindness, insight is seeing into what has been invisible. Yeats joins this metaphor with his own imagery of sunlight and moonlight. Sleep, dreams, the subjective "lunar" insights at first appear suspect. "There's nothing," Wise Man declares, "but what men can see when they are awake." But he soon doubts whether his pupils really share his world of learning. They merely give him back his own words, just as he sees the Fool mime his speech:

> Well, there are your four pennies—Fool you are called,
> And all day long they cry, 'Come hither, Fool.'
> > [*The Fool goes close to him.*]
> Or else it's 'Fool, be gone.'
> > [*The Fool goes further off.*]
> Or, 'Fool, stand there.'
> > [*The Fool straightens himself up.*]

85. Yeats used this kind of imagery in *The King's Threshold*:

> SEANCHAN: *But why were you born crooked?*
> *What bad poet did your mothers listen to*
> *That you were born so crooked?* (133)

86. At this time, Yeats was preparing a version of *Oedipus Rex* for a proposed Abbey Theatre production. Mircea Eliade discusses the traditional metaphors of sight and blindness in *Myth and Reality*, trans. Willard R. Trask (New York 1963), pp. 114–38.

Or, 'Fool, go sit in the corner.'
                    [*The Fool sits in the corner.*]
                    And all the while
What were they all but fools before I came?
What are they now but mirrors that seem men
Because of my image? Fool, hold up your head.
                    [*The Fool does so.*] (307)

When Fool claims he has been followed by an angel, Wise Man
muses on such foolish tales of spirits who

> Would solidly out-stare
> The steadiest eyes with their unnatural eyes,
> Aye, on a man's own floor. (307)

An Angel enters,[87] and for a moment the stage is filled with three
kinds of seeing. The Angel, with "unnatural eyes" of Craig's mask,
is seen at once by the Fool. He had said that he could catch sight of
angels whenever he was so quiet "that there is not a thought in one's
head. . . ." Wise Man is still wrapped in his own thoughts,

> . . . haunted by the notion
> That there's a crisis of the spirit wherein
> We get new sight. . . . (308)

The Fool calls for quiet, and the Wise Man turns to see the Angel.

Yeats continued to revise the dialogue at this point to get the
words in line with the stage movement. The 1911 prose version contained these lines:

> WISE MAN: I have denied and taught the like to others.
>   Believing nothing but what sense has taught,
>   And the mind's abstract.
> ANGEL: It is too late for pardon.
> WISE MAN: Had I but seen your face as now I see it[88]

In the verse version printed in *Responsibilities* (1914), the emphasis

87. The Angel had long been a problem, though the shallow stage at the
   Abbey helped to prevent the mistake of his wearing a large pair of
   wings. In 1930, Yeats recalled that a French etching of an old, wingless,
   elongated angel armed like a knight had been his source for the angels
   in the early final scene of *The Countess Cathleen*. *Explorations*, pp. 305–
   06. Yeats wrote of Craig's idea for the angel, that "Craig evidently wants
   to keep what is superhuman from being inhuman." *Letters*, p. 554.
88. *Variorum Plays*, p. 601.

in these lines has been changed from recollection—"what sense had taught"—to the immediate act of seeing:

> WISE MAN: I have denied and taught the like to others.
> But how could I believe before my sight
> Had come to me?
> ANGEL: It is too late for pardon.
> WISE MAN: Had I but met your gaze as now I meet it. . . . (309)

Wise Man learns he is to die within the hour. Like those in Dante's *Inferno*, he will take on the shape of his learned critical language:

> Hell is the place of those who have denied;
> They find there what they planted and what dug,
> A Lake of Spaces, and a Wood of Nothing,
> And wander there and drift, and never cease
> Wailing for substance. (309)

Una Ellis-Fermor has described the Wise Man's development as a rejection of reason and renunciation of self in order to rediscover "the mood by which truth is perceived and the processes by which the knowledge of it could have grown. . . ."[89] Wise Man's discovery of these limits of his language is also a discovery of his resemblance to the Fool. The Angel's comments link the two characters. Wise Man can be spared, he explains, only if he can find a believer,

> One fish to lie and spawn among the stones
> Till the great Fisher's net is full again. . . . (310)

The Fool appears, with the long pair of shears [pl. 17] which Craig designed for him. Earlier, when the Wise Man asked about the shears, the Fool said,

> Every day men go out dressed in black and spread great black nets over the hills, great black nets.
> WISE MAN: A strange place to fish in.
> FOOL: They spread them out on the hills that they may catch the feet of the angels; but every morning, just before the dawn, I go out and cut the nets with the shears and the angels fly away.
> (305)

89. *The Irish Dramatic Movement* (London 1939), pp. 108–09. The author suggests that the play's kinship lies not with allegorical moralities of the middle ages, but with the modern symbolic morality plays, such as the final act of *Peer Gynt* and parts of *Everyman*.

Though Wise Man scoffs at the tale, he soon finds it a curious version of the effect of his own learning. The great Fisher's net, the Angel explains, has been empty since he opened school. In the 1911 prose version, Yeats made the connection between the Fool and the great Fisher explicit:

> Fisherman lets me sleep among the nets in his loft
> in the winter-time because he says I bring him luck[90]

In subsequent versions, "Fisherman" becomes "fishermen," perhaps because the new costume made such lines redundant.

This analogy—between the Wise Man emptying the Fisher's net and the Fool freeing angels from men's nets—works in several ways. The emptying of nets is similar to the Fool's mimes of the Wise Man's words as well as his mime of the pupils' lectern. Wisdom, in this familiar paradox, appears foolish. Yet the resemblance has another effect. The Fool's wisdom is wisdom of the body. He claims his presence has brought luck to fishermen, and he can see the Angel before the Wise Man does. In this way, what had been the Fool's nonsense—his story of the nets—is now the Wise Man's freedom. A story, an image, have shown him his preoccupations better than all his arguments.

To be saved, the Wise Man must find one believer, and once again the Fool mimes the action. Clutching his large money bag, the Fool refuses to admit any belief:

> I will not speak. I will not tell you what is in my mind. I will not
> tell you what is in my bag. You might steal away my thoughts.[91]
> (322)

In the prose version, a pupil had asked, "Teigue, will you give us your pennies if we teach you lessons?" Once again, Wise Man sees his own desire. Collecting words—and it is a confession of belief he needs, not just a believer—is like saving up pennies. Now he needs no words:

> The stream of the world has changed its course,
> And with the stream my thoughts have run

90. *Variorum Plays*, p. 584.
91. The Fool's money bag is similar to the Amadan's "shining vessel of some
    enchantment or wisdom or dream too powerful for mortal brains. . . ."
    "The Queen and the Fool," p. 192. The bag becomes the "pitchers" in the
    final lyric of *A Full Moon in March*.

Into some cloudy thunderous spring
That is its mountain source—
Aye, to some frenzy of the mind,
For all that we have done's undone,
Our speculation but as the wind. (323)

He bids the Fool be silent, and he dies.[92]

The final stage picture is part of Yeats's new dramatic style. He wanted to represent a kind of knowledge not depicted in the more popular problem play. "Wisdom and beauty and power may sometimes," he wrote, ". . . come to those who die every day they live, though their dying may not be like the dying Shakespeare spoke of."[93] Gordon Craig had dismissed realistic drama as "inhuman" and had written, in sympathy with Yeats, of a drama which could present that "mysterious, joyous, and superbly complete life which is called Death. . . ."[94] This is the kind of death presented at the close of *The Hour-Glass*. On stage there is an angel, a fool, and a dead man. "The self," Yeats believed, "which is the foundation of our knowledge, is broken in pieces by foolishness. . . ." Such foolishness, he suggested, "may be a kind of death."[95]

The Angel carries away the butterfly soul of the Wise Man, and the Fool closes the curtain, inviting the audience to watch him:

He is gone, he is gone, he is gone, but come in, everybody in the world, and look at me.
   I hear the wind a-blow,
   I hear the grass a-grow,
   And all that I know, I know.
But I will not speak, I will run away. [*He goes out.*][96] (324)

92. This episode was Yeats's revision of a part of the play he disliked: ". . . when the Wise Man abused himself before the Fool I was always ashamed. . . . Now I have made my philosopher accept God's will, whatever it is, and find his courage again. . . ." *Variorum Plays*, pp. 645–46.
93. "The Queen and the Fool," p. 193.
94. "The Actor and the Über-marionette" (1907) reprinted in *On the Art of the Theatre*, p. 74.
95. "The Queen and the Fool," p. 192.
96. Yeats recalled this scene in "Another Song of a Fool":

> *This great purple butterfly,*
> *In the prism of my hands,*
> *Has a learning in his eye*
> *Not a poor fool understands.*
>
> *Once he lived a schoolmaster*
> *With a stark, denying look;*

This use of lyric, similar to the use of the faery song which ends *The
Land of Heart's Desire*, is a technique Yeats will develop in his dance
plays. Here, the Fool—like the old hermit in "The Three Hermits"
—gives not an argument but a song for his thought. "I had not
learned what sweetness, what rhythmic movement," Yeats wrote in
Discoveries, "there is in those who have become the joy that is themselves."[97] In that poem, while two hermits argue, the third hermit

> Giddy with his hundredth year,
> Sang unnoticed like a bird.

When Yeats wrote the poem in 1913, he was staying with Ezra
Pound at Stone Cottage, Sussex. Their work on the Japanese plays,
which Pound was editing, is part of the story of Yeats's own dance
plays. But in the meantime, Yeats almost joined Craig's theatre
school in Florence as a literary adviser.[98] Craig discouraged him—
"You could learn nothing there. What you've learnt you've learnt
already"[99]—but in *The Mask* he acknowledged his collaboration

> *A string of scholars went in fear
> Of his great birch and his great book.*
>
> *Like the clangour of a bell,
> Sweet and harsh, harsh and sweet,
> That is how he learnt so well
> To take the roses for his meat.*

The Collected Poems (London 1965), pp. 191–92.
97. *Essays and Introductions*, p. 271.
98. *Letters*, p. 577. At the same time Yeats hoped to go to Florence to begin
a "big scheme of poetic drama," he was urging his publisher to bring out
an edition of his theatre criticism with drawings by Craig and Robert
Gregory: "Coming at this moment when people have in their memories
the Reinhardt productions, the scenery and costumes of the Russian
ballet, the Barker productions of Shakespeare—all examples of the new
decorative method—it would probably get considerable attention. It
would contain the only serious criticism of the new craft of the Theatre.
It is the exact moment for it." *Letters*, p. 579. Such a volume did not
appear until *Plays and Controversies* (1923) and then only with illustrations of the dance plays.
99. Quoted in Joseph Hone, *W. B. Yeats: 1865–1939* (London 1943), p. 252.
In 1912 a group had been formed which called themselves "The Society
of the Theatre," with such members as Yeats, Craig, Augustus John,
William Poel, J. Martin Harvey, Constantin Stanislavski, Tomasso
Salvini, Cecil Sharp, and Ezra Pound. A prospectus, possibly written by
Craig himself, announced that the Society

with Yeats: "I have myself acted as a most willing aid in the interpretation of the drama of Yeats and it has been one of the special
happinesses of my life to have been connected with his poetic dramas
in Dublin . . . but only as a servant . . . seeing his as a 'brother
art'. . . ."[100] Though Craig was more interested in a "mimo-drama"
of mime and movement, he admitted, in *Towards a New Theatre*
(1913), that "My friend W. B. Yeats says that the scene is by no
means disconnected with the art of poetry."[101] Yeats's next drama
was based on the Japanese Noh form, but his skill in fitting dialogue
to movement was a skill he had learned from Craig. As he wrote to
Craig in 1913, "Your work is always a great inspiration to me.
Indeed I cannot imagine myself writing any play for the stage now,
which I did not write for your screens."[102]

> *aims at creating a dramatic movement which shall appeal to the
> theatrical rather than to the literary aspects of drama. By
> "theatrical" is meant that form of stage production which makes
> an appeal to the senses through the imagination rather than to
> the intellect.*
>
> > *The Society has adopted the idea of Gordon Craig, and is
> formed to promote discussion of that idea, and to try to establish
> a School for the Art of the Theatre, with Gordon Craig as
> authoritative director.*

Allardyce Nicoll, *English Drama: 1900–1930* (Cambridge 1973), pp.
103–04.

100. "Is Poetic Drama Born Again?," *The Mask*, V (1912–13), p. 291. It is
interesting to note that this volume contains two articles by Jack B.
Yeats on how he produces his plays written for children, using a
miniature stage with standing figures similar to those Craig used.

101. *Towards a New Theatre*, p. 68.

102. 29 July 1913, Gordon Craig Collection, Bibliothèque de l'Arsenal,
Paris, quoted in Bablet, *Edward Gordon Craig*, p. 130. In 1913, Yeats
arranged the Dublin exhibition of Craig's theatre designs, including the
model for the famous 1911 production of *Hamlet* in Moscow. Miller,
"W. B. Yeats and Stage Design," p. 60.

Assimilation and Accomplishment: Nō Drama and An Unpublished Source for At the Hawk's Well

Richard Taylor

It has become almost a critical commonplace to refer to Yeats's assimilation of Nō technique, but the assertions are generally made on rather inadequate, and often false, information; indeed, with little real knowledge or understanding of classical Japanese drama itself, and with no attempt to ascertain the exact measure of that influence. Recently, however, some of those translations which were among Ernest Fenollosa's papers, but not included by Ezra Pound in *'Noh' or Accomplishment,* have become available, and it is now possible to compare all four of Yeats's dance plays with their Japanese models. I propose to compare *At the Hawk's Well* with its Japanese source, and as a preliminary to examine the nature of Nō drama and its transmission to the West.

The object of Nō is to suggest the truth of idealized action, and active participation through imagination is demanded of the audience. The play is always based on a familiar incident closely associated with a famous place, and it is performed by a single character with only the most essential dramatic foils. The action itself is kept at a distance by avoiding realistic imitation. The focus of interest is the quality of experience involved, not the actual event, and the central incident is presented through various levels of recollection, dream, and vision, as well as aesthetic stylization. The text is often more poetic than dramatic in its dependence on patterns of imagery and connotations of literary and historical allusion. Ultimately, the performance succeeds by virtue of its rhythm and form, not by the logic or interaction of events. One cannot emphasize enough that the drama of Nō is a function of the theatrical presentation, rather than of the dramatic quality of the poetic text. Nō is not a literary form; it only comes fully to life in performance, where the experience of the spectator is primarily visual and aural, a direct experience very like listening to music, and one which is altogether inimical to the intervention of intellectual analysis. Considering the limits of his familiarity with Nō, it is no wonder that Pound should have found the form slight, or intellectually inconsequential. A text, by itself, does not adequately reflect the inherent power and beauty of a given play, and one must understand something of choreographic effect and musical composition to appreciate its possibilities, especially in the case of a purely congratulatory piece.

On the Nō stage the projection of emotion depends largely on elements of mimetic dance, and every motion of the body is measured in time and space; none are imitations of normal human motions, but are rather expressive movements of abstract purity and restraint which approach the condition of dance, introduce elegant ritual action, and suggest universality. The actor does not attempt to imitate the actions of the fictional character, but rather stands outside the role, giving a stylized indication of those actions which is extremely precise. The discrepancy between the performance and the action imitated involves the spectator imaginatively in the completion of the ideal action suggested and in the recognition of its significance. Neither realistic projections of voice nor facial expression are permitted, and acting is purely a question of bodily movement within a fixed vocabulary of positions, as in classical ballet. Motion is inordinately slow and powerful in the performance of Nō, never so fluid as to become ordinary dancing. A basic posture or attitude of the body is common to all movement; the feet are aligned and the knees bent, while the trunk is carried rigidly, chest forward, chin back, and elbows held in with hands resting along the upper thigh, palm inward. In this position the body is perfectly balanced and easily controlled, giving the outward appearance of serenity and immobility while visibly containing the dynamic potential for movement. When "walking," stockinged heels never leave the polished floor, and in order to preserve balance, the foot is arched up from the heel at the end of each glide and placed flat on the stage again as the body weight is shifted for the next "step." The visual impact of this movement is amazing; since the bent knees take up the bobbing motion of normal walking and the mechanical motion of the legs is hidden in the voluminous, richly coloured robes, the solitary, heroic figure seems to glide and sweep over the stage, uncannily freed from resistance, deliberate and graceful as a gull over the sea. It is as though the physical laws of the temporal world are suspended, and the effect of a sudden gliding run against a seemingly endless, static posturing can be stunning.

The set dances are equally anti-realistic and either demonstrate a lyric intensity appropriate to the character and action when accompanied by flute and drums, or serve to emphasize the narration of an accompanying choral chant. Dances are carried out with great solemnity and economy of movement; the more spiritual the representation, the fewer and simpler the movements. The smallest gesture is enough to call up a force of feeling already present in the context. In a play of two acts, where the main character first appears in disguise, relates the familiar story, and later returns to reveal his true identity and relive the emotions of the original action, two or more dances are common. Each is exactly suited to the nature or quality of the character; the first is generally lyrical and subdued, a sympathetic re-creation of emotion rather than of the occasion itself, while the second is immediate and climactic, rather than the manifestation of an attitude toward the action. The two dances are usually contrasted in mood, as well as in tempo, and the first may be omitted altogether in order to focus attention on the inner state of the motionless character.

The rhythm of movement in basic patterns of mime, and especially when mime is raised to the level of dance, also forms a part of the elaborate musical structure which informs Nō drama. Music is the very soul of Nō and shapes the feelings of the audience to the point of imaginative acceptance and participation. Besides the musical accompaniment of drums and flute, which provides a background of rhythmic variety and simple melody, the vocal styles for chanting the lyric poems which, in turn, constitute the dramatic text, are the basis of the play's composition and structure. It is not so much that the form of a Nō play is effective because the formal entrance speech of the secondary character, or dramatic foil, is followed by a passage describing his journey or surroundings, but because a patterned, prosaic style of delivery is gradually developed into a vocal line of relaxed and lyric beauty, and so on. Each lyrical unit has a more or less fixed literary form, subject matter, and rhetorical ornamentation, and associated with each is a general voice style, ranging from pure speech, a figured or heightened recitation, through melodic patterns based on varied rhythms, which are usually chanted by the main and secondary characters, to those of fixed and emphatic rhythm which are generally employed by the chorus. The pitch range of the different styles may vary from "high" to "very low," depending on the effect desired and also shift from the "weak" tonal scale (which employs the full octave range of four main tones and numerous semi-tones) to the "strong" tonal scale (which depends for effect on accent, dynamic stress, tone colour, and a special technique of accomplishing upward movement by intense straining of the vocal chords rather than melodic inflection). In the "strong" system pitch intervals are inexact and unstable, and only two main tones are distinguished. Lyrical and emotional passages are normally sung in the "weak" style, while descriptive and powerful sections are intoned in the "strong" mode.

The composition of any given play is, of course, unique, and highly complex, but in general the development consists in an intensification of feeling with varied literary forms and vocal styles, leading to a sustained melodic section of complex rhythm, a scene of quiet grace and beauty in which the first dance or posturing is performed. The climax follows as a brief sequence dominated by an impelling, regular rhythm and ecstatic dance. Through the musical modification of the poetic forms, emotion is communicated as sense imagery, and the spectator experiences the integration of both dance and poem into a musical flow which is itself the movement of the play's basic emotion or mood.

The general arrangement of lyric passages within a text is fixed to a large extent by tradition and has a certain inherent power. Much of the structural detail, however, is varied within the flexible framework; the form impresses a definite rhythm on the unfolding of events and directs attention toward the metaphysical implications of the ritual. The opening section of a typical play is dominated by a slow and regular rhythm, solemn and powerful, which finds its most characteristic expression in the lyrical description of the secondary character, usually a priest, pilgrim, or court official on some sort of journey, who has arrived at a place associated with a famous legend or historical incident. The development section begins with the entrance of the protagonist, often disguised as a local person, who introduces a different pitch and faster tempo. His encounter with the deuteragonist brings about a recounting of the legend or incident and mutual reflection of the sorrow inherent in the human condition. Having induced the audience into a scene of imagined action, the deuteragonist retires to a seat at the front-right corner of the stage, while the protagonist recreates the significant mood of the original incident through mime and dance. If the principal character has been disguised up to this point, he exits and changes costume for the brief climax of the piece which is characterized by a fast and irregular rhythm. The second entrance of the protagonist reveals his identity and former condition, while the dance performed recreates the crisis or intense passion of the experience itself and provides a vivid contrast in nature and character with the earlier dance. Neither the use of transformations nor the "time machine" technique, however, is absolutely essential to the success of Nō. Rather it is the expressive method of representation through dance and mime, music and chant, which evokes an idealized reality. Instead of the direct representation of a dramatic action Nō recreates an intense emotion or psychological state through a single actor who creates a paradigmatic world of time, space, and energy.

The literary forms of traditional Nō structure are an exact counterpart of the musical composition. The formal announcement of subject, situation, or circumstance by the deuteragonist is followed by a statement of his name, social condition, and present intention. The travel-song which ends the introductory section normally describes the journey he is undertaking and introduces much seasonal imagery with its heavy burden of emotional overtones in Japanese culture. The formal entrance speech of the protagonist opens the development section and leads to a description of place or state of being, depending on the subject matter of the play. A dialogue between the two characters establishes the feelings which motivate them and leads through a relevant narration of past happenings to the protagonist's account of the significant action or experience. The crisis of the development section opens with a maxim or principle of religious doctrine relevant to the central experience, and in discoursing on its application to present circumstances the protagonist dances out the intensity of the emotion or experience which has been recreated in imagination. The climax of the play opens with a temporizing reintroduction by the deuteragonist, a waiting song for the appearance of the transformed protagonist which leads directly to a narration accompanying the climactic dance of the main character, who now relives the emotion or experience in his own person. A choral finale concludes the performance.

From such an outline it is obvious that in the western sense of the word, the ritual of Nō is not really dramatic. There is no conflict of any sort, and whatever progression does exist, is determined by associations of feeling and emotional states, not by cause and effect. Nō always opens in objective exposition; the deuteragonist announces himself as a real person, in a given time and place, with a particular intention that brings him to a famous spot. The audience accepts this reality imaginatively through the imagery of the poetic forms and proceeds to accept the reality of the protagonist on his first appearance, although in a majority of plays this figure is somewhat mysterious and incompletely explained. At this point the narration focuses attention on a spiritual quality or emotion connected with the famous incident that had occurred locally, and the shape-changing potential of the protagonist becomes evident in his discourse with the deuteragonist. The strangeness of replies made by the chief character and his unexplained presence lead the deuteragonist to voice the doubts of the audience as to the figure's true identity, and the very nature of Japanese language lends a further element of flexibility. With neither pronouns nor inflectional endings indicating persons, there is no distinction between a third person narration and one delivered in the first person. In talking about the emotion associated with the legendary incident, the narrator merges his identity with that of the original participant, and the progress of the literary form directs attention from the character experiencing the emotion to the quality of the emotion itself. As the deuteragonist withdraws from the action altogether, and seats himself in a reverie at one corner of the stage, the audience is left unconcerned by the fact that the dramatic reality of the action on-stage recedes into a shadowy region of dream or vision. As the protagonist focuses more intently on the central emotion and its religio-philosophic significance, the music builds towards a climax and stylized bodily movement extends itself into dance which projects abstract states of being as concrete images. The poetry of the text, as well as the extended patterns of images and allusions which abound in Nō, also tend to universalize the protagonist's emotion, and the end-result is a demonstration of depersonalized moral sensibility.

Richness of language and density of rhetorical texture often contrast with the general austerity of Nō and constitute a major technique for conveying maximum meaning economically. The honorific speech patterns of antique court usage are extensively employed, along with extra-grammatical syntax, liberal inversion, weighted vocabulary, and repetition of lines. Such an oblique and arbitrary language of formal elegance tends to render even a fairly simple thought rather complex and vague. With its involved flectional structure Japanese is capable of suggesting tone and mood with almost minute precision and of defining states of mind in close detail; poetic usage is given to indirectness, vague suggestion, free association of images, and symbolic expression. The very regular syllabary of Japanese provides a high incidence of spontaneous assonance and alliteration; sound images abound and are often used in constructional patterns. Conventionalized epithets introduce important lines or ideas, ennobling them with allusive associations, and frequent punning integrates disparate images. The limited number of sounds and combinations brings homonyms into prominence, and words of unrelated meaning may be associated through echoes of sound and endlessly played upon. The most characteristic poetic device of Nō is the "pivot word" which links together separate phrases of different lexical fields and is rightly construed on different levels in each. The first phrase often has no logical ending, the second, no beginning, and the effect is one of surrealistic dissolution and sudden transformation of thought. Complex patterns of images, "related words" run through entire passages and tend to unify them, as well as to raise the whole section to the level of symbol, and further reinforce the shifting, turning, thought-patterns of the protagonist, the floating, free-associations of his reverie. Liberal quotations from both profane and sacred literature, as well as cultural allusions of all sorts abound in Nō texts, extending the dimensions of reference which might otherwise limit the particular experience portrayed. As with the more plastic elements of performance and lyrical composition, the literary texture of a Nō play is specifically designed to suspend reason and carry the spectator on an aesthetically disciplined flow of pure feeling and connotation.

Unfortunately, it is almost impossible to preserve even a semblance of the surface texture of Nō in translation to so alien a language as English, and the Fenollosa-Pound versions are but a pale reflection of the originals.

Ernest Fenollosa (1853–1908) lived and worked in Japan from

1878 to 1890 and again from 1896 to 1901. His versions of Nō plays, probably worked out with the assistance of an interpreter, were left in an unfinished state at his death. The rough drafts amounted to little more than a literal line-for-line redaction into English.

Fenollosa had originally gone to Japan to take up an appointment as professor of political economy and philosophy at the newly founded University of Tokyo. Trained in philosophy and theology at Harvard, he had also studied painting and music. He was fascinated by Japanese thought and aesthetics. He embraced Buddhism and became expert in Oriental art. During his holidays he travelled widely to examine famous paintings and sculptures, piecing together something of the history and development of Chinese and Japanese art and collecting masterpieces at public sales. As a respected foreigner, Fenollosa was in an excellent position to lead the crusade against the craze for Western art-training, with its direct imitation of nature, and to impress upon the Japanese the superiority of their art in its representation of the ideal. As a leader of the national revival in the arts, Fenollosa left the University to become Commissioner of Fine Arts in the Imperial government in 1886. He resigned the post in 1890, returning to America to become Curator of Oriental Art at the Boston Museum of Fine Art, but a divorce scandal forced him to resign that post in 1895. A year later he returned to Japan, where he taught English at a Tokyo school and, continuing his studies of Japanese culture, made a special study of Nō drama.

In 1901 he returned again to America and lectured on Oriental aesthetics and culture with the same success he had met on earlier tours. His life was active and the only writing complete before his untimely death in 1908 was a draft of *Epochs of Chinese and Japanese Art*, later edited by his wife and published by William Heinemann (London 1912).

Fenollosa's study of Nō was made in fortunate circumstances: his understanding of the aesthetics of idealism and of the techniques of stylized construction in Chinese and Japanese art was thorough; he also trained as an amateur performer under the direction of one of the great masters of Nō, Umewaka Minoru, making invaluable notes on historical tradition and on the production methods of the professional performances which he attended. Fenollosa's research pre-dated the development of modern scholarship in Nō research, but in his day *Yōkyoku Tsukai, The Complete and Annotated Edition of Nō Plays*, edited by Ōwada Tateki (Tokyo 1892), was available, a reasonable text from which to work. The fact that many of the translations in *'Noh' or Accomplishment* are heavily-cut versions, sometimes so truncated as to be almost unintelligible, may be due to the fact that amateurs were often taught only the famous passages or "arias."

Ezra Pound, the literary executor chosen by Mrs. Fenollosa, had no first-hand knowledge of either Nō or of Japanese culture, and had no way of discriminating between fragmentary and complete texts. Knowing that music and dance accompanied the libretto in performance, he made too generous allowance for obvious incompleteness, nor was he in any position to compare the rough drafts with originals, nor to identify allusions and quotations, most of which were suppressed in the edited versions. More importantly, Pound had no conception of Nō construction, and his division of the texts into prose or verse is arbitrary and ill-conceived. Nevertheless, his poetic reconstructions of Fenollosa's drafts are effective: at times his imagery and poetic perception closely approximate to the intention of the Japanese, and his versions, with all their faults, are marked improvements on the more scholarly efforts of earlier translators. With the exception of *Kakitsubata*, where some extraneous material from Fenollosa's marginal commentary was incorporated, Pound appears to have been scrupulously faithful to Fenollosa's text, except for occasional attempts to heighten the language. His presentation of Fenollosa's notes on the Nō and his own observations show little grasp of the art form, and concentrate on the historical development of Nō rather than on critical analysis and description, though he makes several perceptive generalizations.

Mrs. Fenollosa and Pound had met in London several years earlier, either through William Heinemann or Laurence Binyon, the oriental art historian, and by the winter of 1913 the manuscripts had arrived from America. There can be no doubt that Yeats had access to all of the material then in Pound's possession, and there is much internal evidence of Yeats's voice in *'Noh' or Accomplishment*. Among Fenollosa's papers were a number of translations from the Nō which, for one reason or another, were later excluded from the 1916 edition. The originals themselves are not now available for study, but in March and April 1960 Mrs. Pound transcribed the texts of six plays: *Adachi ga hara (Kurosuka), Ikuta Atsumori,*

Kanehira, Semimaru, Yōrō, and *Youchi Soga*; these copies give an adequate representation of the untouched translations as they came into Pound's hands.[1] Four of the plays are accompanied by Fenollosa's marginalia and commentary on production method, and all are remarkably complete texts. It is clear that even these copies do suffer in minor ways from the illegibility of Fenollosa's handwriting and Mrs. Pound's lack of familiarity with Japanese culture. In a letter dated 15 November 1969 Mrs. Pound wrote to me as follows: "I must tell you that the hand-copied material is not absolutely complete, as there were places, but very few, where I could not decipher, & one or two very rough characters I could not follow." The inconsistencies are as obvious as they are negligible.

The most important of these texts is the Kami Nō, *Yōrō*, "The Sustenance of Age," which is obviously the model from which Yeats constructed *At the Hawk's Well*. The play was written by Motokiyō Zeami (1363–1443), master performer and theoretician who is believed to have perfected the form of Nō drama as we know it today, and the Fenollosa translation compares well with the far more scholarly version of Gaston Renondeau, and the recent English translation by Chifumi Shimazaki.[2] The text was undoubtedly rejected by Pound because of its nature: the god play has much less appeal for a conventional audience than any other type of Nō, and not a single example was included in the Fenollosa-Pound edition. The god play depends more completely than any other type on choreography and musical composition as paradigms of the emotion to be evoked, and much less sympathy is aroused than in the presentation of a youthful warrior's tragic death, a beautiful woman's thwarted love, or the pathetic derangement of a mind unbalanced by human suffering.

The text of *Yōrō* presented below, follows exactly the transcription made by Mrs. Pound other than the silent correction of transliterated Japanese. Parentheses, italics, and punctuation are presumed to be Fenollosa's; the purity of textual reconstruction is of little import. My present intention is to demonstrate its general relationship to Yeats's first dance play, *At the Hawk's Well*.

1. For the texts of *Adachi ga hara, Kanehira, Semimaru,* and *Youchi Soga* see Richard Taylor, "The Notebooks of Ernest Fenollosa," in *Literature East and West*, XV, 4 (December 1972), pp. 533–76.

2. See "Choix de pièces du théâtre lyrique japonais," *Bulletin de l'Ecole française d'Exertme-Orient*, XXVII (1927), pp. 12–43. Reprinted in Renondeau, *Nō*, premier fascicule (Tokyo 1953), pp. 1–33. See also Chifumi Shimazaki, *The Noh*, I (Tokyo 1972), pp. 171–201.

YŌRŌ*

(name of the waterfall in Mino)

by Motokiyō

1ST SHITE a father
TSURE his son
WAKI an imperial messenger
2ND SHITE God of Mt. Temple

Scene in Mino

WAKI: (*sings*) Winds are calm—All the leaves & branches are quiet. (reign is prosperous) (Kotoba) I am a subject to the Emperor Yuriaku. Some one told him that a wonderful fountain is in this province of Motosu in Mino. So I received his order to see it quickly. So I am now making haste to Motosu.

(Michiyuki) It is peaceful—the land is wealthy, and the people are rich. There are roads everywhere. The gates of the passes are opened. Passing the way of Mino which I heard far in the country I came to the fall of Yoro.

SHITE & TSURE: How the water is clear! Under the shade of the pines! in the mountain of Mino! which pines have passed so many years!

TSURE: The hill of age who is familiar to me—

TOGETHER: How quiet are our hearts to pass!

SHITE: My old friends were already awakened from their dream of the world (or dead). and I passed the flower time of less and more.

SHITE & TSURE: My heart longs for the moon of a thatched house; and my body floats like the frost on a wooden bridge. Though the clouds of white head gather now, the water of the fall which consoles age will make clear my heart. (Yōrō = yō = feeding & consoling—rō = age)

(*Sing*) Is this the custom in the deep valley of far off mountains? However I dip the water, it is not extinguished. In the house of Chosei (long living) is the gate which will not become old (this refers to the gates of some Chinese temple Choseiden, and Furōmon).

*© 1975 by the Trustees of the Ezra Pound Literary Property Trust.

But here, living in this mountain, under the shade of a pine tree, and using the water of the fountain as medicine, and prolonging our age, how hopeful are we, how happy our prospects!

WAKI: I have something to ask of the old man there.

SHITE: You mean me? What's the matter?

WAKI: Are you the father & the son of whom I heard so much?

SHITE: Yes. We are a father & a son.

WAKI: I am the imperial messenger.

SHITE: O how thankful! To receive the words of the Emperor whom I see far up in the sky with this wretched body, how thankful it is! We are father and son.

WAKI: Someone told the Emperor that a wonderful fountain pours from Motosu. He ordered me to go quickly and see it. So tell me in detail why it is called Yōrō.

SHITE: Yes. This is my son. In the morning in the evening, he goes to the mountain, and takes fuel, and feeds me. Once, being weary of mt. road, he dipped this water in his hand and drank it, but strangely his heart was quite refreshed, and he recovered.

TSURE: Thinking the medicine water of the house of Sennin will be such, I went home dipping the water and carrying it, and gave to the father and mother.

SHITE: We drank it, and unconsciously we forgot our age.

TSURE: From that it was not difficult to get up so early in the morning.

TOGETHER: It was not so solitary even when we were awakened from dreams in the night. Some vigor and courage came to us: and as this true clear water consoles our age unceasingly, it is called the Fall of Yōrō.

WAKI: Indeed! How grateful! I think there is some special place in this river where the water of medicine pours out.

SHITE: Look. It is the fountain of water from the rock. A little on this side from the basin below.

WAKI: Then is this the fountain. So saying he approached and looked at it. He found it was very clear.

SHITE: The small pebbles becoming rocks having coverings of moss.

WAKI: The happy example which continues to a thousand generations.

SHITE: I see here in this medicine of waters

WAKI: Truly this!

SHITE: Consoles the age.

CHORUS: If it consoles (invigorates) age, then it will be the best medicine to the people of ripe age, And their lives will not end, forever. O how happy is this fountain! Indeed, as this of the reign which is clear on the upper Emperor part of the gem (source) water, so even we who are in the very end (mouth) of the stream (people) can live happily.

CHORUS: (Kuru) Indeed as the island of Yomogi (Horai) is very far in this age, though we search it, how can we find such example? The medicine of Life, water upon water, it is quite inexhaustible.

SHITE: Though the course of water which flows is not extinguished, but it is not the water of the old! (famous quotation from Kamo no Chomei's Hōjōki)

CHORUS: The bubbles which float on this stream they disappear and they come again. O how clear is this colour.

SHITE: Specially this is of the moment of summer. unparalleled.

CHORUS: And who found this happy sign, to make water as medicine? We will dip the water! We will dip the water! The bamboo leaves of a jar will glow in shade (ehikuyo = sake). The Tekika (flowers of ashi = reed) beside the hedge dips the autumn of the forest leaves. (obscure in origin) The pleasure of 7 sages of Shin as the play of Ryunhakurin (he was one of the 7 sages, who made a famous essay on plays of sake) all are in this water, O dip! O dip! This medicine. I will offer to you the cup floating on the winding water (kiokusin = narrow stream (palace garden)) (on the feast called Kiokusin en) will strike against a rock and will be very slow (to drink)! So I will dip it with my hands, and through the whole night I will dip the moon.

CHORUS: (Rongi) Who was invigorated? By the water & the deep mountain.

SHITE: We hear that it was by virtue of water that Hoso by the vigor of dew of the chrysanthemum lived for 700 years.

CHORUS: Indeed, while I dipped the water of kiku in that very short space, (hearing it was a medicine) (kiku = hear Tsuyu no ma = little space) (double play of double meaning)

SHITE: We passed a thousand years.

CHORUS: Heaven & Earth opened, and even the grass & plants—

SHITE: blossomed and bore fruit.

CHORUS: Season after season

SHITE: Only by the blessing of rain and dew.

CHORUS: By nursing the old man which is like the dew and rain, the parents of flowers were invigorated. And I became familiar to this water. My sleeves were torn, and the shadow of my hands dipping the water is clearly seen in this mountain well. As to think this a medicine, so my figure of old age seems to me as young water. O how happy!

WAKI: O how wonderful, this water! I will go back to my lord quickly and tell him.

SHITE: (That young water is the water of the New Year) The old man felt very grateful for these blessings.

WAKI: The imperial messenger fell in tears. How wonderful that I met such a thing!
(sings) As he did not finish this saying—strange! a light gleaming from heaven, the thunder of falls became quiet, music was heard, and flowers rained. It was not thought a common thing.

2ND SHITE: O how grateful! As the custom of the peaceful reign the mountains, the river, the grass, and the peasants are calm. Winds on every 5th day and rain on every 10th day. The shining sun is lovely in the sky and the fountain of medicine of that green water will not fail. O how grateful are men!

CHORUS: Even I who guard this reign, where the water is inextinguishable—

SHITE: I am the God of the Temple of this mountain (Kami & Buddha are the same)

CHORUS: Or you may call me Yorin (willow) Kuanon Bosatsu

SHITE: The God Kami

CHORUS: The Buddha Hotoke.

SHITE: These are only separation of names.

CHORUS: And are the voice of means to save the people.

SHITE: The storm of the mt., the water of the valley.

CHORUS: The sound goes in harmony. The sound of music makes clear the heart of the falls. O the Shadow of many heavens!

SHITE: The green of the pine tree seems to have passed 1000 years.

CHORUS: The clear clear well of the mt.

SHITE: The water flows & flows, and the waves are calm. The lord of the peaceful reign is the ship—

CHORUS: The lord is the ship, the subject is the water. The water will make the ship float. The subject looks up and reverences the lord. Such a reign will be eternal. Led by the lord of gem water the subject on the lower part becomes clear too. O a good reign! O a good reign! I will repeat this, as the waves on the full basin come back.

Yeats was as unfamiliar as Pound with the conventions of Nō drama, but he saw far greater possibilities in the Fenollosa texts. The instincts that had prompted his earlier experiments with poetic drama, with non-naturalistic acting and stage techniques, were not only confirmed and given the authority of an ancient tradition but a radically compressed form of drama was also demonstrated, capable of both lyric intensity and symbolic depth. The association of Sun God and Emperor in *Yōrō* may have suggested Cuchulain, and Yeats could not but be attracted by the myth on which the play is built. The miraculous waters of regeneration are a recurring symbol of supernatural intervention in the natural world, a means through which man transcends human limitations and renews his spirit. The Celtic counterpart is the myth of Connla's Well, overhung with the berries of nine rowan trees (hazels in some versions). Yeats responded to the symbolism of Well and Tree, representing regeneration, wisdom, and poetic inspiration; he had earlier admired it in Morris's medieval romances, *The Well at the World's End* and *The Water of the Wondrous Isles*. The Japanese rendering of the myth emphasizes the presence of a venerable pine which forms the background of every Nō production: "But here, living in this mountain, under the shade of a pine tree, and using the water of the fountain as medicine, and prolonging our age, how hopeful are we, how happy our prospects?" Yeats's vision of the human condition is much bleaker. Instead of a celebration of order in the universe and harmony between supernatural and temporal powers, *At the Hawk's Well* projects an image of man's fall from the state of undivided being through conflict between the heroic aspirations of the individual and the threatened unity of godhead. The myth is inverted; the Trees are stripped, the Well is dry and guarded against trespass.

In production the miraculous but inaccessible waters are admirably symbolized by a square of brilliant blue cloth upon the floor, a device inspired by a folded kimono which represents the Lady Aoi's sick bed in *Aoi-no-ue*.

The Yeatsian dance play, although an inversion of the myth, follows the outline of Zeami's dramatic construction closely. Yeats carries over from the traditional Nō the device of setting the ritual action in a naturalistic scene evoked through the poetic text. In the Japanese play the Imperial messenger, on his way to the pine-covered mountains of Mino, passes through a peaceful and prosperous land, but Yeats's play depicts a barren mountain landscape, windswept and barbarous, a rough and desolate spot vaguely suggested, but recognizably the coast of Scotland where Aoife leads her troops: Cuchulain identifies himself to the Old Man who has never heard his name: "It is not unknown. I have an ancient house beyond the sea."[3] The pathetic fallacy in the *finale* of the important lyric movement at the end of the first act of *Yōrō* (the act break is not marked in the Fenollosa text) is echoed by Yeats's counter-imagery. In the Japanese play the strange light gleaming from heaven, the suspension of the falls' thunder, music filling the air, and flowers raining down, suggest the benevolence of divine providence, whereas the presence of the supernatural in the Yeats play is accompanied by war-cries and the clash of arms, swords beaten upon shields. The revelation of deity in the Japanese play is through direct godhead dances; in Yeats's play a veil is interposed; the Guardian of the Well is possessed by the god and dances, seducing the hero from the object of his quest, frustrating his desire and foretelling his ultimate destruction.

Another feature of the Nō which Yeats imitated was the removal from the stage of the hero at a crucial moment in the ritual. On the Nō stage the action must be broken for practical reasons: the actor must change costume before returning to reveal himself in his former condition and glory which contrasts sharply with his first appearance. In Yeats's play, however, the least satisfactory element is perhaps the exit of Cuchulain as he follows the Guardian of the Well as if in a dream, and his return after the crucial moments when the waters of regeneration have flowed. There is no need for this, since the opposition between Cuchulain's attraction to the ideal and the

3. *The Variorum Edition of the Plays of W. B. Yeats*, ed. Russell K. Alspach (London 1966), p. 403.

conditions of his humanity is realized in the climax of the play where he is drawn off into the pursuit of Aoife, the incarnation of the ideal in the physical world.

The intervention of the Musicians at the moment of the Guardian's possession by the goddess is also a remarkable instance of assimilation. As in Nō, the dynamic addition of massed voices is enormously effective in raising the level of tension, and Yeats also uses the device to narrate the dance and offer commentary which would not be appropriate to any of the characters. In addition, Yeats has given his Musicians a far more dramatic role, associating them closely with the supernatural order from the very beginning. *At the Hawk's Well* opens with richly textured lyric verse delivered by the seemingly omniscient and mysterious chorus, who set the scene and accomplish the induction of the audience into the imaginary reality of the action, and their song is further emphasized by the ritual unfolding and folding of a cloth. Instead of a gradual withdrawal from actuality, as in Nō, we are introduced immediately to another level of reality which is underlined by the counterpoint of their freer and ornamented lyricism with the more austere and objective formality of the longer pentametres used by the characters themselves. The sudden intervention of the chorus as the Guardian of the Well dances is particularly effective as it reintroduces their more freely musical and heightened speech with all its connotations of the supernatural world, and closely follows the practice of Nō where the chorus functions mainly as an extension of characterization or as an external commentator, substituting for the single actor at the climax of his emotional experience.

Indeed, *At the Hawk's Well* is a very accomplished piece of assimilation in that it overcomes the technical problems of infusing the action with dramatic tension, which in the original had been provoked by orchestrating rhythmic patterns of movement, music, and density of rhetorical texture as sanctioned by established convention. Yeats's creation differs from traditional Nō, which recreates the emotional quality of an incident or experience through the ritualized induction of the spectator's imagination, in both the immediate realism and essentially dramatic convention of its conception. It is true that the "eye of the mind" speech of the Musicians calls on the spectator to recreate the scene in imagination, but the action itself is then played out objectively and directly rather than by having its quality or nature suggested and surmised from the privileged narration of an intermediate consciousness. Realistic action is not unknown in Nō tradition, although it is of late and decadent development, but the idea of sub-plot or secondary conflict, let alone plotting itself, is certainly alien. Besides the active conflict between godhead and man which forms the basic antithesis in Yeats's inversion of *Yōrō*, there is also conflict between types of men. Instead of retaining the secondary character, *Waki*, who acts only as an interlocutor and remains objective and unrelated to the central incident, while serving as a kind of catalyst for the recreation of action, Yeats divided the dramatic function of the role between the Old Man and the Youth who were suggested by the Father and Son of *Yōrō*, and set them in opposition to one another. They share a common purpose, but differ dramatically in temper: the timid Old Man has given in to the limitations of his human condition and withers as he lies in wait for the miraculous waters, warming himself by the meagre fire he barely manages to maintain. The impulsive Young Man, on the other hand, seizes the moment to control his own fate and mounts a heroic assault against godhead itself, his avowed object being nothing less than to hood the Hawk, to grow immortal.

> Some burn damp faggots, others may consume
> The entire combustible world in one small room
> As though dried straw.[4]

Stripped of its original function as deuteragonist in *Yōrō*, the figure of the Imperial Messenger is recast in Yeats's conception of the play as the agent of deity, the Guardian of the Well. Significantly enough, Yokomichi Mario's adaptation of Yeats's play for performance on the Nō stage assigns the role of protagonist to the Old Man, that of deuteragonist to the Young Man, and reduces the Well's Guardian to the status of companion or follower.[5] So drastic a reinterpretation according to Japanese conventions of priority demonstrates how far Yeats had moved from traditional character relationships in Nō; yet, in discussing the progress of the manuscript versions, Curtis Bradford has shown that Yeats did suppress the overt particularization of his characters in favour of the more de-

4. *The Variorum Edition of the Poems of W. B. Yeats*, ed. Peter Allt and Russell K. Alspach (New York 1957), p. 327.
5. See Tsukimura Reiko, "A Comparison of Yeats's *At the Hawk's Well* and Its Nō Version *Take no izumi*," *Literature East and West*, XVI, 4 (1967), pp. 385–97.

personalized descriptions, Old Man and Young Man, which tend to universalize the action by directing attention to its allegorical possibilities.[6] In the same way, the mute and mysterious Guardian of the Well provides a persistent and vividly concrete reminder of the supernatural presence against which the lesser opposition of Old Man and Young Man plays itself out. The success of the device in heightening tension is fully realized in that dramatic moment when the brooding figure is possessed by deity and reveals itself as the Hawk, dancing out its seductive beauty and rapaciousness. The dance itself must reflect the essential ambiguity of the supernatural world, as does the image of the Hawk, and concentrates on the projection of creative power, violence, and sexuality as analogues of the universal relationship between godhead and man.

Dame Ninette de Valois very kindly described to me the Hawk's dance as she performed the role under Yeats's direction in Itō Michio's original costume for the second revival of the play at the Abbey Theatre on 22 July 1933. She danced barefoot in the modern style then known as abstract expressionism, and the choreography was created to express the emotional content of the mask through stylized forms. Both movement and maintained emotion were determined by the fact of the Hawk's hood, and the dance progressed from an evocation of brooding power, through suggestive seduction, to the violent ecstasy of a wild bird. From the snatches of description that have been preserved, photographs of Itō in costume, and what is known of his later dance style, it is quite certain that his concept of the Hawk's dance was much closer to that of Dame Ninette than to the classical choreography of Nō.

At any rate, Yeats did conceive of the climactic dance borrowed from Nō drama as a ritualizing force, a stylized projection of transcendent human passions which shifts interest from objective plot development to a perception of universal relationships or conditions. In the first of the dance plays the hero who looks into the unmoistened eye of the Hawk is seduced and his degradation assured; the fallen man who evades confrontation continues in withering self-despite. The ambiguity of the supernatural world's beauty, its attraction and antagonism, is responsible for man's fall from the ideal of undivided being, and the opposition of spirit and nature, as that between the ideal human condition and man's fallen state, is not

6. See *Yeats At Work* (Carbondale, Ill. 1966), p. 190.

so much resolved by the action of the play as it is placed in balanced perspective. Pity is aroused by the futility of man's exertions and the inevitability of his fall; there is both grandeur and mockery in the Young Man's final assertion of heroic identity: "He comes! Cuchulain, son of Sualtim, comes!"[7]

The success of *At the Hawk's Well* can hardly be attributed to its use of a revolutionary form or structure derived from the Nō. As one can easily see, the play is founded in ostensibly realistic action and dramatic conflict. For the first time, however, Yeats had found a synthesis of dramatic techniques which adequately objectified and rendered concrete the ideas he wanted to project without calling attention to either their own existence or their relationship to conventions of naturalistic reality. The dramatic power of the Hawk's dance, for example, is eminently theatrical and effective, whereas poetry alone lacks sufficient theatricality to evoke the nature of the supernatural and its relationship to man. The depersonalization of characters in *At the Hawk's Well* renders them representative types and focuses attention on the universal rather than the particular. The figures take on symbolic overtones while the play avoids the static monotony of *The Shadowy Waters* by establishing a pattern of action which is itself a dynamic image of universal forces. The aesthetic and moral orders are made to coincide. The use of the Blind Man and Fool in *On Baile's Strand* had been a groping toward this kind of effect, but the conception was not pursued far enough to break the hold of Renaissance forms and naturalistic representation. In *Deirdre* Yeats had also experimented with visual stage images which served as paradigms of the dramatic conflict, but the division of action between hearth and chess board, together with the highly textured verse failed to focus attention beyond the traditional dramatic elements of characterization, conflict, and circumstance. *Deirdre* remains a very personal tragedy, and the symbolic interplay of ideas is largely obscured by rhetoric. In *At the Hawk's Well* character and action together constitute the meaning, forming objective images whose interaction assumes symbolic significance through abstraction and insistence on the independence of its own reality.

The failure of Yeats's earlier attempts at Romantic drama had been brought about by his inability to transcend the stage conventions of naturalistic theatre. Instead of creating a counter-reality, the

7. *Variorum Plays*, p. 412.

earlier experiments had either projected a recognizable illusion of insubstantiality, a never-never land of conventional fantasy which could not carry the burden of his vision, or the intervention of such a fantastic world in a naturalistic setting. The dance of the fairy in *The Land of Heart's Desire* is no more credible than the angel and butterfly of *The Hour-Glass*, and *The Shadowy Waters*, however effective as a symbolist poem, has not a single objective or theatrical element in its make-up. *Cathleen ni Houlihan* alone, of all the early works, creates a life of its own and sufficient intensity of feeling to be taken seriously as the concrete projection of an abstraction, but that may well have as much to do with the political significance of the myth as with the aesthetic achievement of the play. The bolder experiments of *On Baile's Strand* and *Deirdre* still had not solved the problem, while the techniques of Nō did lead Yeats to construct a play as he would a lyric poem, using patterns of objective images in a composition which evoked an independent reality. Replacing the stage altogether by a bare space before a wall in any drawing room or studio, he avoided all association with illusionism, and lighting was to be no more artificial than that of normal circumstances lest the suspicion of illusionism rob the action of both its autonomous reality and meaning. Masks insisted on the presence of archetypes and obviated character investigation or development, while stylized movement and gesture further differentiated the action from naturalistic reality. Dance itself projected meaning concretely where words alone might fail, and abstracted stage properties, such as Tree and Well, acted as independent images, almost personages, carrying their full weight of significance throughout the play. Simple musical accompaniment heightened the lyric verses which framed the action, setting it off from that of the mundane world, and language was returned to a stylized simplicity and matter-of-factness, underlining the imaginative reality of the action projected. A chorus of musicians was used to set the scene, while conventional exposition and logical development were omitted as encouraging the vulgarity of naturalistic realism. Only the passionate climax of the incident was shown, its economical intensity emphasizing the outcome as a paradigm of universal order. When produced according to this rubric, *At the Hawk's Well* is amazingly forceful and effective, in the same way that Cocteau's vision of Death is frighteningly real and powerful on film in *Orphée*, but as soon as the action is separated from the immediate apprehension of the audience by the artificial barrier of stage or proscenium, theatrical lighting, or eerie music, it becomes nothing more than an embarrassing and fantastic Hallowe'en charade.

What Yeats gained from the Nō was a substitute for worn-out and meaningless stage conventions, a valid means of objectifying the life of the spirit and restoring ritual drama to the theatre. His first experiment in the new form had followed the outline of the Japanese model rather closely, while freely assimilating its techniques to his own ends. The success of *At the Hawk's Well* paved the way for further experiments with his perennial themes: the limitations of the human condition, the ideal of heroic action, and the transcendence of the spiritual world as projected through images of aesthetic creation, war or violence, and sexuality.

W. B. Yeats in
Seanad Éireann

David Fitzpatrick

By the early twenties W. B. Yeats had decided to take his colour in the game of politics—"a roulette wheel with various colours." His alter ego might still be "so uncertain about everything," for there was so much to be said on every side;[1] but the poet could endure social isolation no longer, and determined to play his part in moulding the new Free State. As a respectable public figure he was learning when asked about Ireland to answer always:

> ... that if the British Empire becomes a voluntary Federation of Free Nations, all will be well, but if it remains as in the past, a domination of one, the Irish question is not settled. That done with, I can talk of the work of my generation in Ireland, the creation of a literature to express national character and feeling but with no deliberate political aim.[2]

He deplored what he perceived among his compatriots, "a stronger desire than England ever knew to enslave and be enslaved,"[3] yet still found "a delight in the minds of the country people."[4] And he thought that at last he had found a means of promoting the values in which he delighted, and of confuting such damaging accusations

1. "Compulsory Gaelic: A Dialogue," in *Irish Statesman*, II (1924), p. 652.
2. *Autobiographies* (London 1955), p. 534. This passage relates to Yeats's interviews with Scandinavian pressmen in December 1923.
3. "Compulsory Gaelic ...," p. 651.
4. Speech at a Dublin vicarage; see *Irish Times*, 30 June 1923.

of capriciousness and betrayal as those once expressed by Seumas
O'Sullivan:

> I too, with Ireland, loved you long ago
> Because you sang, as none but you could sing,
> The cause we held the dearest; now I know
> How vain your love was, and how mean a thing.
>
> And not to you, whose heart went anywhere
> Her sorrow's holy heritage belongs:
> You could have made of any other air
> The little careful mouthfuls of your songs.

In December 1922 Yeats was offered nomination to Seanad
Éireann, the upper chamber of the Free State's new Oireachtas.
President Cosgrave, eager to placate apprehensive Anglo-Irishmen,
had agreed to nominate half the sixty members of the Seanad "with
a view to the providing of representation for groups of all parties not
adequately represented in the Chamber" (that is, Dáil Éireann).[5] So
dutifully did Cosgrave carry out his promise that in this first Seanad
in a land of Catholic commoners sat twenty-four non-Catholics and
fifteen titled persons.[6] Former nationalists of every persuasion scarcely outnumbered former Unionists, many of whom had fought tooth
and nail to preserve the Union only a few years earlier.[7] What more
celebrated representative than Yeats could the President invite to
join the Seanad? The minister for external affairs, Desmond Fitz-
Gerald, who had a decade before "ascribed his national feelings and
convictions to the influence of Yeats's poetry," was determined "that
Yeats should be invited to become a member. His proposal en-
countered no opposition in the Cabinet and Yeats was enrolled as a
Senator."[8]

5. Motion in Dáil Éireann, 25 October 1922, quoted in D. O'Sullivan, *The
   Irish Free State and Its Senate: A Study in Contemporary Politics*
   (London 1940), p. 90.
6. See J. L. McCracken, *Representative Government in Ireland, 1919–48*
   (London 1958), p. 138.
7. Of the senators 1922–28, 7 were Labour Party members, 19 former
   Home Rulers, Land Leaguers, Sinn Feiners or members of the National
   Liberal Club, and 20 former Southern Unionists, "Independent" Senators
   (excluding Yeats) or members of the Kildare Street Club. Yeats and 32
   others I could not classify according to political affiliation.
8. See F. MacManus ed., *The Yeats We Knew* (Cork 1965), p. 73, for
   Earnán de Blaghd (Blythe) (former minister for local government), on

For Desmond FitzGerald and the cabinet, Yeats was a nostalgic reminder of the old unpractical Nationalism, the unlikeliest of all senators to use politics for his own ends or lobby for interest groups. But Yeats, in accepting nomination, had other ideas. He had no intention of merely adding his patronage to official handbooks and amusing visiting dignitaries. Though by no means contemptuous of the honour done him by the State, nor unmoved by his promised stipend,[9] his first motive in accepting nomination was to pursue specific political aims. At last he hoped to regain his political influence. The second chamber had been "so arranged as to put power into the hands of able men who could not expect election in the ordinary way," and Yeats expected them to get "much government" into their hands.[10] Full of hope and cunning, Yeats prepared immediately to fight for an Irish Academy and a state theatre.[11] In the longer term he resolved to cast his influence behind the more enlightened faction within the government, and behind the government within the nation. After his first remark in the Seanad, he wrote to Olivia Shakespear: "I shall speak very little but probably intrigue a great deal to get some old projects into action. . . ."[12]

Despite its unpopular character, Yeats found the Seanad an alien assemblage. Whether speaking or intriguing, the poet could never fully accustom himself to the merchants, lawyers, and bankers who dominated it.[13] When he spoke he would confuse his hearers with

FitzGerald's role in Yeats's nomination. Cf. *The Memoirs of Desmond FitzGerald: 1913–1916* (London 1968), pp. 3–4. For conflicting but less reliable accounts of Yeats's support within the government see O. St. J. Gogarty, *William Butler Yeats: A Memoir* (Dublin 1963), p. 13; D. Pearce, *The Senate Speeches of W. B. Yeats* (London 1961), pp. 14–15; J. M. Hone, *W. B. Yeats: 1865–1939* (London 1962), p. 350; A. N. Jeffares, "Yeats as Public Man," in *Poetry* (Chicago), XCVIII (July 1961), p. 261; W. Starkie, "Yeats and the Abbey Theatre," in *Homage to Yeats* (Los Angeles 1966), p. 31.

9. In 1928 Yeats felt qualms about losing this stipend (eventually fixed at £360 per annum). See *Letters*, ed. Allan Wade (London 1954), p. 745 (30 July 1928).
10. *Ibid.*, pp. 681–82 (May 1922); pp. 693–94 (December).
11. *Ibid.*, p. 678 (March 1922).
12. *Ibid.*, p. 694 (December 1922).
13. Of the 79 senators who sat between 1922 and 1928 I have traced the occupations of 74. Of these 7 were bankers and railway executives, 16 merchants and manufacturers and 13 professional men (though of these only Glenavy and Brown were practising lawyers).

discourses upon the aesthetic qualities of Irish lace or stained glass,
discomfort them with apologies when he forgot that he was occasionally a politician and remembered that he was always a man of letters;
or irritate them by admitting to "no great knowledge of procedure."[14]
Although on occasion an old acquaintance might be won over by his
eloquence, or a dreary debate enlivened by the recitation of some
old poem of his, those qualities which he himself called "outrageous"
repelled the senators.[15] In most of his short, unorthodox speeches
his only interlocutor would be the chairman—correcting him on
points of order. For the Seanad's head usher his "kindly but in-
offensively condescending" manner evoked "responsive feelings of
protective affection;" but among his "betters" irritation or indifference were commoner reactions.[16] Nor was Yeats more at home in
private intrigue than he was in public debate. Remembering in 1934
those private meetings of the "Independent" group in the Seanad
where the "real work of legislation" was done, meetings dominated
by those "old lawyers, old bankers, old businessmen, who . . . have
begun to govern the world," he warned Ezra Pound against becoming a senator: "the ten minutes they can grant you, after discussing
the next Bill upon the agenda for two hours with unperturbed
lucidity, will outlast your self-confidence."[17] If Yeats ever felt at
home amidst political intrigue, it was during the Army "Mutiny" of
March 1924 when, according to Hone, he was the principal trans-
mitter of political secrets to the Independents, his informers being
anonymous but "usually young men, and always dark in complexion,
who called upon him late at night."[18]

However, Yeats made a great effort early in his term to contribute

14. See Seanad Éireann, *Díospóireachtaí Páirliminte . . . Tuairisg Oifigiúil*
[hereafter *Debates*], I, col. 979 (April 1923).
15. See for instance *ibid.*, VIII, col. 608 (March 1927); VII, cols. 1043–44,
1058 (July 1926). Yeats refers to his and Gogarty's "outrageous" conversation in *Explorations* (London 1962), p. 413.
16. See W. B. Stanford, "Yeats in the Irish Senate," in *A Review of English
Literature*, IV (July 1963), pp. 76, 80.
17. *A Vision*, (New York 1961), pp. 26–27.
18. Hone, *W. B. Yeats*, p. 382. Cf. Hone, "Yeats as Political Philosopher,"
in *London Mercury*, XXXIX (1939), p. 494: the Independents often
"sought his advice on practical matters;" Blythe, in MacManus, *The
Yeats We Knew*, p. 73: "I should not say that his opinion carried great
weight amongst them on general issues. But when he was on his ground
he could, of course, bring the majority with him."

seriously to the work of the Seanad. By 1925 he had headed extra-parliamentary committees on Irish manuscripts and an Irish "Federation of the Arts."[19] He had argued coolly and persuasively for the assignation of a modest £5,000 for the editing and cataloguing of ancient texts and the investigating of Irish dialects; and, more ambitiously, had called for an academy like Sweden's to oversee all aspects of the national language and culture.[20] His parliamentary work *in camera* extended also to at least five committees, some confined to the Seanad and others joint select committees of Seanad and Dáil, dealing with such disparate matters as the Garda Siochána bill and the nomination of personnel for the Seanad's standing committee.[21] Yeats was not to blame if the government ignored his reports and made light of the joint committees on which he served.[22]

Although Yeats spent on average only three hours in the chamber every fortnight,[23] he missed fewer sittings and spoke oftener and upon a wider range of topics than most of his fellow senators in the first triennium.[24] He protested that he did not like to speak in that house unless on things he had studied, letters and art, yet found these studies wide enough to enable him to speak on censorship and contraceptives, divorce and partition, prison conditions and public

19. See Pearce, *Senate Speeches*, p. 18; *Debates*, I, cols. 992–95 (April 1923); III, cols. 161–71 (June 1924).
20. Yeats finally established an Irish Academy of Letters in 1932. For his earlier plans for an academy see *Letters*, pp. 678 (March 1922); 704 (January 1924); 716–17 (July 1926); 732 (November 1927).
21. Yeats may have served on select committees other than those known to me, since after the formation of the Special Committee on Standing Committees (a standing committee to which Yeats was elected in January 1923), the membership of certain committees was no longer recorded in the Debates.
22. The treatment by the Dáil of select committee reports became increasingly cavalier. The Dáil never established another joint select committee after June 1925 when the copyright committee of which Yeats was a member forced the withdrawal of a bill. (See O'Sullivan, *Irish Free State and Its Senate*, pp. 520–21).
23. See *Debates*, I–X; Seanad Éireann, *Imeachta* [hereafter *Proceedings*], 1–8 (Dublin 1923–28).
24. Yeats attended 65 per cent of sittings compared with the mean 60 per cent; taking 100 as the mean for all senators 1922–28, the frequency of his remarks was 114, the range of subjects which he discussed 125. See *Proceedings* and indices to *Debates*, and O'Sullivan, *Irish Free State and the Senate*, pp. 629–30.

safety.[25] As the Boundary Commission floundered towards its in-glorious end, Yeats declared his conviction that Ulster would one day return to a united Ireland. When the rumour spread in 1923 that the parliamentary oath might soon be removed, Yeats intrigued for its abolition. When Republicans attacked British soldiers at Cobh in 1924, it was he who gave notice of a motion of protest.[26] But in each case his ambivalent attitude towards politics and mere "opinion" was manifested in the sequel. He failed to appear to pro-pose the motion, which was sponsored in the end by Clayton Love; when his role in the oath affair was made public, he ambiguously denied taking any official part in the negotiations; and after rising to the motion on Partition, he was careful, speaking "as an artist and a writer," to relate his arguments to the most general issues of Irish "culture."[27] Thus even as a senator and public man Yeats betrayed his lifelong social dilemma. The loyal Anglo-Irishman who almost denounced the Cobh outrage is an image of the estranged poet grasping, then baulking at commitment.

How far did Yeats achieve that commitment while a senator? Let us analyse Yeats's experience as a spokesman for Anglo-Irishmen in society, and for the authoritarian principles in politics which he espoused during the twenties.

Out of the Irish revolution two groups of Anglo-Irishmen emerged undaunted. One had identified itself with the Republican cause, hoping to find there the vigour and cohesion which the fragmenting Protestant community no longer possessed. But Yeats now turned to those other patriots—the "Southern Unionists." The latter had first organized themselves as the Irish Unionist Alliance, which from 1893 till Carson's heyday was mainly independent of the Ulster

25. See Pearce, *Senate Speeches*, for a selection of Yeats's remarks on all subjects.
26. See *Letters*, p. 704 (January 1924); *Debates*, III, cols. 86–88 (October 1924); D. T. Torchiana, *W. B. Yeats and Georgian Ireland* (Evanston 1966), pp. 206ff.; *Debates*, II, col. 1167.
27. For the Cobh affair see *Debates*, II, col. 1257; cf. Stanford, "Yeats in the Irish Senate," p. 72. Yeats gave notice of the motion at 3:05 p.m. but Love did not move it till 7:40 p.m., after dinner. Yeats was still in the chamber at 4:05 p.m. (col. 1185). Did he wine and dine too well? For Yeats on the oath and on partition, see Torchiana, *Yeats and Georgian Ireland*, pp. 207, 209; *Debates*, III, col. 1060. *Cf.* O. Edwards, "W. B. Yeats and Ulster; and a Thought on the Future of the Anglo-Irish Tradi-tion," in *Northman*, XIII (winter 1945), pp. 17, 21; Edwards calls Yeats a "southern partitionist."

Unionists and constituted a small but influential propagandist group concerned more with the English than the Irish public.[28] The triumphs of Orangeism in the North and post-war dislocation in the South led to the decline of the Alliance, the former leader of which (Lord Midleton) condemned Southern Unionists in 1919 for restricting themselves "to the easy task of attending meetings in Dublin and voting strong resolutions which they expected the British Government to respect."[29] By 1921, however, Midleton, Bernard, and Jameson had reinvigorated the movement by forming a private pressure group which O'Higgins called "representative Southern Unionists . . . rather than representatives of the Southern Unionists."[30] With remarkable effect, these Anglo-Irishmen set about rallying Protestant energies behind a campaign to win social and political influence in the Ireland about to emerge from chaos and warfare.[31] Their campaign took them in October to the lobbies of the London peace conference, where they extracted from Griffith the promise that he would advocate the establishment of a senate, about the constitution of which they would be consulted.[32] Seven months later a closed conference of Unionists and delegates of the Provisional Government drew up Heads of Agreement on a Senate, which were largely incorporated into the new Constitution.[33]

In December 1922 a score of former Southern Unionists entered Seanad Éireann, eager to participate in government and to defend their wealth, status, and social identity. Yeats was immediately accepted into this group of senators, now known as "Independents." True to the social outlook which such a group affiliation entailed, Yeats resigned from the "Liberators" old club, the St. Stephen's Green, to join the Kildare Street Club, an institution so reactionary that its dining hall would empty whenever Martyn, a founder of the

28. See P. J. Buckland, "The Southern Irish Unionists, the Irish Question, and British Politics 1906–14," in *Irish Historical Studies*, XVI (1967), pp. 233ff.
29. *Ibid.*, pp. 232–33.
30. Quoted in O'Sullivan, *Irish Free State and Its Senate*, p. 75.
31. In April 1921 Jameson set up an Irish Businessmen's Conciliation Committee to seek negotiations between Lloyd George and de Valera, and in July Midleton and others conferred with de Valera at the Mansion House concerning the projected peace talks.
32. See *Irish Times*, 21 October 1921; O'Sullivan, *Irish Free State and Its Senate*, p. 75.
33. *Ibid.*, pp. 77–81.

club who had grown radical in his last years, entered.[34] But although Yeats was eager to make known his over-all commitment to the group, he was determined to retain his independent judgment on specific questions of policy. He joined it convinced that its leader, his father's old friend Jameson, would leave him free to speak his mind.[35] He was not disappointed. Though Keane and Douglas were called "leaders" of the group, Yeats voted against Keane in one division of every four, and against Douglas in two of every five.[36] He remained an "Independent" indeed.

In view of his persistent political individualism, why did Yeats choose to join this "non-party party" in the Seanad? Indeed, he shared with the Independents their alienation from the masses, their loss of a social identity early in the century, and their desire after the revolution to find a new place in society. But these analogies in mode of social experience would not alone have been enough to cause Yeats to join the former Unionists: his experience was as disparate from theirs in substance as it was similar in mode. The poet's pre-war alienation had been bitter, whereas the Unionists had shown only "cynical indifference" to "Nationalist abstractions;" he had been a popular Nationalist leader, they his unpopular political enemies; for Yeats, entry into the Seanad was a move towards conservatism, for them it was a concession to progress.[37] But for Yeats, these disparities in experience were outweighed by a stronger bond than life could ever tie or untie—the bond of birth. For Yeats had come to believe that both he and the Independents were representative Anglo-Irishmen, that both must struggle together for the preservation of their class.[38] Further, he believed that their class urgently

34. See A. N. Jeffares, *W. B. Yeats: Man and Poet* (London 1949), p. 231; P. Colum, *Arthur Griffith* (Dublin 1959), pp. 85–86.
35. *Explorations*, p. 412.
36. Senator O'Farrell, the Labour leader, dubbed the Independents the "non-party party" after being corrected for calling Keane the "leader" of the Cumann na nGaedheal and Farmers' Party in the Seanad; see *Debates*, I, col. 1855. Frequently the Independents did not vote en bloc, so that Yeats was able to vote against Douglas five times as often as against Jameson or Brown. See Seanad Éireann, *Vótálanna*, 1–8 (Dublin 1923–28).
37. See *Autobiographies*, p. 234. For Unionists conceding to progress see Archbishop Gregg (December 1921) quoted in *The Years of the Great Test 1926–39* (Cork 1967), p. 96; and Sir Horace Plunkett in *Debates*, II, col. 64 (October 1923).
38. See Torchiana, *Yeats and Georgian Ireland*, p. 80.

desired its own preservation, that common factors in the mode of its social development made it more liable than any other class to pursue a common social mission. They were his people, and they wanted and needed his commitment to them.

In his youth, Yeats had been inhibited in identifying himself with the Anglo-Irish aristocratic tradition by his relatively low birth. But as his craving for a settled place in Irish society intensified, his imagination began to give forth comfortable sophistries. "Birth" became for him a metaphysical matter, the process of assuming the "historical mask" of some previous era—in his case the Irish Eighteenth Century.[39] Moreover, he had decided that the Anglo-Irish gentry and he held in common a quality which transcended traditional class cleavages: the love and possession of leisure. By 1923 he was calling himself a "crusted Tory" concerning the preservation of the gentle life: he was "of the opinion of the ancient Jewish book which says 'There shall be no wisdom without leisure.' "[40] But this happy solution of the problems of lineage and political affiliation with former Unionists was soon undermined. For the Unionists proved to care little for Yeats's cherished ideals and he lost his political allies. Moreover the Anglo-Irish community gradually lost cohesion and social significance, and with them its attraction for the spokesman for some great social class. In old age Yeats was to retain only the remnant of his vision—the conviction that the Anglo-Irish and he shared nothing but solitude.

Even at the height of his vision of himself as a representative Anglo-Irishman, Yeats did not entirely ignore the contradictions between vision and observation. In February 1925 his myth of a cultivated Anglo-Irishry, endowed with gentle and leisurely values, already seemed a dream: "I think that in early Byzantium, maybe never before or since in recorded history, religious, aesthetic and practical life were one. . . ."[41] Yeats could not repress his misgivings about all these three aspects of Anglo-Irish life. His social affiliations tugged him towards the Church of Ireland, but he had never learned to accept the Protestantism of his childhood which for all its taste, courtesy, and decency "seemed to think of nothing but getting on in the world."[42] In 1928 he would often sit in St. Patrick's Cathedral,

39. *Ibid.*
40. *Debates*, I, col. 724 (March 1923).
41. *A Vision* (1961), p. 279.
42. *Autobiographies*, pp. 101–02 (December 1914).

Dublin, as he had sat a decade earlier in All Souls' Chapel, Oxford, but never at service time: he had often wondered if it was but timidity come from long disuse that kept him from the service.[43] Nor did the aesthetic life of the Anglo-Irish accord with Yeats's ideal. Among contemporary Anglo-Irishmen there were perhaps more "decayed survivals" of the eighteenth century's "reckless braggadocio" than intellectual descendants of Swift, Burke, Berkeley, or Goldsmith, and maybe fewer decayed survivals than unimaginative businessmen.[44] The more Yeats met Anglo-Irishmen in "practical life," the more he chatted with his titled friends in the Kildare Street Club, the less distinct seemed his vision of the man of leisure with his ancient and universal faith. In the lineaments of what Leinster landlord could he discern the features of Castiglione's Courtier? How could he hope for the emulation in Ireland of "that splendid spectacle," the Swedish court?[45] He abhorred in 1938 as in 1890 the "West British minority with their would-be cosmopolitanism and actual provincialism."[46] Residual misgivings inhibited Yeats's complete identification with the Anglo-Irish class. He kept his social independence within Anglo-Ireland. He took his stand with merchants and gentlemen, but when they shrank away he held his ground alone.

For decades Yeats had dreamed of a cultured Ireland, wisely governed by an enlightened few. By 1922 he had come to rejoice in the prospect of promoting, through the good offices of some enlightened ruler, those values which he thought the Anglo-Irish had preserved in spite of the rude masses. Like Gogarty, he feared "the enormity of the vote," and prayed that strong rulers would suppress the tendency of the ignorant mob to stampede towards destruction.[47] Like Swift, his "historical mask," he believed that "the People are much more dexterous at pulling down and setting up, than at pre-

43. See *A Vision*, pp. 6–7. Cf. Hone, *W. B. Yeats*, p. 444; M. A. Mohr, "The Political and Social Thought of William Butler Yeats" (Ph.D. diss., State University of Iowa 1964), p. 165.
44. See *Letters to the New Island* (Cambridge, Mass. 1934), pp. 90–91; *Explorations*, p. 297.
45. Cf. *Autobiographies*, p. 572.
46. *Letters to the New Island*, p. 109; conversations with Richard Hayes, 1938, recounted in Hayes, "His Nationalism," in *The Arrow* (W. B. Yeats Commemmoration Number, 1939), p. 10.
47. Speech congratulating Yeats on his Nobel Prize, *Debates*, II, cols. 159–60 (November 1923).

serving what is fixed," that as soon as power had reached its balance, one should oppose the "first steps of popular encroachment."[48] Yeats accepted the necessity in modern states for "some kind of expert government firm enough, tyrannical enough if you will, to spend years in carrying out its plans."[49] He gloated over the aura of "inevitability" which pervaded the growth of authoritarianism in the twenties. Far from expressing an "increasingly pessimistic outlook," or for that matter an "emotionally neutral attitude of mind," Yeats showed increasing excitement at the prospect of the coming times.[50]

What man or party could be entrusted with the sacred task of imposing the national good upon the reluctant nation? Communism Yeats rejected as "the spear-head of materialism and leading to inevitable murder;"[51] Fascism, with its great popular leaders trampling upon the "decomposing body of the Goddess of Liberty," was far more attractive[52]—but in the twenties Ireland had neither its Mussolini nor its Gentile. Yeats decided that the time of violent revolutions was fast disappearing, and determined to throw his weight behind the Free State government, which he expected to develop autocratic methods of governing, despite its democratic form.

The government which Cosgrave led after the murder of Collins in August 1922 did promise at first to approach Yeats's ideal of authority. It seemed open to enlightened external influences, it was solid and sane, and it included at least one hero. In January 1924 Yeats wrote in optimistic mood: "Dublin is reviving after the Civil War, and self-government is creating a little stir of excitement. People are trying to found a new society. Politicians want to be artistic, and artistic people to meet politicians, and so on."[53] The

48. "Discourse on the Contests and Dissensions between the Nobles and Commons of Athens and Rome" (1701), in *Prose Works* . . . (London 1907), I, pp. 255ff.
49. Interview with *Irish Times*, 16 February 1924.
50. For the "pessimistic" interpretation see A. Zwerdling, *Yeats and the Heroic Ideal* (London 1966), p. 115, who claims that Yeats worshipped "not victory, but defeat"; Mohr, "Political and Social Thought of Yeats," p. 159 (referring to the years 1921–26).
51. *Letters*, p. 656 (April 1919).
52. Speech at public banquet, Taillteann Games, which Yeats had helped revive as chairman of the Games committee of peers and baronets. Quoted in R. Ellmann, *Yeats: The Man and the Masks* (London 1961), pp. 248–49. See also U. O'Connor, *Oliver St. John Gogarty, A Poet and His Times* (London 1964), p. 210.
53. *Letters*, p. 702.

government's sober mode, which according to "A.E." would later inspire "a half-cynical, but rather cheerful materialism,"[54] gave promise of that long-term planning without which no government could be truly "authoritative." And planning it all was the hero— Kevin O'Higgins. This man was "the one strong intellect in Irish public life,"[55] a fit symbol for the virile government of the future.[56] As vice-president and minister for justice, O'Higgins was the dominant voice in Cosgrave's cabinet, like Parnell

> . . . a tall pillar, burning
> Before us in the gloom . . .

Yeats never lost his respect for the Cosgrave government's unostentatious effectiveness, but his enthusiasm for it waned during the later twenties. The lesser luminaries in the government left him ill at ease: they seemed no more heroic than the hoary bankers in the Seanad. The two or three ministers with whom the Yeatses mixed in 1924 were able, courageous, but unimaginative, "honest modern-minded men swimming still in seas of conspiracy of others' making." Later he recollected: "They seemed men of skill and mother-wit, men who had survived hatred. But their minds knew no play that my mind could play at; I felt that I could never know them. . . . No, neither Gogarty nor I, with our habit of outrageous conversation, could get near those men."[57] Furthermore, the government, however admirable its leaders might be, had been democratically elected and could scarcely remain immune to the mediocrity of middle-class mentality. The mob howled at the door: the mob who were taught by their Mothers and Sisters Superior that Yeats was intent on destroying Dublin, who packed the Abbey Theatre to riot against *The Plough and the Stars*.[58] And the Dáil which sat behind the door seemed in many ways a microcosm of the mob. To every Protestant

54. "Twenty-Five Years of Irish Nationality," in *Foreign Affairs*, 7 (1929), p. 220. *Cf.* W. K. Hancock, *Survey of British Commonwealth Affairs* (London 1937), I, p. 324.
55. *Letters*, pp. 726–27 (July–August 1927).
56. See interview with *Irish Times*, 15 November 1923.
57. *Letters*, p. 705 (May 1924); *Explorations*, p. 413.
58. For Yeats, Mothers and Sisters Superior, see *Letters*, p. 747 (October 1928); Lady Gregory, *Journals, 1916–1930* (London 1946), p. 319. For the Abbey riots of February 1926 see *ibid.*, pp. 87ff; *Letters*, p. 711; U. Bridge, ed., *W. B. Yeats and T. Sturge Moore: Their Correspondence 1901–1937* (London 1953), p. 83.

there were ten Catholic members; hardly three-fifths of the T.D.s had completed secondary school; and in the course of the twenties the commercial classes gained representation at the expense of professional men.[59] Not surprisingly, Dáil Éireann took less and less notice of the Seanad's rare pleas for the minorities whose interests the upper chamber had been established to protect. It was soon evident that enlightened "authoritative" government through such a legislature would be an uphill task.

Yeats was aware of the levelling tendency in Irish politics, but he trusted O'Higgins's ability and determination to suppress it. He saw also that the government, despite its obnoxious democratic basis, had been proven legitimate by "the only effective test: it has been permitted to take life."[60] He and all Irishmen were bound to adhere to the Constitution once validated, and for this Yeats had the authority of no less a writer than Burke who had declared, in Yeats's "political bible": ". . . there is no power existing of force to alter it, without the breach of covenant, or the contract of all the parties."[61] Yeats, therefore, supported the severe public safety measures which seemed to foreshadow the forthcoming oppression of the ignorant.[62] However, he was no readier to forego his independent judgment out of regard for his governmental allies than for his Independent allies in the Seanad. Even in the first triennium he was no stooge of O'Higgins. His defence of the judiciary against the control of "every executive whatever" and, more trivially, his reluctance in the case of the fire hazard to the National Museum "to take the opinion of a board which is under the influence of the Government," testify to his critical spirit.[63] In his second triennium criticism was transformed into defiance.

From June 1925 the latent contradictions in Yeats's social outlook

59. See McCracken, *Representative Government*, pp. 31–34, 92–93, 96–99.
60. That is, the life of its (Republican) citizens. See "Ireland, 1921–1931," p. 137; cf. *Explorations*, pp. 338–39.
61. "An Appeal from the New to the Old Whigs" (1791), in *Works* (London 1852), IV, p. 458. Cf. Torchiana, *Yeats and Georgian Ireland*, p. 169.
62. Of the sixteen Public Safety and related Acts passed between 1923 and 1928 Yeats suggested amendment to only one, when in 1923 he demanded proper prison inspection and the reduction of police powers of summary arrest. See H. Hanna, *The Statute Law of the Irish Free State 1922 to 1928* (Dublin 1929), pp. 37ff.; *Debates*, I, cols. 1440–41, 1579, 1638–39; and passim.
63. *Ibid.*, II, col. 715 (February 1924); III, col. 67 (June 1924).

began to explode into his conscious mind. After his celebrated oration on divorce he learned at last that neither government minister nor Anglo-Irish senator cared for or understood his dreams of an Ireland in which the validity of Anglo-Irish values would be acknowledged. In his second triennium he attended Seanad Éireann almost as often as before; he worked hard for an elegant coinage and an enlightened school curriculum; but he longed increasingly for freedom from senatorial pomposity.[64] He began to seek "some measure of sweetness and of light, bird songs of an old man, joy in the passing moment, emotion without the bitterness of memory."[65] Weary in body and weary of a Seanad which no longer counted for anything in the government of the nation, Yeats was happy to inform his colleagues in July 1928 that his name was not listed on the panel of candidates for election.[66]

The speech which set off this chain of reactions was Yeats's most unequivocal declaration of his "Anglo-Irishry." Divorce *a vinculo matrimonii* was in practice impossible in Catholic Ireland, and his address had little relevance to the subject on notice—indeed, he did not "expect to influence a vote in this House."[67] He spoke deliberately as a "forerunner" of élitist rule and an enemy of the majority: "If we have not lost our stamina then your victory will be brief, and your defeat final, and when it comes this nation may be transformed."[68] Believing that the bulk of Protestant Ireland was behind

64. Despite recurrent illness, Yeats in his second triennium attended 64 per cent of sittings, only 1 per cent less than in his first. But the frequency of his remarks fell from 114 to 35, and the range of his subjects from 125 to 44 (mean for all senators 1922–28 = 100). Cf. n. 24 above.

65. *Letters*, p. 737 (February 1928).

66. *Debates*, X, col. 1097. The Constitution (Amendment No. 6) Act, 1928, ended both the nomination and popular election of senators, and withdrew the right of retiring members automatically to be included in the final panel from which the two Houses were to elect senators. The retiring chairman, Glenavy, assured Yeats that he could be co-opted at the first vacancy; but Yeats had no desire to return to the "frigid atmosphere of isolation" of the impotent Seanad. See O'Sullivan, *Irish Free State and Its Senate*, pp. 208, 228ff., 466–67; also *Letters*, pp. 744–45; Torchiana, *Yeats and Georgian Ireland*, p. 172; Pearce, *Senate Speeches*, p. 175.

67. Yeats spoke "against" a compromise motion by Douglas intended to reconcile Seanad and Dáil, which had been (and were long to remain) in deadlock over the standing orders relating to Private Business, Matrimonial Matters; but it went against his heart to oppose the motion, which was passed (with his help) by 15 votes to 13 with five hard-line Protestant abstainers. See *Debates*, V, cols. 426–31, 434–82.

68. *Debates*, V, col. 443.

him, he discarded his personal values, to some extent, that he might argue as a "typical man of that minority;"[69] he poured scorn on the majority and called his chosen minority to battle.

The majority showed no signs of weakening, and Yeats's speech only increased his alienation from the Cosgrave government. The government in fact was infuriated by Yeats's diatribe, while Yeats on his part increasingly identified the government with the hated mob. It is true that in the final version of his address Yeats removed all direct reference to Cosgrave and his bad faith, and still hoped that the government might educate the people out of their mediocrity, that while the nation was still ignorant it might retain something of its plasticity.[70] But he had already published the earlier draft of his speech outside the Seanad. The murder of O'Higgins in July 1927 removed Yeats's last inhibitions. He spent much of his last year in the Seanad denouncing "the Censorship Bill Holy Church has forced upon the politicians," revelling in the anonymous diatribes sent him by angry Catholics and celebrating the new unity of the enlightened: ". . . our men and women of intellect, long separated by politics, have in the last month found a common enemy and drawn together."[71] Yeats sang no more of the "might of the Church and the State":

> That were a cowardly song,
> Wander in dreams no more;
> What if the Church and the State
> Are the mob that howls at the door!
> Wine shall run thick to the end,
> Bread taste sour.[72]

But the divorce speech provoked a response still more significant for Yeats than the Church's or State's. For the class with which Yeats had identified himself, in whose interests he had sworn to fight, rejected his advocacy with contempt. The last thing the Anglo-Irish

69. *Ibid.* Yeats wrote in 1931: "I spoke in the Irish Senate on the Catholic refusal of divorce and assumed that all lovers who ignored priest or registrar were immoral. . . ." *Essays and Introductions* (London 1961), p. 400.
70. In a version of the speech prepared for an earlier debate which was ruled out of order, and which Yeats published in *Irish Statesman*, IV (March 1925), pp. 159–60, he had accused Cosgrave of breaking "the religious truce in Ireland."
71. "The Irish Censorship," in *The Spectator*, 29 September 1928, quoted in Pearce, *Senate Speeches*, p. 175.
72. The poem "Church and State" was written in August 1934.

could afford was confrontation with the majority: "A poet may sing of broken hearts; but the task of mending the bruised hearts that seek relief from tragic wedlock in the Free State needs qualities of steadiness and compromise that are found more often in plainer men."[73] With this response ended Yeats's noble vision of the Anglo-Irishry. As long as he remained a senator, Yeats supported the Independents; in his second triennium those old bankers seemed the "most able and the most educated" of the Senators, better at least than that "youthful chimpanzee," the "typical elected man."[74] Yeats still celebrated Anglo-Irish values, but no longer did he attach those values to any particular class of men then alive. In 1925 he had defiantly declared: "We are the people of Burke; we are the people of Grattan; we are the people of Swift, the people of Emmet, the people of Parnell. . . ."[75] But bitter experience had limited the scope of that "we" to himself, his father, a few friends. By 1930 his mind had come to dwell upon the solitary virtues of those few, the true sons of their fathers; it dwelt upon Berkeley—

> When I think of him, I think of my father, and of others born into the Anglo-Irish solitude, of their curiosity, their discourse, their spontaneity, their irresponsibility, their innocence, their sense of mystery as they grow old, their readiness to dress up at the suggestion of others though never quite certain what dress they wear. . . .[76]

And Yeats himself had found Anglo-Irish solitude, "a solitude I have made for myself, an outlawed solitude."[77]

"The wheel swings full circle."[78] In old age, a lifetime of social involvement behind him, Yeats came to accept what a part of him had always known: that he must confront the world naked. "An-

---

73. *Irish Times*, 12 June 1925. Cf. *Round Table*, XV (1925), p. 756.
74. *Explorations*, pp. 412–13. Yeats actually voted more consistently with the Seanad majority in his second triennium (31 divisions of 36) than in his first (47 of 59)—perhaps because he had despaired of converting the majority to his views.
75. *Debates*, V, col. 443.
76. *Explorations*, p. 325. In a slightly later version of this passage "Anglo-Irish solitude" was, significantly, displaced by "Irish solititude." See *Essays and Introductions*, pp. 399–400.
77. *Explorations*, p. 308.
78. Gogarty's comment on Yeats's return to "Fenian" Anglophobia. Quoted in *Yeats and Patrick McCartan: a Fenian Friendship*, ed. J. Unterecker (Dublin 1967), p. 397.

archic as a sparrow," he revelled at last in uninhibited caprice.[79] He
had flitted from Fenianism to Fascism and back, from back-room
politicking to conspicuous privacy.[80] But the poet could never have
attained that passionate condition of solitary freedom had not his
social experience introduced him to "all classes of men." For among
them, and not before the mirror, he had learnt the measure of his
power, the uniqueness and variety of his genius. All his attempts at
social participation had failed in their explicit aims, but all had
enriched his social being. For he learned at last to live unmasked
among his friends, and to hate the rest of the world without shame.
When young he had dreamed of lonely indolence on an uninhabited
Lake Isle, but now his solitude was shared by many friends; his
indolence was turned to frenzy. Much had changed while the wheel
swung. . . .

> Swift has sailed into his rest;
> Savage indignation there
> Cannot lacerate his breast.
> Imitate him if you dare,
> World-besotted traveller; he
> Served human liberty.

79. *Letters on Poetry to Dorothy Wellesley* (London 1940), p. 157.
80. An account of these fluctuations is given by C. C. O'Brien in *In Excited
    Reverie: a Centenary Tribute to William Butler Yeats 1865–1939* (Lon-
    don 1965), pp. 207–78.

The Words upon the Window-pane
and *Yeats's Encounter*
with *Jonathan Swift*

Douglas N. Archibald

In 1927 W. B. Yeats wrote "Blood and the Moon," his first poem explicitly devoted to Swift and his contemporaries, and most memorable for those vivid and titanic portraits of them in the second section. The opening stanza, immediately following "A Dialogue of Self and Soul" in *Collected Poems*, extends the blessings of that poem to Thoor Ballylee and elliptically defines two paradoxical relationships that had recently preoccupied Yeats: the dependence of grace and order upon power and violence which he had explored in "Meditations in Time of Civil War;" and the dependence of a nation upon those great intellects that master and utter its ethos and yet who, in their turn, are dependent upon the national spirit which they articulate. The stanza anticipates Yeats's commentary on Swift's idea of liberty and suggests his appreciation of Swiftian scorn. It is also an instance of his deceptively casual incorporation of Swift legend. In *Conjectures on Original Composition* Edward Young had recalled an episode that was to become part of Dublin's ample lore about the Dean:

> I remember, as I and others were taking with him an evening's walk, about a mile out of Dublin, he stopt short; we passed on; but perceiving that he did not follow us, I went back; and found him fixed as a statue, and earnestly gazing upward at a noble elm, which in its uppermost branches was much withered, and decayed. Pointing at it, he said, "I shall be like that tree, I shall die at top."[1]

1. Edward Young, *Conjectures on Original Composition*, ed. Edith J. Morley (Manchester 1918), p. 29.

Yeats converts the anecdote, as Swift had converted so much of his own experience, into an attack on modernism:

> Blessed be this place,
> More blessed still this tower;
> A bloody, arrogant power
> Rose out of the race
> Uttering, mastering it,
> Rose like these walls from these
> Storm-beaten cottages—
> In mockery I have set
> A powerful emblem up,
> And sing it rhyme upon rhyme
> In mockery of a time
> Half dead at the top.

Swift is a compelling force in the conception and execution of "Blood and the Moon." It is difficult to believe that Young's recollection and Yeats's reading do not hover somewhere behind and within that powerful emblem around which the poem is organized. It is more difficult, however, to determine the degree of self-consciousness with which Swift's grim prophecy is invoked, the precise dimensions of his figure in the poem, or his more general significance to Yeats in 1927. One does not know quite what to do with the presence of Swift in the consciousness of Yeats—how to chart it, or assess it, or participate in it. It brings us right up against large questions of literary influence, literary history, and all their attendant problems.

Like other readers, I have thought about these problems and ways of coping with them, and have tried to suggest a more capacious and flexible language than we ordinarily use. It is possible, I believe, to discover patterns of literary relationship: patterns of confrontation (Hemingway "takes on" Balzac and James, Auden parodies, Wilde steals); of mediation (facing Nature, Dorothy stands for Wordsworth's younger self, Coleridge—briefly but crucially—for an older and wiser self); of resonance (often, to alter Thoreau's metaphor, writers march to the tune of the same drummer); and of encounter (the confrontation that is consummated or sublimated). The exploration of these and other patterns can liberate us from a vulgar positivism, mitigate the anxiety of subjectivism, and lessen the burden of the past. It can serve to remind us of something we all more or less sense, that when we are reading well, we exist in a kind of imaginative present, attending to the truth and value of yesterday and to the experience and needs of today. Our understanding inevitably involves some circularity: we must begin empirically, with the terms and issues provided by the authors we are reading. In this essay I should like to explore once again—because I do not think critics have approached it properly—Yeats's encounter with Jonathan Swift.[2]

Yeats recalled in 1931 that when he was a young man he had

> turned from Goldsmith and from Burke because they had come to seem a part of the English system, from Swift because I acknowledged, being a romantic, no verse between Cowley and Smart's *Song to David*, no prose between Sir Thomas Browne and the *Conversations* of Landor. But now I read Swift for months together, Burke and Berkeley less often but always with excitement, and Goldsmith lures and waits. . . . Swift haunts me; he is always just round the next corner.[3]

Yeats must have known some Swift as a schoolboy, read more for essays written or planned in the nineties, and again around 1910 when he was being considered for Edward Dowden's chair at

2. "Yeats's Encounters: Observations on Literary Influence and Literary History," *New Literary History*, 1: 3 (Spring 1970), pp. 439–69. The full-length studies which most adequately recognize the importance of Swift are Joseph Hone's *W. B. Yeats: 1865–1939* (2nd ed. rev.; London 1962), Richard Ellmann's *Yeats: The Man and the Masks* (New York 1948), and T. R. Henn's *The Lonely Tower: Studies in the Poetry of W. B. Yeats* (London 1950). Donald T. Torchiana's *W. B. Yeats and Georgian Ireland* (Evanston 1966) contains a thorough investigation; it is limited by the shortcomings of most conventional influence studies and never quite brings together the two minds it discusses; it does assemble some previously unavailable or disparate information and all subsequent studies, including this one, are in its debt. The best discussion of Yeats and Anglo-Ireland is Thomas R. Whitaker's *Swan and Shadow: Yeats's Dialogue with History* (Chapel Hill 1964), especially ch. IX. The essays include D. E. S. Maxwell, "Swift's Dark Grove: Yeats and the Anglo-Irish Tradition," *W. B. Yeats 1865–1965: Centenary Essays on the Art of W. B. Yeats* (Ibadan 1965), pp. 18–32; Thomas Flanagan, "A Discourse by Swift, A Play by Yeats," *University Review*, V (Spring 1968), pp. 9–22; and Peter Faulkner, "Yeats and the Irish Eighteenth Century," *The Dolmen Press Yeats Centenary Papers*, ed. Liam Miller (Dublin 1968), pp. 85–124. A useful antidote to some and warning to all is Ellmann's "Yeats Without Analogue," *Kenyon Review*, XXVI (1964), pp. 30–47.

3. *Explorations*, pp. 344–45.

Trinity.[4] By 1930 his knowledge of the man and his work was extensive, and deep. He had read or read in: *The Contests and Dissensions in Athens and Rome, The History of the Last Four Years of the Queen*, the *Journal to Stella*, much of the *Correspondence, A Tale of a Tub, The Battle of the Books, Gulliver's Travels, The Drapier's Letters*, and *A Modest Proposal*. It is reasonable to assume that he read in or about the *Bickerstaff Papers, An Argument Against Abolishing Christianity in England, A Letter to a Young Gentleman Lately enter'd into Holy Orders*, and some of the *Sermons* and *Thoughts on Religion*. He knew enough of Swift's verse to claim that Stella was a better poet; this probably included, along with the three or four well-known pieces, "Cadenus and Vanessa," some of the poems to Stella, and some of the scatalogical verse.[5]

4. *The Letters of W. B. Yeats*, ed. Allan Wade (London 1954), pp. 154n., 156, 550, 555, 557; Whitaker, p. 189; Torchiana, p. 124.
5. I infer Yeats's knowledge of the Bickerstaff papers from his general awareness of Swift's life and his appreciation of the debunker [e.g. *Essays and Introductions* (London 1961), p. 398.]. I infer his knowledge of the religious writings from comments and allusions; e.g., Yeats writes [*Explorations*, p. 334] that Swift "looked upon himself, he says somewhere, as appointed to guard a position"; "somewhere" is *Thoughts on Religion, The Prose Works of Jonathan Swift*, ed. Herbert Davis (14 vols.; Oxford 1939–68), IX, p. 262—hereafter cited as *Prose Works*; Yeats's speculations about Swift's religious beliefs [e.g., *Explorations*, pp. 314–17, 356] depend, in part, upon *Thoughts on Religion*, pp. 259–64 and upon *A Letter to a Young Gentleman, Prose Works*, IX, pp. 61–81; Yeats begins one sentence [*Explorations*, p. 349]: "In 1730 Swift said from the pulpit. . . ."
   Yeats's references to the other Swift titles can be more positively identified: see "Ireland, 1921–31," *Spectator*, 148 (30 Jan. 1932), p. 137; "The Irish Censorship," *Spectator*, p. 141 (29 Sept. 1928), p. 391; *W. B. Yeats and T. Sturge Moore: Their Correspondence, 1901–1937*, ed. Ursula Bridge (London 1953), p. 160; *The Senate Speeches of W. B. Yeats*, ed. Donald R. Pearce (London 1961), p. 178; *A Vision* (New York 1961), p. 4; *Explorations*, pp. 243–63, 289, 292, 294, 313, 315; *Letters*, pp. 664, 773, 818–19, 876, 892.
   Yeats used Thomas Sheridan's edition (17 vols.; London 1784) and read his *Life* (vol. 1) as well as Dr. Johnson's. He also read Richard Ashe King's *Swift in Ireland* (Dublin 1896) and reviewed it for *Bookman* (June 1896), Shane Leslie's *The Skull is Swift* (London 1928), and Lecky's chapter on Swift in *Leaders of Public Opinion in Ireland* (Dublin 1861). His library included, in addition to the Sheridan edition, Sir Harold Williams's edition of *Gulliver's Travels* (London 1926) and his

Between 1926 and 1932 the references to and invocations of Swift begin to accumulate. A substantial portion of the diary Yeats kept in 1930 is devoted to thoughts about Swift and the lessons his writings and example hold for modern Ireland, as are several letters, parts of an essay on Bishop Berkeley, and a section of his introduction to Brian Merriman's *The Midnight Court*. Yeats translated Swift's epitaph in 1929 and in 1930 wrote *The Words upon the Window-pane*, a brilliant play about his relationship to Stella and Vanessa, with an "Introduction," written in the following year, about his philosophy, presence, and importance.[6] Two poems of the period, "Blood and the Moon" and "The Seven Sages," explicitly invoke Swift and his Anglo-Irish contemporaries, and he is a pressure behind the outlook and accent of others, most notably "The Tower" and the "Crazy Jane" series of *Words for Music Perhaps*. Yeats had already decided, as a matter of doctrine, that "there is scarcely a man who has led the Irish people, at any time, who may not give some day to a great writer precisely that symbol he may require for the expression of himself,"[7] and Swift was assuming an increasingly large role in his personal and national mythology. He meant something to Yeats as a man, perhaps as a poet, certainly as a creative force and possessor of a unique and intense vision of life. The idea

---

Dean Swift's Library (Cambridge 1932), F. Elrington Ball's *Swift's Verse* (London 1929), and Stephen Gwynn's *The Life and Friendships of Dean Swift* (London 1933). These books would have made Yeats familiar with Swift's life and writings, and we cannot be sure that his mention of a title indicates first-hand knowledge. Yeats read Mario Rossi's essay, "An Introduction to Swift" and Hone and Rossi's *Swift: or the Egotist* (London 1934) after making his major pronouncements, but he always felt indebted "to Joseph Hone's understanding of the eighteenth century" [the "Introduction" to Hone and Rossi's *Bishop Berkeley* (London 1931), p. xxix, a "Postscript" not reprinted in *Essays and Introductions*; *Explorations*, pp. 361–62; *Letters*, pp. 791, 818; Hone, *W. B. Yeats*, pp. 423–24; Torchiana, pp. 121–22n., and T. L. Dume, "William Butler Yeats: A Survey of His Reading" (Ph.D. diss., Temple University 1950)].

6. "The Midnight Court," *Explorations*, pp. 281–86; *Pages from a Diary Written in Nineteen Hundred and Thirty*, *Explorations* pp. 289–340—hereafter cited as *1930 Diary*; "Bishop Berkeley," *Essays and Introductions*, pp. 396–411—hereafter cited as "Berkeley"; "Introduction" to *The Words upon the Window-pane*, *Explorations*, pp. 343–369—hereafter cited as "Swift." The play itself appears in *Collected Plays* (London 1960), pp. 597–617.

7. *Plays and Controversies* (London 1923), p. 95.

of Swift also carried political and philosophical meanings. Yeats characteristically draws all the meanings together into "the half-symbolic image of Jonathan Swift."[8]

Part of Swift's appeal lay in the contours of his life and the abundant and vivid lore about it. His position—an Anglican Ascendancy dean in a Catholic country—anticipated Yeats's frequent feelings of isolation as an Anglo-Irish Protestant writer misunderstood and maligned by Catholic middle-class Ireland. He saw in Swift the same self-imposed "Anglo-Irish . . . outlawed solitude" that he found in Augustus John's portrait of himself.[9] The enigmatic relationship of Swift to Varina, Stella, and Vanessa must have recalled Yeats's own situation—at once complex, strained, and tender —with Maud Gonne and "Diana Vernon," as well as delighting his sense of intrigue and esoteric. Swift's alleged sexual irregularities were, Yeats says, "folklore all over Ireland;" and one suspects that Yeats, already flirting with the idea of being a "wild, old wicked man," was at least as interested in this sort of folklore as he was in Lady Gregory's other stories from the Kiltartan peasantry.[10]

Addison said that Swift was "the most agreeable companion, the truest friend, and the greatest genius of his age."[11] We are inclined to overlook his loyalty, his conviviality, and his practical jokes: *Vive la bagatelle* was one of his favourite phrases. Those who worry that Yeats, had he not been the greatest poet, would have been the greatest charlatan of the century,[12] and those who insist on the

8. "Berkeley," p. 397.   9. *1930 Diary*, p. 308.
10. The story about Swift's man bringing a black woman off the streets and into his master's bed appears in *The Kiltartan History Book* (London 1926), p. 56; Yeats repeats it in his introduction to "The Midnight Court," which he suggests, following Robin Flower, "is founded upon *Cadenus and Vanessa*" [*Explorations*, pp. 281–82]. Some of Yeats's ideas about Swift's life, and some of the details of the last scene of *The Words upon the Window-pane*, may have been suggested by Shane Leslie's rather frantic speculations in *The Skull of Swift*, chs. X and XIII. For a thorough summary of Swift lore see Mackie L. Jarrell, " 'Jack and the Dane': Swift Traditions in Ireland," *Journal of American Folklore*, LXXXVII (1964), pp. 99–117; reprinted in *Fair Liberty Was All His Cry: A Tercentenary Tribute to Jonathan Swift*, ed. A. N. Jeffares (New York 1967), pp. 311–41.
11. Quoted by Herbert Davis, "Jonathan Swift," *Major British Writers*, gen. ed. G. B. Harrison, 2 vols. (New York 1954), I, p. 526.
12. Most recently and notably, Harold Bloom, throughout his *Yeats* (New York 1970).

veracity of *A Vision* or the logic of its geometry, might remember
the Scriblerus Club and Isaac Bickerstaff. Like Swift and with his
example, Yeats could be intimidating and aloof, but he was also
witty, loyal, and convivial. He was not a genuine satirist, but he was
often an ironist, slippery and unpredictable—at times puckish. A.E.
maintained that "an impish humour" partly animates *A Vision*,[13]
and fuller recognition of this fact would make Yeats studies more
pleasant as well as more accurate.

"I cannot discover truth by logic unless that logic serve passion,"
Yeats wrote in his diary, and it is not the satirist in Swift that most
compelled him, but the public figure whose "convictions came from
action and passion"—"passion ennobled by intensity, by endurance,
by wisdom." As the *Examiner* and spokesman for the Harley-St.
John ministry, as the *Drapier* and Dean, Swift was a public force
who, unlike most modern literary men, had consequence in the
practical world. He and his Anglo-Irish colleagues "spoke as it were
sword in hand, . . . played their part in a unique drama, but played
it, as a politician cannot though he stand in the same ranks, with the
whole soul."[14] In *The Words upon the Window-pane*, Swift stands
for a society in which mind meant power and for an age in which
the life of the intellect and the life of the state could still coalesce.
John Corbet, the young scholar and Yeats's spokesman in the play,
is writing an essay which proves that "in Swift's day men of intellect
reached the height of their power—the greatest position they ever
attained in society and the State, that everything great in Ireland and
in our character, in what remains of our architecture, comes from
that day; that we have kept its seal longer than England."

That characteristic opposition—Swift *and* Ireland set against
England—raises the tangled question of Swift's Irish patriotism,
indeed of his "Irishness" itself. Conor Cruise O'Brien has suggested
that "Irishness is not primarily a question of birth or blood or
language; it is the condition of being involved in the Irish situation,
and usually being mauled by it." On that sensible definition, as
O'Brien observes, "Swift is more Irish than Goldsmith or Sheridan,
although by the usual tests they are Irish and he is pure English."[15]
Yet Irishness of that kind is not the same thing as loyalty, or even

13. *The Living Torch*, ed. Monk Gibbon (London 1937), p. 254.
14. *1930 Diary*, p. 301; "Swift," p. 348; *Letters*, p. 776.
15. Conor Cruise O'Brien, "Irishness," *Writers and Politics* (London 1965),
    pp. 98–99.

responsibility, to Ireland; and "the question of Swift" has elicited violent reactions from Irishmen (and from mere readers) during his lifetime and ever since. It is said that Swift considered himself an Englishman unfortunate enough to have been born in Ireland and who looked on Ireland as a place of exile and on most of its inhabitants with contempt,[16] and that he condoned the disenfranchisement of the Catholics and dissenters under the most atrocious penal laws and acts of exclusion in English history. In 1698, Molyneux had anticipated Swift's position in speaking for "the true English people of Ireland," a significant phrase from the fourth *Drapier's Letter*, in the strong case which he made for legislative independence: the Anglo-Irish community had, before Swift spoke, not only objected to English colonialism and mercantilism, but specifically to Wood's coinage, the immediate cause of the *Drapier's Letters*. Swift effected, this view continues, no real change in the English administration of Ireland. A more extreme view is that his politics were always dictated by personal animosity, that he was not concerned with an Irish or even an Anglo-Irish cause, but influenced by "disappointment acting on a nature singularly fierce, gloomy, and diseased," and by his "bitter animosity" against Walpole and the Whigs.[17]

Swift's more moderate defenders argue that there were mitigating circumstances about his admittedly ambiguous relationship to Ireland, that his nationalism, love of liberty, and sympathy for human suffering are genuine, but repressed and limited by the assumptions and attitudes of his church, his class, and his party. Swift saw each public issue primarily if not exclusively from the point of view of the established church. His insistence on the Sacramental Test, his persistence over the First Fruits, his complacence about Catholic

16. For these opinions I have relied most heavily on: Vol. I of W. E. H. Lecky, *A History of Ireland in the Eighteenth Century*, 7 vols. (London 1892), and *Public Opinion in Ireland*; Edmund Curtis, *A History of Ireland* (London 1936), pp. 275–352; Constantia Maxwell, *Dublin Under the Georges* (London 1936) and *Country and Town in Ireland Under the Georges* (Dundalk, Ireland 1949); Herbert Davis, "Introduction" to his separate edition of *The Drapier's Letters* (Oxford 1935), pp. ix–lxvii; Harold Williams, "Introduction" to *Prose Works*, X, pp. ix–xxxi; Rossi and Hone, *Swift*, pp. 251–81; Ricardo Quintana, *The Mind and Art of Jonathan Swift* (London 1953), pp. 246–72; and Oliver W. Ferguson, *Jonathan Swift and Ireland* (Urabna 1962).

17. Lecky, *Ireland in the Eighteenth Century*, I, p. 457.

disabilities, and his efforts to exclude dissenters from any voice in party or state should be seen as rigorous clericalism rather than English intolerance. We should not blame Swift for the "singular condition" of eighteenth-century Ireland.[18] Disenfranchisement, legislative disabilities, commercial restrictions, and wholesale confiscations had been English policy in Ireland for centuries; if Swift sinned it was because he, like everybody else, took them for granted. Nor should we hold his realism against him; if he was infuriated by Irish stupidity, jobbery, and lethargy as much as by English rapacity, he had good cause.

Swift scholars, at least in Ireland, increasingly appear to believe that the Dean not only needs no apology, but that he was, positively and emphatically, an Irish patriot. The energy and the sheer bulk (approximately 65 titles and 800 pages in the *Prose Works*) of his Irish tracts indicate that his nationalism was no occasional exercise in misanthropy. Their range, especially as seen in the prescriptive tracts of 1728–29, written after Wood had been defeated and his coins banished, refutes the charge that he used Ireland only to battle against Walpole and the Whigs. His countless anonymous acts of generosity to the Dublin poor attest that his hatred of injustice and sympathy for human suffering extended, except perhaps where the interests of his church were concerned, to all the Irish. He did not merely repeat the Molyneux principle; he gave it its most direct, eloquent, and passionate statement, and, in the fourth *Drapier's Letter*, raised it to a universal principle: "I have digressed a little, in order to refresh and continue that spirit so seasonably raised amongst you; and to let you see, that by the laws of GOD, of NATURE, of NATIONS, and of your own country, you ARE and OUGHT to be as FREE a People as your brethren in England."[19]

He taught the Irish, his advocates insist, the principles of the boycott and home consumption—burn everything from England except their coal[20]—and so anticipated, in method if not in doctrine, Sinn Fein. If only for a moment, "he succeeded," Lecky writes, ". . . in uniting that people for great political ends. He braced their energies; he breathed into them something of his own lofty and

---

18. The phrase is from Swift's *Letter to the Archbishop of Dublin, Concerning the Weavers, Prose Works*, XII, p. 65; Oliver Ferguson has aptly made it the title of ch. 1 of *Swift and Ireland*.
19. *Prose Works*, X, p. 63.
20. *Prose Works*, IX, pp. 15–22.

defiant spirit; he made them sensible at once of the wrongs they endured, of the rights they might claim, and of the forces they possessed; and he proved to them, for the first time, that it was possible to struggle with success within the limits of the constitution."[21] His class, in spite of all their faults, did establish the country's first real public elegance, its first sense of nationalism, and its first effective political intelligence. In 1782, forty years after Swift was declared insane and almost sixty years after the *Drapier's Letters*, the Declaratory Act of 6 George I was repealed, permitting the short-lived but great eighteenth-century Irish Parliament. On the day the repeal was announced Henry Grattan proclaimed on the floor of the Commons: "Spirit of Swift! Spirit of Molyneux! Your genius has prevailed!"

Furthermore, in 1724–25, the Dean of St. Patrick's was, with whatever logic, protected, revered, and claimed kin by "the whole people of Ireland" whom he had significantly and self-consciously addressed in the fourth *Letter*. When the Irish Privy Council offered a reward of £300 for the discovery of the author of the "wicked and malicious" *Letter*, though the author was widely known and Dublin full of poverty, no one could be found to betray him. The answers of the "men, women and children" was instead to demand that Swift be given "the Freedom of the City in a Gold-box," and to memorize and repeat in the streets a verse from the first book of *Samuel*: "And the people said unto Saul, Shall Jonathan die, who hath wrought this great salvation in Israel? God forbid: as the Lord liveth, there shall not one hair of his head fall to the ground, for he hath wrought with God this day. So the people rescued Jonathan, that he died not."[22]

It is an exhilarating and moving episode—a moment (I believe the only moment) when Swift, so frequently at the ear of power and more often attacking its abuses, fully and successfully participated in the life of a political community. As he well knew, it could not last. Arrangements were soon made to compensate Wood for his lost patent, and a pension of £24,000, secretly negotiated and issued to a fictitious "Thomas Uvedale, Esq.," was drawn from funds in the Irish establishment. "In the years to come," the most

21. Lecky, *Ireland in the Eighteenth Century*, I, p. 458.
22. From a private letter of Mr. Tickell, secretary to Lord Carteret, Lord Lieutenant of Ireland, quoted by Harold Williams, "Introduction" to *Prose Works*, X, pp. xix–xx.

thorough student of Swift and Ireland has observed, "he was to
labour as hard in Ireland's cause as he had in 1724–25, but he was
to find only frustration, failure, and, in the end, despair."[23]

Troubles accumulated very rapidly: Stella died in 1728; Swift
suffered increasing fits of giddiness; there were crop failures in the
three harvest seasons of 1726–28, causing famine severe even for
Ireland. In March 1728 Swift wrote *An Answer to a Paper Called
a Memorial to the Poor Inhabitants, Tradesmen, and Labourers of
the Kingdom of Ireland*, one of the seven tracts of that period. It is
an angry essay, but not an ironic one, without the familiar persona.
It is nevertheless a revealing prologue to Swift's most ferocious
satire. Swift rejects the anonymous memorialist's proposal for the
massive importation of corn, and seriously discusses Irish agri-
cultural and economic problems. There are hints of the depth of his
anger and range of his imagination—when he calls for "some regu-
lation in the price of *Flesh*, as well as *Bread*," or when he suggests
that the poor should be exported like any other salable commodity,
and so mocks the mercantile assumption that "people [are the]
riches of a country"—but such notes are not sustained. Then,
suddenly, at the close of his argument, all reserve gone, he explodes
with biblical authority and prophetic rage:

> If so wretched a state of things would allow it, methinks I could
> have a malicious pleasure, after all the warning I have in vain
> given the public, at my own peril, for several years past; to see the
> consequences and events answering in every particular. I pretend
> to no sagacity: what I writ was little more than what I had dis-
> coursed to several persons, who were generally of my opinion:
> And it was obvious to every common understanding, that such
> effects must needs follow from such causes . . . *Wisdom crieth in
> the Streets; because I have called and ye refused; I have stretched
> out my Hand, and no Man regarded. But ye have set at nought all
> my Counsel, and would none of my Reproof. I also will laugh at
> your Calamity, and mock when your Fear cometh.*[24]

Six months later the first edition of *A Modest Proposal for Prevent-
ing the Children of poor People in Ireland, from being a Burden to
their Parents or Country; and for making them beneficial to the
Public* appeared in Dublin.

23. Ferguson, p. 138.
24. *Prose Works*, XII, pp. 17–25. The biblical source is Proverbs I, 20–33;
    Swift's version is more compact and powerful.

The *Drapier*'s moment of victory and unity in 1725 defines Swift's one experience of community, an experience that was to beguile and frustrate Yeats all of his life. The second moment, the full *saeva indignatio*, is as terrible as any other expression of the "singular condition" of "this one individual Kingdom of Ireland" that so preoccupied both writers. Mark Van Doren once said that Swift's is "a story of fire in a language of ice."[25] Swift, too, knew "enough of hate / To say that for destruction ice / Is also great / And would suffice."

During the late 1920s the figure of Swift—*Drapier* and Jeremiah to the whole people of Ireland—appealed to Yeats because of the power of his imagination, the drama of his life, and the mystery of his personality. The Irishness of Swift—those remarkably strained ambiguities of attitude, that vacillation between triumph and despair, community and alienation—fascinated the poet and suited the public purposes of the senator. For most of his life Yeats had wanted to "preserve that which is living and help the two Irelands, Gaelic Ireland and Anglo-Ireland, so to unite that neither shall shed its pride." Yet the differences between the Ireland he had dreamt of and the Ireland he saw developing around him led to estrangement and disenchantment: first, between 1900 and 1910, with the Celtic Twilight, the Gaelic League, Catholic nationalism, and the forces those movements represented; then, during the Troubles and the Civil War, with the whole fabric of Irish life. The Irish Renaissance, as a literary force, was spent, Synge dead, Lady Gregory aged, the Abbey a burden, and Yeats interested in other matters. The "heroic period" of Irish history and legend seemed increasingly inadequate, and the nineteenth century (Yeats borrowed a phrase from Swift) "a dark insipid period." Ireland was at last independent, but at the expense of the kind of integrated, living culture Yeats had hoped to achieve.[26]

The Dean of St. Patrick's could serve as a counter against the

25. *Swift* (New York 1930), p. 3.
26. *1930 Diary*, p. 337; "Swift," p. 353. A representative expression of the desire to reconcile the two Irelands is found in a talk Yeats gave to the Irish Literary Society in 1925, "The Child and the State," *Senate Speeches*, pp. 168–74. The earlier disenchantment is most evident in *Estrangement* and *The Death of Synge* (in *Autobiographies*), the later in letters and *The Tower*.

"devout Catholicism and enthusiastic Gaeldom" that depressed and angered Yeats. An Irish patriot savagely defending liberty, he was yet politically conservative and spokesman for the Protestant hegemony. If opinion about Swift's patriotism varied, and if that patriotism itself vacillated, so much the better. He not only teaches the virtues of national commitment and consciousness, but the lesson that scorn, indignation, and aloofness are necessary complements to patriotism. If earlier in his life Yeats had attempted to find a voice expressive of the Celt, he is now preoccupied with finding a voice for the Anglo-Irish minority, with trying to bring the Ascendancy "back into the tapestry" of Irish life, and urging the new state "to base some vital part of its culture upon Burke, Swift and Berkeley." Characteristically, Yeats is most militant and oracular when, in his peroration to the Senate Speech on Divorce, he feels that his position, or that of the minority he represents, has been severely and unjustly threatened:

> This is a matter of very great seriousness. I think it is tragic that within three years of this country gaining its independence we should be discussing a measure which a minority of this nation considers to be grossly oppressive. I am proud to consider myself a typical man of that minority. We against whom you have done this thing are no petty people. We are one of the great stocks of Europe. We are the people of Burke; we are the people of Grattan; we are the people of Swift, the people of Emmet, the people of Parnell. We have created the most of the modern literature of this country. We have created the best of its political intelligence.[27]

This may be more snobbery than politics or history, and the whole speech, on the floor of Seanad Éireann, was certainly tactless ("Alas, poor Ireland, who shall teach thy very Senators wisdom?" John Wesley complained in 1787);[28] but Yeats does transform it into the assured poetry of section III of "The Tower"; and it is a perception upon which he strenuously insists between 1925 and 1932. Swift has become the central figure of a new national mythology:

> The battle of the Boyne overwhelmed a civilisation full of religion and myth, and brought in its place intelligible laws planned out upon a great blackboard, a capacity for horizontal lines, for rigid

27. *1930 Diary*, p. 338; *Essays and Introductions*, p. 517; *Letters*, p. 779; *Senate Speeches*, pp. 98–99.
28. Wesley's *Journal*, quoted by Maxwell, *Dublin*, p. 61.

shapes, for buildings, for attitudes of mind that could be multiplied
like an expanding bookcase: the modern world, and something that
appeared and perished in its dawn, an instinct for Roman rhetoric,
Roman elegance. It established a Protestant aristocracy, some of
whom neither called themselves English nor looked with contempt
or dread upon conquered Ireland. Indeed the battle was scarcely
over when Molyneux, speaking in their name, affirmed the sover-
eignty of the Irish Parliament. No one had the right to make our
laws but the King, Lords and Commons of Ireland; the battle had
been fought to change not an English but an Irish Crown; and
our Parliament was almost as ancient as that of England. It was
this doctrine that Swift uttered in the fourth *Drapier Letter* with
such astringent eloquence that it passed from the talk of study and
parlour to that of road and market, and created the political
nationality of Ireland.[29]

The antithesis is familiar: the rigid rules of rhetoric, Roman
elegance, and national pride set against religion and myth. Yeats is
almost always ambivalent about the eighteenth century. He dislikes
the Enlightenment and neoclassicism; "that hated century" is usually
dismissed because it is dry and mechanical, scientific and material-
istic, commercial and vulgar, ridden by abstractions and weakened
by timidity, with an art that is merely "external, sentimental, and
logical."[30] But he endorses conservatism and reveres (and needs)
Swift, Berkeley, and Burke; so he usually establishes a double
perspective, setting the dryness of Augustan England against the
power, passion, and fecundity of Georgian Ireland. In Yeats's system
the eighteenth century includes that moment when mechanism over-
takes organism; for personal and patriotic as well as historical and
theoretical reasons, he maintained that the capitulation had already
taken place in England—led by Bacon, Newton, and Locke—but
that eighteenth-century Ireland contained "a Renaissance echo,"
fragile and combative, still struggling to keep the seal. With genuine,
if wayward, historical accuracy and with great imaginative conviction, he celebrates the Anglo-Irish Augustans as outsiders, rebels
against the orthodoxies and inadequacies of their time, who "found
in England the opposite that stung their own thought into expression
and made it lucid."[31]

29. "Swift," pp. 347–48.
30. See *Autobiographies* (London 1961), pp. 169, 175, 358, 537; *Explorations*, p. 432; *A Vision*, p. 296f.; *Essays and Introductions*, p. 510.
31. "Swift," p. 345; *A Vision*, p. 297; "Berkeley," p. 402.

So Yeats found Georgian Ireland by exclusion as well as by instinct and design. England and Europe were too distant, alien, and formidable for him to endorse; Romantic Ireland was not quite dead and gone, but it had paled since the turn of the century. Hence Swift, Berkeley, and Burke momentarily replace Cuchulain, Deirdre, and Cathleen ni Houlihan. If the Free State is to discover its national identity, and if that identity is to be of any worth, Yeats says over and over again during this period, it must accept the position of such figures in the development of the nation and heed the wisdom and force of their example.

Yeats is most systematic about the "scheme of intellectual nationalisms," which he found defined by Swift and his contemporaries, in the *1930 Diary* and in the "Introduction" to *The Words upon the Window-pane*, which is addressed to the "Cellars and Garrets" of Dublin and which begins with this fundamental question: "What shall occupy our imagination?" "We must," he answers, ". . . decide among these three ideas of national life: that of Swift; that of a great Italian of his day [Vico]; that of modern England [progressivist, postivistic, materialistic]." All three ideas originate, for Yeats, in philosophies of history, which lead him to a consideration of *The Contests and Dissensions in Athens and Rome*. He calls it "Swift's one philosophical work," which is no doubt a curious judgment but not an absurd one, and Yeats's reading is perceptive and substantially correct. He endorses Swift's view of the past as drama and personal experience and contrasts it with the modern historian's tendency to see only a conflict of material interests, a kind of analysis which Yeats finds lifeless and desiccating.[32] He approves of Swift's negative idea of history—"Swift seemed to shape his narrative [of *Athens and Rome*] upon some clairvoyant vision of his own life, for he saw civilization pass away from comparative happiness and youthful vigour to an old age of violence and self-contempt"—and aligns it with his own and Vico's cyclical theories, against the modern historiography of "Anglo-Saxon nations where

---

32. *Letters*, p. 779; *1930 Diary*, pp. 289–90; "Swift," p. 343f. Some of the *1930 Diary* is later used in the Swift essay; because they were written so nearly at the same time and show no significant change of substance or attitude, I do not always distinguish them in my text. For a rough test of the accuracy of Yeats's reading of *Contests and Dissensions*, cf. Quintana, *Mind and Art*, pp. 130–36.

progress, impelled by moral enthusiasm and the Patent Office, seems a perpetual straight line":

> I suggest to the Cellars and Garrets that though history is too short to change either the idea of progress or the eternal circuit into scientific fact, the eternal circuit may best suit our preoccupation with the soul's salvation, our individualism, our solitude. Besides we love antiquity, and that other idea—progress—the sole religious myth of modern man, is only two hundred years old.[33]

Swift would have been bemused by *A Vision*'s philosophy of history and scornful of its heterodoxy; and Yeats has to do some juggling to incorporate *Contests and Dissensions* into it. Yet the essential burden of the negative idea of history—that the task of the cultivated man is to fight the rising tide of barbarism and chaos—was close to Yeats's instincts and ideas at this time. His invocations of Georgian Ireland are also attempts to justify and provide a heritage for unpopular politics. The persisting gap between the Anglo-Irish gentry and Roman Catholic people was clearly widening, and the gentry was becoming less powerful and more anomalous. So Swift, Berkeley, and Burke are set up against popular democracy and socialism as well as against devout Catholicism, enthusiastic Gaeldom, and English materialism. They "dreaded a return of public disorder," Yeats writes with an eye on Irish and European events, and so "demand[ed] for the State the obedience a Connacht priest demands for the Church"; they restored "European spirituality" and "European order" and "re-created conservative thought."[34] As with his speech on divorce, Yeats's view of the political ideas of

33. "Swift," pp. 353–55; *1930 Diary*, pp. 313–15; *A Vision*, p. 50. The interpretation of history in *Dove or Swan* (*A Vision*, pp. 267–302) is symbolized by a double cone. As one age expands towards its ultimate, inevitable disintegration, it both counteracts the preceding age and lays a foundation for the next age to counteract in its turn. Thesis and antithesis occur simultaneously, and the process of expansion and contraction—or "winding" and "unwinding"—takes about 2,000 years. Yeats located Swift in the nineteenth phase when the disintegration first became visible and the modern man in the twenty-second, only two phases away from the destruction of their common epoch. Because civilization will begin again, Yeats's theory is cyclical; because it is now whirling towards the end of one cycle, Swift's negative idea is compatible with and can be absorbed into a system of "eternal circuits."
34. "Swift," p. 363, *1930 Diary*, pp. 292–93, 318, 337; *Senate Speeches*, pp. 171–72.

Augustan Ireland includes more than a little "sublimation of the old Ascendancy feeling,"[35] and some darker impulses as well. While much of what he says about the politics of Swift and Burke is accurate and acute, Yeats is also prejudiced and wilful. Where he misunderstands or misappropriates he is likely to convert their conservatism into reactionary and authoritarian rage. Thus his reading of *Contests and Dissensions* permits an aggressively oversimplified summary of Swift's career and his madness:

> His ideal order was the Roman Senate, his ideal men Brutus and Cato. Such an order and such men had seemed possible once more, but the movement passed and he foresaw the ruin to come, Democracy, Rousseau, the French Revolution; that is why he hated the common run of men,—"I hate lawyers, I hate doctors," he said, "though I love Dr. So-and-so and Judge So-and-so"— that is why he wrote *Gulliver*, that is why he wore out his brain, that is why he felt *saeva indignatio*, that is why he sleeps under the greatest epitaph in history.[36]

Yeats's most famous homage to Swift is his translation of that epitaph; he also called it, and Berkeley's *Commonplace Book*, "the greatest works of modern Ireland":[37]

> Swift has sailed into his rest;
> Savage indignation there
> Cannot lacerate his breast.
> Imitate him if you dare,
> World-besotted traveller; he
> Served human liberty.

"World-besotted" is Yeats's English, not Swift's Latin, the only significant addition; it is probably there to further the symbolic association of Swift with Shelley, Milton, and Yeats himself—at

35. John Eglinton noticed this in *Reveries over Childhood and Youth*: "Mr. Yeats's *Autobiographies*," Dial, LXXXIII (August 1927), p. 93.
36. *The Words upon the Window-pane, Collected Plays*, pp. 601–602. In his "Introduction" Yeats endorses this speech. The most useful discussion of the dark side of Yeats's politics is Conor Cruise O'Brien's "Passion and Cunning: An Essay on the Politics of W. B. Yeats," *In Excited Reverie: A Centenary Tribute to William Butler Yeats*, ed. A. N. Jeffares and K. G. W. Cross (New York 1965), pp. 207–278; the most balanced observations occur throughout Whitaker's *Swan* and *Shadow* (e.g. pp. 71–75), the most hostile in Bloom's *Yeats*.
37. *Moore Correspondence*, p. 141.

work, solitary, in a tower, while the timid and uncomprehending world passes by; still, it has an uncomfortable ring. Swift did serve human liberty; Yeats appreciated his lesson and was steady and bold in his defences of artistic and intellectual freedom. Nevertheless, in the "Introduction," Yeats again revises Swift's conception (essentially the Christian Liberty of *Areopagitica*), giving it a special, and dangerous, turn:

> What was this liberty bought with so much silence, and served through all his life with so much eloquence? . . . That *vox populi* or "bent and current" [of a people historically considered, a topic of *Contests and Dissensions*], or what we even more vaguely call national spirit, was the sole theme of his *Drapier Letters*; its right to express itself as it would through such men as had won or inherited general consent. I doubt if a mind so contemptuous of average men thought, as Vico did, that it found expression also through all individual lives, or asked more for those lives than protection from the most obvious evils. I remember J. F. Taylor, a great student of Swift, saying "Individual liberty is of no importance, what matters is national liberty."[38]

In his *1930 Diary* Yeats wrote that "all great literature at its greatest intensity displays the sage, the lover, or some image of despair."[39] In letters, in the Swift essay, and in his diary, Yeats interprets the sage. In *The Words upon the Window-pane*, although he is celebrated by John Corbet as sage, prophet, and national hero, and loved by Vanessa and Stella, it is the image of the desperate and despairing old man that dominates the play. The "Introduction" is speculative and assertive, but Yeats recognizes that there is no complete and satisfactory solution to the enigma of the Dean of St. Patrick's: "Swift, though he lived in great publicity, and wrote and received many letters, hid two things which constituted perhaps all that he had of private life: his loves and his religious beliefs."[40] *The Words upon the Window-pane* confronts that private life, or part of it, and is properly ambiguous. It creates an intense feeling of Swift's presence and power, but does not commit itself to any single interpretation of his life or to any precise biographical details. It is a most Yeatsian combination of evocation and equivocation.

The scenario, called simply "Jonathan Swift," was more thoroughly worked out and the play went through fewer drafts than

38. "Swift," p. 357.   39. *1930 Diary*, p. 295.   40. "Swift," p. 362.

usual for Yeats, which suggests that the material (Swift, spiritualism, the séance) was fully and vitally present in his mind at the time of composition.[41] He finished it at Coole in October 1930 and dedicated it to Lady Gregory, thereby accentuating a preoccupation that had become a *leitmotif* of the play: the decline of the Big House and of the Anglo-Irish gentry. While writing the play Yeats experienced a dream "which I dream several times a year," where Coole and Sandymount Castle coalesce to remind him of those lost or passing buildings, attitudes, and values. He attributes the dream partly to the imminent demise of "Coole as a Gregory house"and partly to "the impression on my subconscious . . . made in childhood [by a print of Sandymount], when my uncle Corbet's bankruptcy and death was a recent tragedy."[42] Yeats names his spokesman in the play John Corbet, and he too wants to resurrect Swift as a national ideal and as a stay against the decline and corruption of the Anglo-Irish. The action of the play occurs in a fine old eighteenth-century house imprecisely but forcefully associated with Grattan and Curran, Swift and Stella; and the decay of Swift is a parable of larger social and historical disintegration.

The Words upon the Window-pane is an excellent play, and the more remarkable because it is not, except for the conjoint themes of Swift and spiritualism, characteristic Yeats. It is entirely in prose, largely without metaphor, realistic in method and setting, tightly constructed, deft in its rapid characterization of contemporary middle-class Dubliners, urbane and ironic in its treatment of spiritualism—with its argumentative "Introduction," altogether more like Shaw and Ibsen than anything else Yeats wrote. To a séance being held by the Dublin Spiritualists' Association, in addition to Dr. Trench, the president, and Miss Mackenna, the secretary, come Cornelius Patterson, who wants to discover if "they race horses and whippets in the other world"; Abraham Johnson, who wishes to invoke the aid of Dwight Moody for his evangelical preaching in Belfast; and a Mrs. Mallet, who is trying to get her late husband's advice about opening a tea-shop in Folkstone. The only outsider is John Corbet, friendly but sceptical, who discusses Swift with Dr. Trench and is shown some lines of a poem Stella wrote for the Dean's fifty-fourth birthday and that have been cut into the window-

41. The textual information is in Curtis B. Bradford's *Yeats at Work* (Carbondale 1965), pp. 217–36.
42. *1930 Diary*, pp. 318–19.

pane. Dr. Trench also explains that there are no "evil spirits," only "hostile influences," such as the one that has twice previously disrupted the séance. He goes on to say that some spirits, in their purgatorial development, "think they are still living and go over and over some action of their past lives, just as we go over and over some painful thought, except that where they are thought is reality. . . . This spirit which speaks those incomprehensible words and does not answer when spoken to is of such a nature. The more patient we are, the more quickly will it pass out of its passion and its remorse."[43]

When the session begins Mrs. Henderson, the medium, apologizes for the failures, goes into a trance, and speaks in the voice of her "control," "a dear little girl called Lulu who died when she was five or six" (outré enough for any spiritualist, and a happy revision from "Silver Cloud, a little American girl"). She almost succeeds in communicating with Mr. Mallet but is twice interrupted by "that bad old man . . . his face covered with boils." The first time, the spirit of Swift, its presence conveyed by Mrs. Henderson speaking in his voice, which a startled Corbet recognizes, relives an episode with Vanessa. He violently berates her for having written to Stella, for having betrayed—"like some common slut with her ear against the keyhole"—his confidence and perverted the classical education which he had given her. The unfortunate Vanessa declares her passion and demands that Swift reciprocate it, offers him her body and her soul, warns him about the pain of being a childless, solitary old man, and claims that, were they to have children, "the Vanhomrigh blood" would counteract his and make them healthy. Swift is adamant. He begins with the confession: "I have something in my blood that no child must inherit," but is soon frenzied: "What do I care if it be healthy? What do I care if it could make mine healthy? Am I to add another to the healthy rascaldom and knavery of the world?" As the scene closes (or, more accurately, recedes), Mrs. Henderson beats upon the door and shouts in Swift's voice: "O God, hear the prayer of Jonathan Swift, that afflicted man, and grant that

43. Dr. Trench takes his eschatology from the theories of *A Vision*, and *The Words upon the Window-pane* is a signal example of the way Yeats can make his system work for his art. According to the theory, the corporeal form of spirits depends upon the state of their bodies at death; but they relive experiences that had occurred throughout their past incarnation; thus Yeats can present a Swift of different moments and yet have the old man the dominant and controlling image.

he may leave to posterity nothing but his intellect. . . . My God, I am left alone with my enemy. Who locked the door, who locked me in with my enemy?"

It is impossible to prove Swift's celibacy or to account for it by a fear of madness, and Yeats is too shrewd to commit himself wholly to any theory; but it is a dramatically apt and arresting idea; at the end of the play Corbet widens its reference and insists upon its political pertinence: "Swift was the chief representative of the intellect of his epoch, that arrogant intellect free at last from superstition. He foresaw its collapse. He foresaw Democracy, he must have dreaded the future. Did he refuse to beget children because of that dread? Was Swift mad? Or was it the intellect itself that was mad?"[44]

The second interruption is more peaceful, though no less affecting. It dramatizes the observation of Yeats in the "Introduction"—"it seems certain that Swift loved [Stella] though he called it by some other name, and she him, and . . . it was platonic love"—and of Corbet before the séance begins: "How strange that a celibate scholar, well on in life, should keep the love of two such women! He met Vanessa in London at the height of his political power. She followed him to Dublin. She loved him for nine years, perhaps died

44. *Collected Plays*, p. 615. Yeats supports the theory and speculates about its implications in the "Introduction," pp. 360–63. If Swift's alleged celibacy, and his statements that seem to advocate celibacy, have anything to do with politics, they are more likely the result of his seeing everywhere around him in Ireland a people and an economy caught in a relentless mercantile and Malthusian trap. Nine years later, at the close of his life, Yeats modified the theory into the overpowering pessimism of his penultimate play, *Purgatory*. The old man murders his son in a particularly ghastly scene "because had he grown up / He would have struck a woman's fancy, / Begot, and passed pollution on." Both plays deal with purgatorial renactment of episodes from past lives; the old man finally prays to God to "Appease / The misery of the living and the remorse of the dead," an appeasement Dr. Trench hopes to allow the spirit of Swift; but neither are purged. The scene of *Purgatory* is "a ruined house and a bare tree in the background," and one of the climaxes occurs when the house is illuminated. At the end of the Swift essay Yeats gives, as an example of the "limitlessness" of mind and experience, an Irish countrywoman's vision of "the ruined castle lit up," a vision which appears in "Crazy Jane on God," one of a series of poems also associated with Swift. Like Corbet, the old man protests against the deterioration and contamination of the Ascendancy world: ". . . to kill a house / Where great men grew up, married, died, / I here declare a capital offense."

of love, but Stella loved him all her life."[45] The voice of Swift tries
to express his love for Stella (and his stumbling at the beginning of
the scene is a mark of the play's skill and tact), thanking her for
companionship, moral guidance, and sustenance. He is deeply moved
by Stella's birthday poem ("You taught how I might youth prolong /
By knowing what is right and wrong"), which Corbet recognizes as
the words upon the window-pane. He acknowledges his fear of
solitude and instability, and, very tenderly, thanks Stella for the
comfort of knowing that she will outlive him, close his eyes, and see
him safely away. Alas, Stella was to die within eight years of the
moment of the scene, and Swift to struggle on for twenty-four. The
irony of Swift's false hope is part of the strategy of the play. To
Yeats, twice near death between 1927 and 1930, and acutely conscious of "Decrepit age that has been tied to me / As to a dog's
tail," the irony and the quality of Swift's love must have had special
point. Both irony and love account for the fact that, though she
never speaks, Stella is the second most important presence in *The
Words upon the Window-pane*.

The séance ruined, Corbet stays behind to thank Mrs. Henderson
and suggests that she is not an incompetent medium but an "accomplished actress and scholar" who "created it all," confirming his
own theories about Swift. She replies, "Swift? I do not know anybody called Swift," is left alone for the play's final, terrifying
moment, and speaks in Swift's voice the grim injunction from *Job*
which he supposedly reserved for his birthdays:

> How tired I am! I'd be the better of a cup of tea. [*She finds the
> teapot and puts kettle on fire, and then as she crouches down by
> the hearth suddenly lifts up her hands and counts her fingers,
> speaking in Swift's voice.*] Five great Ministers that were my
> friends are gone, ten great Ministers that were my friends are gone.
> I have not fingers enough to count the great Ministers that were
> my friends and that are gone. [*She wakes with a start and speaks
> in her own voice.*] Where did I put that tea-caddy? Ah! there it is.
> And there should be a cup and saucer. [*She finds the saucer.*] But
> where's the cup? [*She moves aimlessly about the stage and then,
> letting the saucer fall and break, speaks in Swift's voice.*] Perish
> the day on which I was born![46]

45. *Collected Plays*, p. 601; "Swift," p. 361.
46. *Collected Plays*, pp. 616–17; on Swift and *Job*, see *Works*, ed. Temple
    Scott (London 1883), XIX, p. 167; and G. M. Berkeley, *Literary Relics*
    (London 1789), p. liii.

The Words upon the Window-pane is difficult to perform, but remarkably effective when done (or read) well. There is great tension between the three images of Swift. The public figure imagined and discussed by Corbet is at the height of his power; the man loved by Stella and Vanessa is past his prime but not yet sunk "into imbecility or madness"; the aged, deformed, and demented apparition is the dying dean of legend and fact. The delineation of Swift's gruesome appearance—dirty, covered with boils, one eye swollen and standing "out from his face like a hen's egg"—is as moving as it is grotesque. The emphasis placed upon his physical location—he "appears" "in a corner, that corner over there"—makes brilliant use of Swift's complaint that he had been left to die in a corner of his deanery "like a poisoned rat in a hole." His Swift is the most powerful, the most fully rendered, of Yeats's images of despair and suffering. Perhaps the immediacy and intensity of his identification with Swift, as well as the sweeping political and historical resonance he gives to it, is best suggested by a passage from the "Introduction":

> Swift called himself a poor scholar in comparison with Lord Treasurer Harley. Unity of being was still possible though somewhat over-rationalised and abstract, more diagram than body; whereas the best modern philosophers are professors, their pupils compile notebooks that they may be professors some day; politicians stick to their last or leave it to plague us with platitudes; we poets and artists may be called, so small our share in life, "separated spirits," words applied by the old philosophers to the dead. When Swift sank into imbecility or madness his epoch had finished in the British Isles, those "elemental forms" had passed beyond him; more than the "great Ministers" had gone.

> I can see in a sort of nightmare vision . . .
> Locke sank into a swoon;
> The Garden died;
> God took the spinning-jenny
> Out of his side.[47]

"In judging any moment of past time," Yeats wrote in the "Introduction," "we should leave out what has since happened; we should not call the Swift of the *Drapier Letters* nearer truth because of their influence upon history than the Swift who attacked in *Gulliver* the inventors and logicians; we should see certain men and women as if at the edge of a cliff, time broken away from their feet."[48] This is the

47. "Swift," pp. 358–59.   48. "Swift," pp. 359–60.

Swift we now need to consider, the figure in isolation, the essential "half-symbolic image."

We can begin with the question of technical or stylistic influence in the conventional sense. This was raised first, I think, by Horace Gregory, who claimed that "the image of Swift's hand guiding Yeats's is all too clear"[49] as early as 1891 in a poem which castigates "Tragic Eire":

> That country where a man can be so crossed
> Can be so battered, badgered, and destroyed
> That he's a loveless man.

But those lines were added in Yeats's revision of 1924 replacing an epithet—"the willow of the many sorrowed world"—much more ninetyish and not at all Swiftian. Gregory argued that the influence is a matter of parallel formal development: both move from ornate and luxuriant to tough, sparse, and direct verse. But Swift was not a lyric poet; Yeats did not think well of his verse; there is little chance that he influenced Yeats's craftsmanship in anything like the way that Pater, for example, influenced his prose or Blake and Shelley his poetry. Any parallel of formal development is surely fortuitous: as a poet (and particularly a poet writing from 1899–1939) matures, he is likely to become less luxuriant. The influence is of a different and more complicated kind, though Yeats does admire Swift's prose —"his animation and his naturalness"—and recognizes his voice:

> I can hear Swift's voice in his letters speaking the sentences at whatever pace makes their sound and idiom expressive. He speaks and we listen at leisure. . . .
> . . . How much of my reading is to discover the English and Irish originals of my thought, its first language, and where no such originals exist, its relation to what original did. I seek more than idioms, for thoughts become more vivid when I find they were thought out in historical circumstances which affect those in which I live, or, which is perhaps the same thing, were thought first by men my ancestors may have known. . . . I have before me an ideal expression in which all that I have, clay and spirit alike, assists; it is as though I most approximate towards that expression when I carry with me the greatest possible amount of hereditary thought and feeling, even national and family hatred and pride.[50]

49. "W. B. Yeats and the Mask of Jonathan Swift," *Southern Review*, VII (Winter 1941–42), pp. 492–509.
50. "Swift," pp. 293–94.

That is the Swift that most deeply matters to Yeats, the complex legacy that shapes an ideal expression. We can pass over some of the early suggestions of the pressure of Swift behind the voice of Yeats (there are several in *Responsibilities*) because they are not, finally, tenable, and move directly into the years when Yeats is most explicitly invoking the Dean.

In 1927 Yeats wrote "Blood and the Moon," his first poem largely devoted to Swift and his contemporaries. He began "A Dialogue of Self and Soul" right after "Blood and the Moon" and finished it in late 1927 or early 1928, after his collapse from lung congestion and influenza. It is, as he wrote to Mrs. Shakespear, "a choice of rebirth rather than deliverance from birth."[51] "Blood and the Moon" seems to impose upon the intellectual or the artist, in his "drunken frenzy" for an impossibly pure world, a Swiftian mockery of a "time / Half dead at the top." But section IV adds, tentatively and precariously, the necessity of living in the present moment—even if it be without wisdom and with the stain of blood. "Self and Soul" is an explicit rejection of the other-worldliness that Yeats had praised, if not quite endorsed, in "Sailing to Byzantium." It is further an acceptance of a life which Yeats first reviles, and then claims the poet can transform. There are a number of ways to account for the acceptance and the transformation. Yeats had been seriously ill, which probably made him less contemptuous of life, less anxious, even metaphorically, to escape from it. He spent most of that winter at Rapallo and no doubt the Mediterranean blows milder winds than the Irish sea. In *A Vision* and elsewhere he was developing schemes for his own and his nation's destiny; and one is always more sanguine when one has a program. But he was also reading Swift; "Blood and the Moon" alone makes clear Swift's hold on his imagination. This forced on him a deep awareness of man's bestiality and folly. Yeats was too honest, and too much affected by Swift's power, to deny that awareness. He once said that Edward Martyn "read Saint Chrysostom, Ibsen, Swift, because they made abstinence easy by making life hateful in his eyes"; he compared "the horror that is in *Gulliver*" to the horror of Oedipus's discovery, of *King Lear*, and of "Les Fleurs du Mal." Unlike most readers Yeats was not willing to discard Swift's cloacal view of the world as diseased misanthropy or frustrated ambition, retarded development or neoclassic commonplace. It is

51. *Letters*, p. 729.

something, Yeats knew, a good deal more intense and less reducible or avoidable. He called it this "Irish hatred and solitude . . . that can still make us wag between extremes and doubt our sanity."[52] So Yeats has a problem: how to affirm life without dismissing Swift?

Yeats wrote the Crazy Jane and Tom the Lunatic series between the spring of 1929 and late 1931. He began while recovering from his first illness when "life returned as an impression of the uncontrollable energy and daring of the great creators." Their composition was interrupted by the writing of *The Words upon the Window-pane*, its "Introduction," and "Swift's Epitaph." He completed the series after his second collapse. Yeats wrote frequently to Mrs. Shakespear about Crazy Jane, which suggests that he was recalling as well as advocating passion, thinking of "Diana Vernon" and perhaps of Vanessa, too: "Sexual abstinence fed their fire—I was ill and yet full of desire. They sometimes came out of the greatest mental excitement I am capable of."[53] He informed them with the same quality and intensity of affirmation that characterizes "Self and Soul," the same dialogue between body and spirit, the same choice of the impure ditches, the same insistence that an integrated personality can make them pure. Both Jane, whose body is "like a road that men pass over" and Tom, "a ranting roaring journeyman" who swears his belief with Lawrentian energy and symbolism, reflect a deliberate earthiness that reinforces the commitment to life.

Perhaps Yeats reduces Jane to a bundle of rags and her idea of love to sexual intercourse for the same reasons that Swift supposedly reduced Vanessa—to make her see that unaccommodated man or woman must be stripped in just this way before wisdom can replace illusion.[54] At any rate, the series is full of glances at Swift. When Crazy Jane talks to the Bishop her concluding stanza begins with a particularly Swiftian quatrain:

> A woman can be proud and stiff
> When on love intent;
> But love has pitched his mansion in
> The place of excrement;

52. *Autobiographies*, p. 386; *A Vision*, pp. 27–28; *Essays and Introductions*, p. 519.
53. "Notes" to *Collected Poems*, pp. 456–57; *Letters*, p. 814.
54. Henn, p. 42.

and ends (except for the pun which Swift would have appreciated) with a particularly Yeatsian couplet:

> For nothing can be sole or whole
> That has not been rent.

The "place" where love has pitched his mansion is defined in *Gulliver's Travels* or in "Cassinus and Peter" or "Celia." It is also defined in Yeats's diary when he writes that "Descartes, Locke, and Newton took away the world and gave us its excrement instead. Berkeley restored the world."[55] The materialists destroy; unaccommodated Jane and Anglo-Irish Berkeley restore. While they are indeed strange bedfellows (the metaphor would please Jane but probably not the Bishop of Cloyne), they do agree about the sanctity of the self and its perceptions; and they recognize the conflict of opposites that underlies love and the necessity of destruction in order to achieve—"sole or whole"—unity of being.

The pattern in that poem, to put it crudely ("more diagram than body"), is "Swift but" or "Swift plus." Yeats seems to be saying that he will grant Gulliver's view of the world, embrace it even, but that he will transform it by adding his own doctrines and perceptions and affirmations. He was quite self-conscious about the process:

> I must not talk to myself about "the truth" nor call myself "teacher" nor another "pupil"—these things are abstract—but see myself set in a drama where I struggle to exalt and overcome concrete realities perceived not with mind only but as with the roots of my hair.
>
> Man can only love Unity of Being and that is why such conflicts are conflicts of the whole soul.
>
> No matter how full the expression, the more it is of the whole man, the more does it require other expressions for its completion.
>
> All that our opponent expresses must be shown for a part of our greater expression, that he may become our thrall—be "enthralled" as they say. . . . When a plant draws from and feeds upon the soil, expression is its joy, but it is wisdom to be drawn forth and eaten.[56]

55. *1930 Diary*, p. 325. Blake's Spectre of Urthona must also be behind Crazy Jane's wisdom: "For I will make their places of love & joy excrementitious." See "Yeats's Encounters," pp. 455–61, for some discussion of the ways in which Swift and Blake come together.

56. *1930 Diary*, pp. 301–303; I have reversed the order of the third and fourth entries.

Between 1925 and 1932 Yeats was finding in Georgian Ireland the "originals of my thought" that helped to shape an "ideal expression." He felt that his thought and expression completed theirs, that his joyous plant was feeding on their wise soil. But it was also a matter of confrontation and conflict; it was necessary to accept Swift's violence and contempt along with his strength, just as it was necessary to accept the violent and bitter men of "Meditations in Time of Civil War" and the paradoxical relationships between wisdom and power, vision and blood in "Blood and the Moon."

Two relatively slight but contemporary poems illustrate the pattern and its development. In "Consolation" (a poem made "not so innocent" by its last two lines),[57] the first stanza repeats Crazy Jane's interest in anatomy; the quatrain of the second stanza recalls Swift, and the couplet could only be Yeats:

> O But there is wisdom
> In what the sages said;
> But stretch that body for a while
> And lay down that head
> Till I have told the sages
> Where man is comforted.
>
> How could passion run so deep
> Had I never thought
> That the crime of being born
> Blackens all our lot?
> But where the crime's committed
> The crime can be forgot.

Swift, the emperor of Byzantium, and the speaker of "A Man Young and Old" have this in common: they urge a rejection (or a scorn and horror intense enough to amount to rejection) of the complexities, depravity, and corruption of this life "fastened to a dying animal." And Yeats was just as conscious of Swift at this point as he was of anybody else. So he embraces "bodily lowliness" as well as "the heart's pride," the inside as well as the outside, the Swiftian reality as well as the appearance, rather than retreating from it or letting it drive him into blind frenzy.

There are any number of strategies Yeats adopts for thus having it both ways. One is the bold assertion of Crazy Jane or "Self and Soul," replacing the obsession with affirmation: the "profane per-

57. *Letters*, pp. 725–26.

fection of mankind" that "Under Ben Bulben" discovers in the
Sistine Chapel. There is the friendly irony of forgetting the crime of
birth in the joy of "Consolation," a topic about which Swift's irony
is never comfortable. There is the transforming ecstasy of fully
realized romantic love. The lady of "A Last Confession" has had
many lovers with whom she has, like Jane with Jack the Journeyman,
"lived like beast and beast":

> I gave what other women gave
> That stepped out of their clothes,
> But when this soul, its body off,
> Naked to naked goes,
> He it has found shall find therein
> What none other knows,
>
> And give his own and take his own
> And rule in his own right;
> And though it loved in misery
> Close and cling so tight,
> There's not a bird of day that dare
> Extinguish that delight.

Yeats later wrote to Mario Rossi that

> Swift's absorption in the useful (the contemporary decline of
> common sense), all that made him write *The Tale of a Tub,*
> compelled his nature to become coarse. The man who ignores the
> poetry of sex, let us say, finds the bare facts written up on the
> walls of a privy, or himself is compelled to write them there. But
> all this seems to me of his time, his mere inheritance. When a
> [man] of Swift's sort is born into such dryness, is he not in the
> Catholic sense of the word its *victim*? A French Catholic priest
> once told me of certain holy women. One was victim for a whole
> country, another for such and such a village. Is not Swift the
> human soul in that dryness, is not that his tragedy and his genius?
> Perhaps every historical phase may have its victims—its poisoned
> rat in a hole.[58]

It is quite special pleading of course, but it is also an acute para-
graph, conforming to Yeats's double perspective on the eighteenth
century and strikingly similar to Matthew Arnold's remarks about
Burke and his epoch of concentration. To see Swift as a victim is
not an afterthought but something that Yeats had felt about him

58. *Letters*, pp. 818–19.

from the beginning. In 1896 he said that Swift had "given the world an unforgettable parable by building an overpowering genius upon the wreckage of the merely human faculties." Thirty-six years later he wrote to Joseph Hone that "there was something not himself that Swift served. He called it 'freedom' but never defined it and thus has passion. Passion is to me the essential." The *Diary* adds that "Swift, who almost certainly hated sex, looked upon himself, he says somewhere, as appointed to guard a position." "Somewhere" is *Thoughts on Religion*; they are not quite Swift's words, but Yeats is right about Swift's sense of himself. Throughout *Words for Music Perhaps* Yeats is confronting and revising that hatred and passion, putting the poetry back into sex without ignoring the privy walls.[59]

There are further answers and appeals to Swift after 1932. The wild old wicked man of *On the Boiler* and *A Full Moon in March*, with his reactionary and sometimes hysterical contempt, recalls the Tory Dean trapped in Dublin and raging in his way against "this filthy modern tide." Indeed that hysteria, with its occasional grim resonance from Swift (as in Yeats's propaganda for selective eugenics or the fury of *Purgatory*) gives a special point to his claim that Anglo-Ireland recreated conservative thought. For Yeats and Swift and Burke do define something we can call the conservative imagination. They define it in its happy and valiant moments, when it seems deeply in touch with communal and historical reality, and in its moments of excess, when it is threatened and out of joint. While it is true that Yeats insufficiently recognizes the balance of Augustan conservatism, it is also true that his reaction to strongly felt threat is similar to Swift's and Burke's, and that the similarity is instructive: a compulsive and emotional attachment to the past and the established, and a corresponding distrust of theory and innovation; a feeling of personal isolation; an intelligence in uncertain relationship to reality; an inclination to seek authoritarian and sometimes violent solutions; a tone obsessive and paranoiac; a vision usually gloomy and often apocalyptic.[60]

Another, relatively late appeal to the Dean occurs when "Ribh Considers Christian Love Insufficient" and so studies "hatred with

59. "The New Irish Library," *Bookman*, X (June 1896), p. 83; *Letters*, p. 791; *1930 Diary*, p. 334; Swift, *Prose Works*, IX, p. 262; Arnold writes about Burke in "The Function of Criticism at the Present Time."
60. "Yeats and the Conservative Imagination" needs to be more adequately discussed, and the proper context is his encounter with Edmund Burke.

great diligence," sounding something like Swift and something like a more learned and slightly reconstructed Crazy Jane. Owen Aherne, thinking also of literary life in Dublin, had already discovered that "Jonathan Swift made a soul for the gentlemen of this city by hating his neighbour as himself."[61] "Under Ben Bulben" is, among other things, Yeats's analogue to "Verses on the Death of Dr. Swift," his last testament, though Yeats is prophetic and imperative (and rather grandiose) where Swift is ironic. Both men wrote their own epitaphs; Yeats translated Swift's and called it the greatest in history; when the time came to compose his own, he could hardly have forgotten those lines "in large letters, deeply cut, and strongly gilded"[62] on the south wall of St. Patrick's Cathedral; and he does invoke Swift's *Abi Viator*:

> No marble, no conventional phrase;
> On limestone quarried near the spot
> By his command these words are cut:
>> *Cast a cold eye*
>> *On life, on death.*
>> *Horseman, pass by!*

The associations, however, are not nearly so numerous or explicit after *The Winding Stair*. The diary entry about completing our opponent's expression continues: "Yet our whole is not his whole and he may break away and enthrall us in his turn, and there arise between us a struggle like that of the sexes. All life is such a struggle." Swift may have been growing unmanageable; Crazy Jane certainly was. In November 1931 Yeats wrote to his wife that he wanted to exorcise that slut whose language had become unendurable, and to Mrs. Shakespear that he had "begun a longish poem called 'Wisdom' in the attempt."[63]

"Wisdom" became "Vacillation" which begins by stating a problem: "Between extremities / Man runs his course." The first five of eight short poems chronicle "All those antinomies": day and night; death of the body and remorse of conscience that had preoccupied him in *The Words upon the Window-pane* and *The Tower*; transfiguring joy and vitality that became *The Winding Stair*'s response; the ascetic and the sensual life; conventional wisdom and its playful antitheses. The third section enjoins the poetic speaker to prepare

61. *Collected Poems*, pp. 284–85; *Mythologies* (New York 1959), p. 301.
62. From Swift's will, quoted by Ferguson, p. 1.
63. *1930 Diary*, p. 302; Jeffares, p. 272; *Letters*, p. 788.

for death by contemplating, among other emblems, the lesson and limitations of Swift and, more immediately, the poet's own experience in confronting him:

> Test every work of intellect or faith,
> And everything that your own hands have wrought,
> And call those works extravagance of breath
> That are not suited for such men as come
> Proud, open-eyed and laughing to the tomb.

The sixth poem faces the antinomies with the bold and precarious humanism, at the edge of solipsism, that had characterized section III of "The Tower," the ego's declarations into the teeth of personal decrepitude and social disintegration. But the ego is muted and solipsism avoided, as they are to be again in "Lapis Lazuli," by a plunge into history. The "great lord of Chou" and the Babylonian conqueror paused to survey the wreckage of time

> And cried to battle-weary men,
> "Let all things pass away."

The equanimity of lord, soldier, and poet depends upon the assertion that all the antinomies—the tree of life that contains them, human history which records their transience, and song which investigates and celebrates them—all, "from man's blood-sodden heart are sprung." That, as a glance back at "Blood and the Moon" makes clear, is a Yeatsian truth to which Swift could hardly attain. Swift went mad "because the heart in his blood-sodden breast had dragged him down into mankind." Yeats has decided that for all its intensity and endurance and wisdom, Swift's dark vision is circumscribed by its failure to comprehend "the fury and the mire of human veins." He could not—or would not—admit that all ladders really do start in "the foul rag-and-bone shop of the heart."

Section VII of "Vacillation" introduces a debate between *Soul* and *Heart* (or *Self*) where *Heart*, predictably, wins a close but real victory:

> THE SOUL. Seek out reality, leave things that seem.
> THE HEART. What, be a singer born and lack a theme?
> THE SOUL. Isaiah's coal, what more can man desire?
> THE HEART. Struck dumb in the simplicity of fire!
> THE SOUL. Look at that fire, salvation walks within.
> THE HEART. What theme had Homer but original sin?

That coal is confusing as well as purifying. In the Old Testament
passage the seraphim flies to Isaiah, places a live coal against his
mouth and says, "Lo, this hath touched thy lips, and thine iniquity
is taken away and thy sin purged." The verses that follow, however,
are less familiar and less comforting; Yeats, acutely self-conscious
about the relationships between poetry, prophecy, and community
must have remembered them too:

> Also I heard the voice of the Lord, saying, Whom shall I send,
> and who will go for us? Then said I, Here am I; send me. And he
> said, Go, and tell this people, Hear ye indeed, but understand
> not; and see ye indeed, but perceive not. . . . Then said I, Lord,
> how long? And he answered, Until the cities be wasted without
> inhabitant, and the houses without man, and the land be utterly
> desolate, And the Lord have removed men far away, and there be
> a great forsaking in the midst of the land.[64]

"*I also will laugh at your Calamity, and mock when your Fear
cometh.*" That is the "reality"—whether articulated by Solomon or
Isaiah, *The Soul* or Swift—that the poet of "Vacillation" has to
confront. He appeals to Homer as a stay against it and as a way of
transfiguring it.

Isaiah's coal is a complex image in another, partly contradictory,
way. In his diary Yeats wrote that "I do not ask myself whether
what I find in Elizabethan English, or in that of the early eighteenth
century, is better or worse than what I find in some other clime and
time. I can only approach that more distant excellence through what
I inherit, lest I find it and be stricken dumb."[65] Literature as well as
the Lord can intimidate the modern poet, inescapably and anxiously
self-conscious about the accomplishments of his titanic predecessors.
Yeats insists upon his Anglo-Irish heritage because it is his, with all
its local embodiments and attachments, and so mitigates the burden
of that distant excellence of the past. Many-sided to the end, the
figure of Swift remains a source of liberation and strength even when
it is being judged.[66]

The last stanza addresses the Catholic scholar and mystic, Baron
Friedrich Von Hügel, who had argued that the Christian vision was

64. Isaiah VI, 6–12.
65. *1930 Diary*, p. 294.
66. Discussions of the burden of the past and some of the ways writers cope
    with it include: Walter J. Bate, "The English Poet and the Burden of the

the artist's. Yeats acknowledges the appeal of Christian doctrine, honours sanctity, and gladly admits his belief in miracles. Still, he plays a "predestined part" and must choose the mixed fortunes of life before the tomb:

> Homer is my example and his unchristened heart.
> The lion and the honeycomb, what has the Scripture said?
> So get you gone, Von Hügel, though with blessings on your head.

Sweetness and light come from terror and destruction. Yeats must also have had Samson's riddle in mind when he composed "Meditations in Time of Civil War" and, in a different mood, when he animated those flamboyant characters from Barrington in "The Tower." He had certainly remembered it in the early twenties, when he recalled the Irish Literary Society and infused it (anachronistically) with the spirit of Swift: "If we were, as I had dreaded, declamatory, loose, and bragging, we were but the better fitted—that declared and measured—to create unyielding personality, manner at once cold and passionate, daring long-premeditated act; and if bitter beyond all the people of the world, we might yet lie—that too declared and measured—nearest the honeyed comb."[67]

"The swordsman throughout repudiates the saint," Yeats wrote Mrs. Shakespear as he revised his poetry in 1932, "but not without vacillation. Is that perhaps the sole theme—Usheen and Patrick— 'so get you gone Von Hügel though with blessings on your head'?"[68] The honeyed comb, Homer's theme and way, this life and original sin—the apprehension of which had caused Swift so much pain and given him so much force—is the poet's choice; just as it was "the crime of death and birth" demanded in "Self and Soul," the "crime of being born" ironically dismissed in "Consolation," and the bad language of Crazy Jane. Yeats does perceive the "concrete reality" of Swift—few men better—but he also knows that it was partial, that it must be measured as well as declared, overcome as well as exalted. Like the mysticism of a saint, a clergyman's disgust is a

---

Past, 1660-1820," *Aspects of the Eighteenth Century*, ed. Earl R. Wasserman (Baltimore 1965), pp. 245–64, expanded into the Alexander lectures in 1969 and published as *The Burden of the Past and the English Poet* (Cambridge, Mass. 1970); Bloom's *Yeats*, chs. 1–6; and "Yeats's Encounters," pp. 461–69.

67. *Autobiographies*, p. 207; Samson's riddle is Judges XIV, 5–18.
68. *Letters*, p. 798.

rejection of the world. Yeats's myth, he said, was rooted in the earth. Self can only bless and be blessed by pitching into "the frog-spawn of a blind man's ditch." Jane must be rent to become whole and the soul which creates light by the lover's union must have a body which is naked and a beast. What Yeats wants—and struggles impressively to attain—is a kind of lay sanctity, a secular beatitude which absorbs and transforms the partiality of Swift's disgust as well as the artificiality of the drowsy emperor's hammered gold and the other-worldliness of Von Hügel.[69]

Yeats observed that "history is necessity until it takes fire in someone's head and becomes freedom or virtue." That achieved freedom attests to the necessity of Yeats's encounter with Swift, results from his arguments, and justifies his revisions—his trans-formation of the historical Dean and *Drapier* into the essential, half-symbolic image. His idea of Swift is always personal and some-times wayward and capricious; his interpretation of Georgian Ire-land is coloured by his own needs, which include the darker political impulses which were then forming and which take such dreary and dangerous shapes by 1933. Yet Yeats is also profoundly right about Swift, corrective of conventional views and fruitful for himself. The years of his immersion in the Anglo-Irish eighteenth century are, after all, the years which produced *The Tower* and *The Winding Stair*. The engagement with Swift, like the "incredible experience" of *A Vision*, contributes to their "self-possession and power."[70]

Yeats almost always knew what he was about (always in poetry and almost, perhaps, in other matters) and a short poem of 1931 widens our reference and casts instructive glances backwards and forwards. It is aptly called "Remorse for Intemperate Speech," and begins with an angry recollection of literary controversy and republican politics:

> I ranted to the knave and fool,
> But outgrew that school,
> Would transform the part,

69. *Moore Correspondence*, p. 114; the conflagration of lover's souls is in "Ribh at the Tomb of Baile and Aillin"; Yeats write to Mrs. Shakespear [*Letters*, p. 807] that we should take seriously Swedenborg's intercourse of the angels: "His vision may be true, Newton's cannot be." Ellmann writes briefly and well about "Vacillation" and lay sanctity in *The Identity of Yeats* (New York 1954), pp. 268–74.
70. *1930 Diary*, p. 336; *A Vision*, p. 8.

Fit audience found, but cannot rule
My fanatic heart.

The second stanza summarizes, with great compression, his exploration of Georgian Ireland.

I sought my betters: though in each
Fine manners, liberal speech,
Turned hatred into sport,
Nothing said or done can reach
My fanatic heart.

The final stanza is plural and historical, invokes Swift and Burke, and declares Yeats's independence as well as his communality. It suggests his awareness of four related facts: that even the Augustans could not overcome their singular Irish condition; that both Swift and Burke were maimed by it; that they must be absorbed, not imitated; and that Yeats himself has no idea of curbing his sometimes glorious intransigence:

Out of Ireland have we come.
Great hatred, little room,
Maimed us at the start.
I carry from my mother's womb
A fanatic heart.

Great hatred, along with elegiac lament, is a decisive quality of Yeats's final years. The attitude they convey often determines the tone of his confrontations with reality, his valedictory blessings, and his personal, historical, and national retrospections. But those concerns are susceptible to other attitudes and different tones; resolution and harmony also provide one of the major chords of *Last Poems*—a chord which must modify whatever we remark about its shrillness. In Yeats's coda several poems try to obliterate politics; one transcends politics.

"Lapis Lazuli," a poem written in 1936 (and "almost the best I have made of recent years")[71] is part of the permanent and preeminent Yeats. It also implies and recapitulates many of his encounters. It is not an Anglo-Irish or Augustan poem; neither is it strictly a response to or resonance of Swift, Berkeley, or Burke. Its relationship to them is not technical or verbal but philosophic and

71. *Letters*, p. 859.

psychological. The view of the world it embodies was partly created by the engagement of Yeats's imagination with their imaginations.

We can consider just one aspect of the poem that reveals the encounter with Swift. In "Poetry and Tradition" Yeats had maintained that tragedy included mockery: "Shakespeare's persons, when the last darkness has gathered about them, speak out of an ecstasy that is one-half the self-surrender of sorrow, and one-half the last playing and mockery of the victorious sword before the defeated world." He also knew the terror of tragedy and the diary entry about the sage, the lover, and the image of despair continues: "When the image of despair departed with poetical tragedy the others could not survive, for the lover and the sage cannot survive without that despair which is a form of joy. . . ." Despair and mockery he had recently confronted in Swift as he had sensed it in Shakespeare. *The Words upon the Window-pane* is Yeats's homage to the Swift who suffered and despaired. The Swift who mocked is evident in "Blood and the Moon," and, in a different key, in a letter Yeats wrote to Dorothy Wellesley five months after finishing "Lapis Lazuli":

> You say that we must not hate. You are right, but we may, and sometimes must, be indignant and speak it. Hate is a kind of "passive suffering," but indignation is a kind of joy. "When I am told that somebody is my brother Protestant," said Swift, "I remember that the rat is a fellow creature"; that seems to me a joyous saying. We that are joyous need not be afraid to denounce. . . . I am an old man now, and month by month my capacity and energy must slip away, so what is the use of saying that both in England and Ireland I want to stiffen the backbone of the high-hearted and high-minded, and the sweet-hearted and sweet-minded, so that they may no longer shrink and hedge, when they face rag-merchants like [an "illbred and dishonest" reviewer]. Indeed before all I want to strengthen myself. It is not our business to reply to this and that, but to set up our love and indignation against their pity and hate.[72]

72. *Essays and Introductions*, p. 254; *1930 Diary*, p. 296; *Letters*, pp. 875–77. In an unpublished passage of the *1930 Diary* Yeats wrote, ". . . if I communicate with the living mind of Shakespeare when I read of Coriolanus among the servants of Aufidius, do I not communicate with the living mind of Swift still in that almost equal moment when discovering that his life or liberty depended upon an unsatisfactory servant, he dismissed him that he might not through fear endure any man's negligence or insolence, & restored him & honoured him when all danger had passed" [quoted by Torchiana, p. 136].

Shakespearean tragedy is the text for the second stanza of "Lapis Lazuli," but Swift's imagination and his life have sharpened Yeats's sense of despair and mockery. Swift has broadened his idea of tragedy and enabled him to make it a concrete part of Anglo-Irish history and his own heritage. He had to come to grips with Swiftian despair and wanted to endorse Swiftian indignation. The encounter with Swift gave Yeats a powerful emblem with which to stiffen his own and his country's backbone; it has also made more urgent his need to face "the desolation of reality" and to transform it, to transfigure dread by gaiety.

More fundamentally perhaps, Yeats achieves the comprehensiveness and equanimity of "Lapis Lazuli" in part because he belongs to the minority. A poet who is at the centre of a tradition is often, like Tennyson or Whitman, bound by the assumptions and horizons of that tradition. But a poet who, like Blake, is outside the conventional and current idea of tradition must discover or create a larger view, a more capacious world. So it is with Yeats, acutely conscious of his anomalous Anglo-Irishry, of the otherness that, he discovered, had already been defined by Swift, Berkeley, and Burke. Tragedy transforms loss, and the self who mocks the now defeated world creates his own tradition. It has special relevance to a poet who so combatively celebrates the alien and moribund society from which he comes.

Yeats's epitaph for Parnell is also his last Swift poem. In its exultation and indignation, in its stance and imagery, "Parnell's Funeral" is its own kind of *Modest Proposal*:

> Come, fix upon me that accusing eye.
> I thirst for accusation. All that was sung,
> All that was said in Ireland is a lie
> Bred out of the contagion of the throng,
> Saving the rhyme rats hear before they die.
> Leave nothing but the nothings that belong
> To this bare soul, let all men judge that can
> Whether it be an animal or a man.

But its concluding couplet, one of Yeats's final glimpses of the Uncrowned King of Ireland and the Dean of St. Patrick's, is autobiography, not political history:

> Through Jonathan Swift's dark grove he passed, and there
> Plucked bitter wisdom that enriched his blood.

Shortly after Yeats's death, the then Dean of St. Patrick's offered interment in the Cathedral not far from the place where Swift and Stella remain. No one had been buried there for over a century. Mrs. Yeats wisely declined to overrule the injunction of "Under Ben Bulben," and her husband was laid in Drumcliff Churchyard, near Sligo. Yeats would have been pleased anyway. He had wanted "Protestant Ireland . . . to bring back the body of Grattan from Westminster Abbey to Saint Patrick's . . . that we might affirm that Saint Patrick's is more to us than Westminster." For him the presence of the past was intensely concrete, and he had once written: "Swift haunts me; he is always just round the next corner."[73]

73. Hone, pp. 478–79; *1930 Diary*, pp. 296–97; "Swift," p. 345.

Yeats's Versions of
Sophocles:
Two Typescripts

David R. Clark
and James B. McGuire

I

The early typescripts of Yeats's versions of *Sophocles' King Oedipus*[1]
and *Sophocles' Oedipus at Colonus*, which are published here for
the first time, may be found in the files of the Abbey Theatre, Dublin.
The interest and value to Yeats scholars of the former was first
noted by James McGuire, of the latter by David Clark. Yeats has
clearly indicated his indebtedness to R. C. Jebb over all other translators of *King Oedipus*,[2] and the first of the two typescripts presented
here will show that indebtedness (as, to a lesser extent, does the
final version). Joseph Hone tells how "Dr. Rynd of the Norwich
Cathedral Chapter, who was on a visit to Dublin, stood over him
with the Greek text while he turned Jebb into speakable English
with rough unrhymed verse for Chorus."[3] This was in the winter of
1911–12. The play "was forbidden by the English censorship on

1. First produced at the Abbey Theatre, Dublin, 7 December 1926. First
   published as W. B. Yeats, *Sophocles' King Oedipus: A Version for the
   Modern Stage* (London 1928). Cf. also p. 246, note 14.
2. "I have gone through translations and find Jebb's much the best. I
   ordered it some days ago." Letter to Lady Gregory, Friday [26 November
   1909]. *The Letters of W. B. Yeats*, ed. Allan Wade (London 1954), pp.
   538–39. Frederic D. Grab's very interesting and useful essay comparing
   "Yeats's *King Oedipus*" with Jebb's translation does not treat the manuscripts. Cf. *JEGP*, LXXI, 3 (July 1972), pp. 336–54.
3. Joseph Hone, *W. B. Yeats, 1865–1939* (New York 1943), pp. 273–74.

the ground of its immorality" and Yeats wanted to make Ireland "proud of her freedom" by a successful performance there. Yeats explained this purpose, his method of work, and how he happened not to complete an actable version until 1926, in a lecture reported in the *New York Times* of 15 January 1933.

> When I got back to Dublin I found a young Greek scholar who, unlike myself, had not forgotten his Greek, took out of a pigeon-hole at the theatre a manuscript translation of *Oedipus* too complicated in its syntax for the stage, bought Jebb's translation and a translation published at a few pence for dishonest school-boys. Whenever I could not understand the precise thoughts behind the translators' half Latin, half Victorian dignity, I got a bald translation from my Greek scholar. I spoke out every sentence, very often from the stage, with one sole object, that the words should sound natural and fall in their natural order, that every sentence should be a spoken, not a written sentence. Then when I had finished the dialogue in the rough and was still shrinking at the greater labour of the choruses, the English censor withdrew his ban and I lost interest.
>
> About five years ago my wife found the manuscript and set me to work again, and when the dialogue was revised and the choruses written, Lady Gregory and I went through it all, altering every sentence that might not be intelligible on the Blasket Islands.[4]

The manuscript which McGuire presents here answers to the description of the one which Yeats worked on in 1911–12 and which, found by Mrs. Yeats, formed the basis of his further work on the play at a later date.[5] The version of the first chorus which McGuire gives after line 106 below answers to the description of "rough unrhymed verse for chorus" which Hone mentions. The second chorus, after line 358, is announced but not supplied; the third chorus, after line 685, is summarized in three prose sentences; the fourth chorus, after line 886, is again announced but not sup-

4. *Letters*, p. 537n. Hone, p. 274, is evidently wrong in saying that the version published in 1928 is "an entirely new work." It obviously grew out of the earlier manuscript, found by Mrs. Yeats. Yeats consulted various translations including one by Gilbert Murray (Hone, p. 274) and one in French by Paul Masqueray (A. Norman Jeffares, *W. B. Yeats: Man and Poet* (London 1962), p. 246). Cf. *Sophocle*, Tome I, Texte établi et traduit par Paul Masqueray (Paris 1922).
5. In spite of Yeats's "five years ago" (1933 minus 5 equals 1928!) he was hard at work on a "material [must mean metrical] version of a chorus" for *Oedipus* when he wrote to H. J. C. Grierson, 21 February [1926]. *Letters*, p. 710.

plied; the fifth chorus, after line 989, although printed as prose, reads like "rough unrhymed verse"; and the final chorus, in fact all of the play after line 1030 below (consisting of the remaining speeches of the Second Messenger, Oedipus' re-entry blinded, his reunion with his children and his colloquy with Creon) is not found in this manuscript.

We are fortunate that at least two other typescripts of the whole play have survived which enable us to trace Yeats's process of revision. Leaving aside the manuscript translation "too complicated in its syntax for the stage" and the crib "for dishonest schoolboys" which we have not traced, there are seven stages to be noted. They are (1) Jebb, (2) the Abbey typescript presented here, (3) a typescript in the National Library, Dublin, numbered MS 8765, entitled "Oedipus," (4) the same typescript, reading all its many manuscript corrections, (5) another, later typescript which David Clark found in the Abbey, very close to (6) the first published version, *Sophocles' King Oedipus* (1928), and (7) the version in *The Collected Plays of W. B. Yeats* (1934). It is interesting to select one or two speeches and follow them from Jebb through the six stages of Yeats's revisions, without comment, so that the reader may trace the process for himself. After Jebb, the six stages are indicated as "Abbey 1"; "NL 8765 TS"; "NL 8765 MS Corrections"; "Abbey 2"; "Wade 161"; "Wade 177." Let us take the first opening of the play.

OEDIPUS. My children, latest-born to Cadmus who was of old, why are ye set before me thus with wreathed branches of suppliants, while the city reeks with incense, rings with prayers for health and cries of woe? I deemed it unmeet, my children, to hear these things at the mouth of others, and have come hither myself, I, Oedipus renowned of all.

Tell me, then, thou venerable man—since it is thy natural part to speak for these—in what mood are ye placed here, with what dread or what desire? Be sure that I would gladly give all aid; hard of heart were I, did I not pity such suppliants as these. (Jebb, ll. 1–13)[6]

6. Sophocles, *The Plays and Fragments, with Critical Notes, Commentary, and Translation in English Prose*, by Sir Richard C. Jebb, Part I, *The Oedipus Tyrannus* (Amsterdam 1966; reprint of the 1914 Cambridge University Press edition), hereafter referred to as "Jebb," with line numbers.

OEDIPUS. My children descendants of Cadmus that was of old time, why do you come before me thus? With the wreathed branches of suppliants, while the city smokes with incense and murmurs with cries of sorrow, prayers for health. I would not hear these from another's mouth, and therefore I have questioned you myself. Answer me, old man. What fear or what desire brings you here? Be sure that I would gladly give all aid. I were indeed hard of heart did I not pity such suppliants as these. (Abbey 1)[7]

OEDIPUS. My children, descendants of Cadmus that was of old, why do you come before me with the wreathed branches of suppliants, while the city smokes with incense and murmurs with prayer for health and cries of sorrow. I would not learn from another's mouth, and therefore I have questioned you myself. Answer me, old man. What fear, or what desire brings you here? Be sure that I would gladly find a remedy. I were indeed hard of heart did I not pity such suppliants as these. (NL 8765 TS)

OEDIPUS. children, descendants of old Cadmus, why do you come before me, why do you carry the branches of suppliants, while the city smokes with incense and murmurs with prayer and lamentations. I would not learn from any mouth but yours old man therefore I question you myself. Do you know of any thing that I can do & have not done How can I, being the man I am, being King Oedipus, do other than all I know [?] I were indeed hard of heart did I not pity such suppliants. (NL 8765 MS Corrections)[8]

OEDIPUS. Children, descendants of old Cadmus, why do you come before me, why do you carry the branches of suppliants, while the city smokes with incense and murmurs with prayer and lamentation? I would not learn from any mouth but yours, old man, therefore I question you myself. Do you know of any-

---

7. We do not give the variants in the indications of the speakers. All typed corrections are brought down to the line in this and the following type-scripts.
8. We have ignored here some cancelled words and some faintly written words which Yeats has written over. In this instance only, manuscript corrections have been brought down to the line.

thing that I can do and have not done? How can I, being the man I am, being King Oedipus, do other than all I know? I were indeed hard of heart did I not pity such suppliants. (Abbey 2)

Abbey 2 thus follows closely the corrections to NL 8765. Wade 161, p. 1,[9] and Wade 177, p. 475,[10] are the same as Abbey 2. The Priest's reply to Oedipus follows.

PRIEST OF ZEUS. Nay, Oedipus, ruler of my land, thou seest of what years we are who beset thy altars,—some, nestlings still too tender for far flights,—some, bowed with age, priests, as I of Zeus,—and these, the chosen youth; while the rest of the folk sit with wreathed branches in the market-places, and before the two shrines of Pallas, and where Ismenus gives answer by fire.

For the city, as thou thyself seest, is now too sorely vexed, and can no more lift her head from beneath the angry waves of death; a blight is on her in the fruitful blossoms of the land, in the herds among the pastures, in the barren pangs of women; and withal the flaming god, the malign plague, hath swooped on us, and ravages the town; by whom the house of Cadmus is made waste, but dark Hades rich in groans and tears.

It is not as deeming thee ranked with gods that I and these children are suppliants at thy hearth, but as deeming thee first of men, both in life's common chances, and when mortals have to do with more than man: seeing that thou camest to the town of Cadmus, and didst quit us of the tax that we rendered to the hard songstress; and this, though thou knewest nothing from us that could avail thee, nor hadst been schooled; no, by a god's aid, 'tis said and believed, didst thou uplift our life.

And now, Oedipus, king glorious in all eyes, we beseech thee, all we suppliants, to find for us some succour, whether by the whisper of a god thou knowest it, or haply as in the power of man; for I see that, when men have been proved in deeds past, the issues of their counsels, too, most often have effect.

On, best of mortals, again uplift our State! On, guard thy fame,—since now this land calls thee saviour for thy former

---

9. W. B. Yeats, *Sophocles' King Oedipus: A Version for the Modern Stage* (New York 1928).
10. *The Collected Plays of W. B. Yeats* (London 1934).

zeal; and never be it our memory of thy reign that we were first restored and afterward cast down: nay, lift up this State in such wise that it fall no more!

With good omen didst thou give us that past happiness; now also show thyself the same. For if thou art to rule this land, even as thou art now its lord, 'tis better to be lord of men than of a waste: since neither walled town nor ship is anything, if it is void and no men dwell with thee therein. (Jebb, ll. 14–57)

PRIEST. Oedipus, ruler of my land! You see our ages who are about your door; some but nestlings, too tender for far flights; some bowed with age; priest as I of Zeus; and these the chosen youth; while the rest of the people are sitting with wreathed branches in the market places, for the city is now too sorely vexed, and can no longer lift up her head from beneath the waves of death. A blight has fallen upon the fruitful blossoms of the land, upon the herds among the pastures; that flaming god the plague ravages the town. It lays waste the house of Cadmus, but our groans and tears enrich dark Hades. Now Oedipus, King, glorius in all eyes; seeing that when you came to the town of Cadmus, you quit us of a tax we paid to the hard songstress; we beseech you, all we suppliants, to find some help for us. Whether you find it by your power as a man or because some god has whispered it. Foremost of men! Uplift our state; think upon your fame; your coming brought us luck—be lucky to us still. Seeing that you rule over this land; and seeing that it is better to rule over men than over a waste place; since neither walled town nor ship is anything if it be empty, and no man dwell within it. (Abbey 1)

PRIEST. Oedipus, King of my country! You can see our ages who are about your door; some but nestlings, too tender for far flights, some bowed with age; priests of Zeus as I am; and these the chosen young men; while the rest of the people are sitting with wreathed branches in the market places, for the city is now greatly troubled, and can no longer hold up her head out of the waves of death. A blight has fallen upon the fruitful blossoms of the land, upon the herds among the pastures; the plague ravages the town. Oedipus, King, glorious in all eyes; seeing that when you first came to the town of Cadmus, you freed us from a toll paid to the hard songstress; we beseech you, all we suppliants, to find some help. Whether you find it by your power as a man or because some god has whispered it. Foremost of men! Uplift our state; think upon your fame; your coming brought us luck—be lucky to us still; remember, that you rule over this land, and remember, that it is better to rule over men than over a waste place, since neither walled town nor ship is anything if it be empty, and no man [d]well within it. (NL 8765 TS).[11]

PRIEST. Oedipus, King of my country! You can see our ages who are about your door; some it may be too ~~old~~ young for such a journey & some too old, priests of Zeus such as I & these chosen young men; while the rest of the people fill the market places with their suppliant branches, for the city stumbles towards death hardly able to raise up its head. A blight has fallen upon the fruitful blossoms of the land, a blight ~~has fallen~~ upon flock and field & upon the bed of marriage; plague ravages the city. Oedipus, King, not god but foremost of living men, seeing that when you first came to this town of Thebes, you freed us from that harsh singer, the Riddling Sphinx, we beseech you, all we suppliants, to find some help. Whether you find it by your power as a man or because being near the gods a god has whispered it. Uplift our state; think upon your fame; your coming brought us luck—be lucky to us still; remember, that it is better to rule over men than over a waste place, since neither walled town nor ship is anything if it be empty, and no man within it. (NL 8765 MS Corrections)[12]

PRIEST. Oedipus, King of my country, you can see our ages who are before your door; some it may be too young for such a journey, and some too old, Priests of Zeus such as I, and these chosen young men; while the rest of the people crowd the market places with their suppliant branches, for the city stumbles towards death, hardly able to raise up its head. A blight has fallen upon the fruitful blossoms of the land, a blight upon flock and field and upon the bed of marriage—plague ravages the city. Oedipus, King, not god but foremost of living men, seeing that when you first came to this town of Thebes you

11. Material supplied by the editors is in square brackets: e.g. "[d]well."
12. Again we have omitted some cancelled matter for simplicity in these preliminary notes.

freed us from that harsh singer, the riddling sphinx, we beseech you, all we suppliants, to find some help. Whether you
find it by your power as a man, or because, being near the
gods, a god has whispered to you. Uplift our State; think upon
your fame; your coming brought us luck—be lucky to us still
—remember that it is better to rule over men than over a
waste place, since neither walled town nor ship is anything if
it be empty and no man within it. (Abbey 2)

Wade 161, pp. 1–2, follows Abbey 2 almost exactly. Wade 177, as
the *Variorum Plays*[13] shows, introduces a substantial change in part
of this speech:

PRIEST. Oedipus, King of my country, we who stand before your
door are of all ages, some too young to have walked so many
miles, some—priests of Zeus such as I—too old. Among us
stand the pick of the young men, and behind in the market-
places the people throng, carrying suppliant branches. We all
stand here because the city stumbles towards death, hardly
able to raise up its head. (Wade 177, p. 475)

It is not our purpose to trace in detail the six stages of Yeats's
departure from Jebb. There would be no space to do that here. Nor
is it our intent here to evaluate Yeats's final text as a version of
Sophocles' play. It will take a book to describe and present the
manuscripts of Yeats's versions of the two Oedipus plays and to
define the value of his final texts. Such a book is projected for
inclusion in the series "Manuscripts of W. B. Yeats."

A few examples may be cited, however, to show that Yeats seems
deliberately to cut down on the metaphoric, ambiguous, and ironic
language of Sophocles which Jebb has made a certain effort to
preserve. Yeats leaves out, for example, lines 337–40 of the Greek
text which Jebb renders:

TEIRESIAS. Thou blamest my temper, but seest not that to which
thou thyself art wedded; no, thou findest fault with me.

OEDIPUS. And who would not be angry to hear the words with which
thou now dost slight this city.

13. *The Variorum Plays of W. B. Yeats*, ed. Russell K. Alspach, assisted by
Catharine C. Alspach (New York 1966), p. 810, hereafter referred to
as *Variorum Plays*. The reader may find here the other, less significant,
changes in the remaining lines of this speech.

These lines would occur between lines 232 and 233 of Yeats's published version. They do not appear in the typescript, i.e. Abbey 1, so that Yeats must have decided immediately that they were too cumbersome to include. Jebb's note to line 337 demonstrates that Yeats did not choose to retain a Sophoclean ambiguity:

> ὁμοῦ ναίουσαν, while (or though) it dwells close to thee,—possesses and sways thee. . . . But (as Eustathius saw, 755.14) the words have a second meaning: 'thou seest not that thine own [τὴν σήν, thy kinswoman, thy mother] is dwelling with thee [as thy wife].' The ambiguity of τὴν σήν, the choice of the phrase ὁμοῦ ναίουσαν, and the choice of κατεῖδες, leave no doubt of this.

It is interesting to see Jebb anticipating William Empson by so many years. Yeats sacrifices irony for swift action.

Similarly when Jebb translates line 379 "Nay, Creon is no plague to thee; thou art thine own," Yeats does not reproduce the metaphor which is relevant to the pestilence from which the city suffers: "Creon is not your enemy; you are your own enemy." (*Variorum Plays*, p. 819, ll. 286-87).

Lines 122–25 of Sophocles' text contain an eerie slip of Oedipus' which Jebb does not note but does translate:

CREON. He said that robbers met and fell on them, not in one man's might, but with full many hands.

OEDIPUS. How then, unless there was some trafficking in bribes from here, should the robber have dared thus far?

Yeats misses Oedipus' Freudian slip of changing "robbers" plural to "robber" singular. Yeats gives:

CREON. He said that they were fallen upon by a great troop of robbers.

OEDIPUS. What robbers would be so daring unless bribed from here?
                                         (*Variorum Plays*, p. 812, ll. 85–88)

Yeats does not always reproduce, in minor passages, the repetition of the verbs "to see" and "to know," verbs relating to the theme of the play which support the imagery of inner and outer sight and blindness. Cf. for example lines 767–68 of Sophocles, which Jebb translates:

OEDIPUS. I fear, lady, that mine own lips have been unguarded; and therefore am I fain to behold him.

In the typescript Yeats first dictates:

> I fear, Lady, that I have spoken folly; and therefore I would look at him.

This awkward attempt to make the sight metaphor idiomatic is then cancelled by the change of "look at" to "speak with." The final version is:

> I fear that I have said too much, and therefore I would question him.
>
> (*Variorum Plays*, p. 830, ll. 606–7)

Sophocles' lines 528–31 are translated by Jebb:

CREON. And was this charge laid against me with steady eyes and steady mind?

CHORUS. I know not; I see not what my masters do: but here comes our lord forth from the house.

Yeats drops the sight metaphor partially in the typescript:

CREON. And had he his right mind saying it?

CHORUS. I do not know—I do not see the things my masters do.

He drops it completely in the final version.

CREON. And had he his right mind saying it?

CHORUS. I do not know—I do not know what my masters do.

> (*Variorum Plays*, p. 822, ll. 380–82)

Sometimes when Jebb has carefully preserved a word order that allows a double meaning, Yeats has altered it, losing the ambiguity. Lines 568–73 as translated by Jebb (the italics are his) preserve both the sight-light metaphor and the "turn of phrase which the audience can recognise as suiting the fact that Oedipus *had* slain Laius," as Jebb puts it in his note to line 572.

OEDIPUS. And how was it that this sage did not tell his story *then*?

CREON. I know not; where I lack light, 'tis my wont to be silent.

OEDIPUS. Thus much, at least, thou knowest, and couldst declare with light enough.

CREON. What is that? If I know it, I will not deny.

OEDIPUS. That, if he had not conferred with thee, he would never have named *my* slaying of Laius.

The typescript plays down the metaphor and ambiguity:

OEDIPUS. And why did not this seer tell out his story then?

CREON. I do not know. Where I lack light it is my custom to be silent.

OEDIPUS. This much at least you know and can speak out.

CREON. What is that? If I know it I will not refuse.

OEDIPUS. That if he had not consulted you he never would have spoken of my slaying Laius.

The final version removes them:

OEDIPUS. And why did he not tell out his story then?

CREON. I do not know. When I know nothing I say nothing.

OEDIPUS. This much at least you know and can say out.

CREON. What is that? If I know it I will say it.

OEDIPUS. That if he had not consulted you he would never have said that it was I who killed Laius.

(*Variorum Plays*, p. 824, ll. 418–24)

Another cluster of images which Yeats reduces in significance is that of the "track" or "trace" of the old crime which relates to the paths of Cithaeron, to the place where the three roads meet, and to the swollen, limping feet of Oedipus. Thus the opening of Oedipus' proclamation to the people, Sophocles' lines 216–23, is translated as follows by Jebb:

OEDIPUS. Thou prayest: and in answer to thy prayer,—if thou wilt give a loyal welcome to my words and minister to thine own disease,—thou mayest hope to find succour and relief from woes. These words will I speak publicly, as one who has been a stranger to this report, a stranger to the deed; for I should not be far on the track, if I were tracing it alone, without a clue. But as it is,—since it was only after the time of the deed that I was numbered a Theban among Thebans,—to you, the Cadmeans all, I do thus proclaim.

In the typescript Yeats changes the metaphor, rendering the passage:

OEDIPUS. You are praying and it may be that your prayer will be answered; that if you give a loyal welcome to my words, you may find help out of all this trouble. I speak all this among you, speaking as one that knew nothing of this ~~report~~ crime till now.

> Had I known of it it had not been long till I found a clue, but it [was] after the time of the deed that I became a Theban among thebans.

In the final version the relevant lines are omitted. All that is retained is:

OEDIPUS. You are praying, and it may be that your prayer will be answered; that if you hear my words and do my bidding you may find help out of all your trouble.

(Variorum Plays, p. 814, ll. 131–34)

One must resist the temptation to give further examples of Yeats's reduction, in his revision of Jebb, of Sophoclean richness. Enough has been shown to demonstrate the importance of the manuscript which McGuire presents here, the first step in Yeats's revision of Jebb towards his own version of *Sophocles' King Oedipus.*

In collating the following typescript we have followed the same basic text—taken from *The Collected Plays of W. B. Yeats* (London 1952)—and the same procedures and rules employed in *The Variorum Edition of the Plays of W. B. Yeats*, pp. 809–51. Obvious minor errors have been silently corrected and some illegible cancelled words silently omitted. The spelling of proper names has been normalized to conform to *Collected Plays*. "Teresias" and "Cythaeron" are consistent misspellings which may be of interest. The spelling "Polybius," used throughout Wade 161 and Wade 177, occurs in the typescript only as an occasional error (Cf. line 613). Elsewhere it is "Polybus". Some strange spellings of other words have been preserved to suggest that possibly the typist is copying written notes by Yeats. (Yeats was a bad speller!) Other evidence indicates that Yeats is standing over the typist dictating: "~~no eye (?) came~~ No, I came." The styling of stage directions has been normalized.

We are indebted to the Directors and staff of the National Library of Ireland and of the Abbey Theatre, Dublin for their courtesy and help and for permission to consult and use the following manuscripts.

OEDIPUS

TITLE   Oedipus
DATE   [lacking]
DRAMATIS PERSONAE   [lacking]
STAGE DIRECTIONS   [lacking]

Act 1.

1 My children descendants of Cadmus that was of old time,
   why . . .
2 . . . me thus? With the wreathed branches
4 . . . with cries of sorrow, prayers for health. I . . .
5 not hear these from another's mouth, and there-
6–9 . . . I have questioned . . . myself. Answer me, old man. What
   fear or what desire brings you here? Be sure that I would
   gladly give all aid. I were . . .
10 . . . suppliants as these.
11–18 Oedipus, ruler of my land! You see our ages who are about
   your door; some but nestlings, too tender for far flights;
   some bowed with age; priest as I of Zeus; and these the
   chosen youth; while the rest of the people are sitting with
   wreathed branches in the market places, for the city is now
   too sorely vexed, and can no longer lift up her head from
   beneath the waves of death. A blight . . .
19 . . . land,
20 upon the herds among the pastures; that flaming god the
21–22 . . . the town. It lays waste the house of Cadmus, but our
   groans and tears enrich dark Hades. Now Oedipus, King,
   glorious in all eyes; seeing . . . you
23 . . . to the town of Cadmus, you quit us of a tax we paid to the
24 hard songstress; we . . .
25 . . . help for us. Whether . . .
26–7 . . . man or because some
   god has whispered it. Foremost of men! Uplift . . .
28 state . . .
29 . . . luck—be . . . still. Seeing that you rule over this Land;
   and seeing that [it] is
30 . . . place;
32 . . . empty, and . . . dwell within . . .
33 . . . what desires

34 bring you and what sufferings . . . endure, yet

35 . . . not one among you

36 . . . mine. Each one of you mourns . . . ,

37 . . . myself and . . .

38 . . . to awaken one who sleeps.

39 No! . . . cried many tears, and

40 gone upon many ways in the wandering of my thought.
And I . . .

41 already acted upon the only hope that came to me

42 my thought; . . .

43 . . . brother to . . . house

44 . . . Phoebus to learn . . .

45 . . . town. (*Chorus moves*) But I . . .

46 . . . be But . . .

47 . . . shall be no true man ~~if I do not all that the god~~ unless . . .

48 . . . god shows.

49 . . . spoken in good season, for at this very moment they are

50 . . . making signs to me that Creon draws near.

51 . . . bring us brighter . . . ,

53 He ~~will be~~ is comfortable to us, for . . .

54 bay!

55 . . . soon; Prince Menoe-

56 ceus, ~~what answer from the god?~~ Son; what news do you
bring us from the god?

57 . . . news; for the most unbearable things, if one find

58 a way to straighten them, may end in peace.

59 . . . oracle—. . . far your words have given me

60 neither fear nor courage.

61 . . . it, with . . . ,

63 . . . sorrow ~~which I bear~~ endure . . .

65 . . . lord,

66 Phoebus, . . .

68 . . . what rite are we to cleanse us?

68a ~~By banishing a man, or by shedding blood in quittance of~~
~~blood.~~

68b ~~And who is this man whose fate He has revealed.~~

69 . . . king . . .

71 . . . knowledge for . . .

73 . . . god . . .

75 . . . we find out the dim track of

76 this old crime? Was it in house . . .

77 field or in some strange land that Laius came to his bloody end?

78 . . . strange land; . . .

81 . . . perished, ~~save~~ but . . . terror,

82 . . . all that . . .

84 . . . things; a small beginning for our hopes.

85 . . . said they . . . by

86 robbers.

87 But how should robbers dare so much unless they had been bribed

88 . . . here.

90 . . . dead, no . . . rose. We . . .

92 . . . had fallen thus . . . trouble

93 . . . have hindered a full search?

94 . . . Sphinx ~~had~~ put ~~all such~~ those dark things. out

95 . . . thought . . .

98–99 plain. Not as though it were for some far off friend, but for my own cause. For whoever it was slew Laius, he might turn as fierce a hand against myself. In doing right by Laius I but serve myself.

101 . . . boughs, and . . .

102–04 . . . hither, and warned that there is nothing I shall leave untried. For with the gods' help we shall make certain of health or ruin.

106 it, and . . . deliverer.

Chorus

107–30 1st. O sweet-spoken message of Zeus!
What comes out of golden Pytho,
From Pytho to far-famed Thebes,
I cry out, O Delian Healer,
In a sacred terror of Thee!
What will you work upon me?
Is it something ever unheard of,
Or something heard of again.
~~Now that i~~
With the return of its season.
O Voice,
Imperishable hope begotten,
Speak to us.

2nd. No one can ever count my sorrows,
Our people stricken with the plague.
No thoughts that are a comfort to us.
The rich earth ripens to no fruit.
No new life coming ~~and~~—the old going,
Ghost after ghost going,
They seem like birds on the wing,
So quickly they flit away
To the god-trodden western shore.

1st. O grant us our prayers,
That the fierce god of Death
Who has come with no brazen shield
Nor cries of embattled men,
Yet wrapping me as with fire,
May flit away from our land
With fair wind to the deeps,
Even of Amphitrite,
Nor those where none find haven
Nor aught but world-folding sea.
O Zeus, O Zeus, our Father,
Master of Thunder-Clouds!
We bid you slay him, O Zeus,
Overturn this god of Death,
Heap upon him the lightning.

131 ... praying and ...

132 ... answered that if you give a loyal welcome to my words,

133 you ...

134 this trouble. I speak all this among you, speaki[ng] as one
that knew nothing of this ~~report~~ crime till now. Had I
known of it it had not been long till I found a clue, but
it [was] after the time of the deed that I became a Theban
among thebans. This is my proclamation, Children of

135 ... amongst ...

136 ... Labdacus was ...

137–39 knows. And if he is afraid I tell him that if he must denounce
himself he shall thereby be in the less danger. No other
harm shall be done to him, but that he leave this land un-
hurt. If anyone amongst you on the other

140 hand, knows that it was the work of a man from another
country,

141 let him . . .
142 . . . thanks with it; but if you keep silent, if anyone keep
      silence from fear
143 . . . all of you what . . .
144 . . . him, or shelter him, whoever he be; nor shall they pray
      with him nor
146 . . . their houses being indeed that which defiles us.
147 . . . god, and . . .
148–52 . . . man. I pray solemnly that the murderer whoever he be,
      whether his guilt is hidden in his own heart, or shared
      among others, may see his accursed life dropping from him
      and wearing away. And for myself I pray, that if ever that
      man be inmate of my house, to my knowledge, I suffer all
      that I have called down on others;
152 and . . . make
153 these words . . . sake and . . .
154 god's . . .
155 . . . god . . . it was not right
156 that you should leave . . .
157 . . . perished; rather were you
158 bound to search it out. And now
159 . . . powers . . .
160 . . . ~~should~~ would have
161 [typist went off the page. Only top halves of letters appear.
      Line seems identical to published version.]
162 [Only top halves of letters of first four words appear.] cause
      and [?] as I . . .
164 . . . gods . . .
167 for you loyal people, who uphold this cause, may the gods
168 be with you for ever.
169 You put me on my oath, and on my oath O King, I will speak.
      I do not know . . .
171 . . . should tell us what man it was.
172 . . . gods do what they
173 will not.
176 . . . lord, Tiresias, is . . .
177 . . . lord, Phoebus, and ~~from~~ through . . .
179 So was I . . .
181 . . . help, we . . .
187 . . . know; but . . .

189 ... and fear ...

190 ... silent ...

192 ... not make afraid ...

193 be afraid now because ...

195 the prophet ...

(*Enter Tiresias, led by a boy.*)

197 Tiresias, whose soul grasps all things; the knowledge that

198 ... be told, and that that is unspeakable; the

199 secrets of heaven and the low things of the earth; you feel,
      though you cannot see it, that the plague is in our State,

200 and ... Prophet, you shall protect ...

201 ... us. But now Phoebus sent answer ...

202 that the plague would not leave ... had found out the

203 ... and killed them or

204 sent them into exile. Do ... therefore, neglect ...

208 ... task comes ...

209 ... has.

210 Alas! how fearful to have wisdom when there is no ~~prophet~~
      profit

211 for those that have it. I knew this well, but if I had not let it
      slip out of my mind

212 I ... come here.

214 ... home. Most easily will you bear ...

215 ... end, and ...

217 ... strange nor kindly to this

218 ... that nurtured you.

220 shut tight ...

223 knowledge: we ...

224 Yes; for you all lack knowledge, but I will not reveal

225 my sorrows that I may not say out yours.

226 ... know the secret and will not tell

227 it? But are minded to betray the State.

228 ... vainly ask ...

230 What, basest ...

231 ... speak it ...

233 ... I cover

234 it in silence.

236 tell me of it.

240 ... will [not?] spare ...

242 ... deed, and short

243 ... hands, to have ...

244 ... would have laid the very doing of it

245 on you also, and on you alone.

248 ... these not [nor?] to ...

250 ... your blustering! ...

253 ... this? ~~Your art has never taught it~~ You ...

259 ~~Did you not understand my~~ You understood ...

260 well enough—you are but tempting me.

261 ~~But~~ No ...

263 ... say you ... the slayer ...

265 Now but [you?] shall ...

266 dreadful words

269 ... will. ~~What are your words to me~~ I will ...

272 ... think that you ...

274 Yes; if ...

275 ... yes; for ... But that strength is not

276 ... you who ...

277 ... speaking taunts ...

278 ... everyone here shall speak of you.

279 Night; endless ...

280 ... can hurt nor me ...

282 ... Apollo was

283 enough; it ...

288–89 O wealth and power and skill set up to throw down skill in
   the rivalries of the world what envy you create! How great
   must it be if for the sake

290 of my ... town a ...

291 ... unsought, trusty ...

292 ... Creon has crept upon me secretely longing to take it

293 ... juggler—

294 this tricky quack—this man who has eyes ...

295 gains alone—~~this prophet [?] blind in his art.~~ Come ...

296 ... seer? Why when the Watcher, the riddling Sphinx was
   here, singing a dark song did ...

297 ... free.

298 Yet ... riddle at least was ...

299 firstcomer ... read; there was need And

301 ... god: ~~no, eye [?] no eye [?] came~~ No, I came; I the
   ignorant Oedipus, and made her silent;

302 it was I ...

303 ... answer ~~by~~ in my mother-wit untaught ...

304 ... that now you pluck ...

306 ... mourn your

307 ... land. Even now, were ...

308 had learnt ...

311–13 ... anger. Little need have we to hear such words, but rather to seek out how best we may obey the gods.

316 ... but Loxias ...

317 ... you since ...

319 ... stand;

320–22 ... ~~live~~ are living nor with whom. Do you not know the stock you come of? Unknowing what you did, you have been your own kin's enemy

323 whether on earth above or in the shades. And one day mother's

328 ... shall yet be ...

329 ~~Begone! May ruin fall upon you~~ Begone ... Get thee

332 ... you would but speak folly.

333 ~~So seem I now to you?~~ I may seem a fool to ...

335 ... Stop! What man among men was my father?

336 ... day you will know ...

340 ... dark speech!

341 And do you ... for the thing that made ...

344 ... go; boy ...

347 ... go; but ...

348 ... you never can destroy me; and I tell you the

349 man you have been looking for this long while—the man you have been

350 threatening, and for whose sake you have proclaimed a search into the murder

351 ... here; seeming so far as looks

352 ... alien; and yet ...

354 ... beggar though

357 ... that; and ...

358 ... no wit in ...

      (*Tiresias is led out by the boy*)

      (*Oedipus enters the Palace*)

                   Chorus

[No draft of this chorus appears in this typescript.]

      (*Creon enters from house*)

369 indignation. If he thinks that in these present troubles he . . .

370 . . . me, or any-

371 . . . that tends to wrong, . . .

372 deed, I were loth to live my full time out enduring blame like
    this. ~~Such slander~~ What

373–74 life is left to me worth having if I am to be called a traitor
    through the town, and by you here and by my best friends.

375 . . . it but in . . .

377 . . . was ~~my counsel~~ I . . .

381 . . . not know—I do not see the things my
    (*Oedipus enters.*)

384 . . . you the . . .

385 assasin of his master . . .

386 crown. Come tell . . . in the [face?] of the gods was

387 it cowardice that you saw in me, or folly, that you

388 . . . see the thing

389 till you had crepped up on me, or . . .

390 . . . off? Now was it not sheer madness . . .

391 . . . followers.

392 Now listen, and hear . . .

394–95 . . . plausible in speech, but teach me as you will you will find
    me but a dunce now that I know you for my malignant
    enemy.

398 . . . are false.

399–400 If you think that senseless stubborness sits well upon you you
    are not wise.

401–2 If you think that you can wrong a kinsman and escape the
    penalty you are not sane.

403 . . . said I . . .

405 . . . or ~~did you~~ not ~~advise,~~ that . . .

406 that reverend seer?

408 . . . it then since Laius?

409 Since Laius? I do not understand.

410 Was carried from men's sight by deadly violence.

411 ~~To count the~~ It would bring you back a long way to reckon
    up those years.

412 . . . this seer of the craft in those days also?

414 At that time did he speak of me at all?

416 . . . you make inquiry into . . .

417 We made the rightful inquiry but . . .

418 . . . did not this seer tell . . .

419 . . . know. Where I lack light it is my custom to be

420 silent.

421 . . . speak out.

422 . . . will not refuse.

423 . . . he never would

424 have spoken of my slaying Laius.

425 . . . know that that is what he said, but I have as much to learn

426 from you as you from me.

427 Learn your . . .

436 Yes; and it is just because of that you . . .

437 . . . so; if you but reason it in your heart as I in mine, and first

438 . . . this: whether you think that anyone would choose to
rule amid terrors

439 . . . than unbroken peace-granting . . .

440 . . . cases. Now I for one have no desire to be a King, rather
than do kingly deeds, nor any other man who keeps

441 a sober mind. For now you give me whatever thing I ask and I

442 have nothing to be afraid of, but were I King myself I should
have to do

443 many a thing that I myself disliked. How then could royalty
be sweeter

444 than painless power and influence? For I am not so great a

445 . . . honours. . . .

446 all wish me joy; now every man has a greeting for me; now all

450 . . . no lover of such plots . . .

451 . . . And if [in?]

452 . . . this first go to Pytho and . . .

453 . . . gods said; and . . . that

454 . . . sooth-

455 . . . me an'kill . . .

456 . . . mouths; my own no less than

457 yours. But . . . corner, ~~because of anger~~ [?] upon . . .

460 . . . friend, . . .

465 . . . well, and as ~~a prudent man~~ one who thinks

466 before he speaks, those that speak quickly

467 are unsure.

468 When the stealthy plotter is coming quickly upon me I must
counter-

469 plot quickly. If I wait in quiet he . . .

474 . . . death; that you may ~~show what envy is.~~ warn men from
envy.

475 ~~will you not listen to reason? I do not think you are sane.~~
You . . .

478 No for . . .

480 . . . rule!

483 . . . also not . . .

484 Cease princes; I . . . Iocasta . . .

485 . . . house in the nick of time; with her to help you will

486 set this quarrell right.
(Iocasta enters)

487 . . . this uproar of

488 words? Are . . . ashamed while the land is lying sick

489 to stir up trouble on your own account.

490 Come, go you into the house; and you, Creon, go

492 . . . petty injury.

493 Oedipus, your lord, is . . .

495 Yes; for . . . have caught him, Lady, working treacherously

496 against my ~~life~~ person.

497 . . . I never set eyes on any good thing but perish accurst

498 if ever I have done any of those things you charge me with.

499 . . . First ~~because of his~~ for

500 . . . oath before the gods, and . . .

501 . . . these who stand before you.

502 (All) Consider! Listen, O my King, I beseech you.

503 What is the favour that you would have of me?

504 That you should not make . . . charge against a friend

505 who has bound himself with an oath, with no more

506 evidence than rumour.

507 Then it is very certain that in seeking for this you are seeking
for my exile or my death.

508–11 No; by Him who is the Leader of the Heavenly Host; no, by
the Sun. May I suffer the utmost doom and die unblest and
unbefriended if I have that thought; but my soul is withered
by the withering of the land, and that ~~these~~ our old sorrows
should be topped by sorrows springing from you two.

514 . . . his that . . . compassion:

515 yet he, wheresoever he be, shall be hated.

519 . . . peace, and

521 . . . go, my way: I have found you without sense, but in

522 ... (*He goes*)

523 ... you delay from taking ... into ...

527 ~~On the one hand,~~ The half ...

528 ~~Upon the other~~ the rest ...

533 ... (*Exit leader*)

534 ... gods ...

539 ... on if ... quarrell

540 rose.

542 As on ... knowledge or ... hearsay from another?

543 No; he . . . mouthpiece, and so can keep his own lips un-
profaned.

544 You have no need to fear ...

545 ... and you will learn ...

547 ... Oracle ...

550 child who should spring from him and me. Now the rumour
is that Laius was murdered at a place where three highways
meet by foreign robbers; and when the child was

551 ... Laius had pinned its ankles together ...

552 ... trackless [ll. 550–552 are repeated with revision.]

550 when his ...

551 ... Laius pinned its ankles together ...

554 ... was, so ...

557 or Laius die ...

560 ... god ...

562 ... Lady, ~~what a tumult of the mind~~ has ~~fall~~ come ...

567 The thing I heard you say that Laius

571 The land is called Phocis and branching roads lead from the
same spot

573 How many years have passed since this thing

574 happened?

575 News was ~~carried to~~ published ...

576 ... came to power in this land.

578a Oedipus, why do you let this thing weigh upon you?

579b Do not ask me yet. But tell me what was Laius' stature,

579c and what years he had.

579 ... tall, the ...

585 I ... dreadful misgiving ...

586 ... will see it ...

588 Indeed though ...

590 ... him? Or ...

595 ... Lady?
596 ~~The one survivor that reached home—a servant.~~ A ...
598 ... he ~~came to~~ [?] found ...
599 ... me with his ... mine
600 that I would send ... cattle, that ...
606 ... fear, Lady, that I have spoken folly; and ...
607 I would ~~look at~~ speak with him.
610 Yes; ... you; now
613 ... Polybius ...
614 Corinth—... Merope and ...
615 held to be the ...
616 ... to wonder at, though ...
617 make one angry ...
618 ... table and ...
619 out at me that ...
625 ... my mother or my father
628 ... terror; ...
632 ... Corinth and ...
633 ... it is by finding its ...
634 ... sought the place where ... the infamous
635 ... me. In my flight I came to
636 those regions where ...
637 king ... Lady ... tell the. ...
638 ... roads I
639 ... herald and ... man sitting like ...
640 described in a carriage drawn by colts. **** ** *** ~~came first and the~~ The man that
641 came in front and ... would have
642 had me pushed from off the path—and in my anger
643 I struck the man that pushed me—the driver. The ...
645 ... then brought down upon my head his two-pronged goad.
         I ...
646 ... full for I struck him from the carriage
647 ... swift blow ... on to ... back and
649 ... Laius is ...
652 ... house, nor is it lawful that any speak to
653 him whom all must drive out of their houses. And no ...
655 ... the world ...
656 ... terror. Yet
657 ... you have got full knowledge from him

658 that saw the deed.

659 . . . have that knowledge I . . . hope—I . . .

661 And when he comes what ~~would you have~~ is . . . hear?

662 . . . yours

665 You said he . . .

667 slayers I . . . slayer. A solitary man is not a band of men. But . . .

668 loneley wayfarer then . . .

670 . . . least it was of robbers

671 he first spoke. He . . .

672 . . . Yet if . . .

676 . . . him

678 . . . not for . . . do so . . .

681 . . . that

684 . . . into . . .

685 . . . [stage direction lacking]

686–700 Ch. The old prophecies concerning Laius are fading. Already men neglect them. Apollo is not honoured—the worship of the gods is perishing.

     (*If no interval a much longer Chorus must be given*)

     [Stage direction, *Jocasta enters from the palace*, lacking.]

701 Citizens of Thebes, the thought has come to me

702 . . . visit the shrines of . . . gods with this wreathed branch in my hand,

703 this dish . . .

704 . . . Oedipus who does not judge the new

705 thing by the old, . . . sense but is . . . the will

706 of the speaker if he but speak terrors . . . that by

707 advice I can do nothing, I come to you Lysian

708 Apollo, because you are the nearest. I . . .

709 . . . prayer that you may find a way to rid us

710 from uncleaness. For . . .

     (*Enter Messenger*)

712 Might I . . .

713 the house . . . Oedipus. . . . still tell . . .

715 . . . house and . . .

716a ~~10. May you have all happiness~~

717 May she be ever happy in a happy home, seeing that

718 she is his heaven-blessed Queen.

719 I wish you like happiness, stranger, in return for your

720 good greeting; but what is it that you have come . . .
721 tell.
722 . . . Lady . . .
725 . . . Corinth and at the message I am about to give
726 you will rejoice doubtless, yet maybe, . . .
729 . . . people, they say, will make him King of the
730 Isthmian land.
731 . . . Is it the aged Polybus . . .
735 If I do not speak the truth I am content to die.
737 O Oracles . . . gods where . . . ? This ~~Polybus~~ is . . .
739 . . . him and . . .
740 . . . Oedipus. ~~but through his own.~~
(*Enter Oedipus*)
741 Iocasta, . . .
743 . . . man and judge as you listen to . . .
744 . . . gods . . .
748 . . . Polybus, no longer lives.
749 How stranger! . . .
751 The first thing is—if I am to tell my story—
753 By treachery or some disease?
755 . . . died it seems of sickness.
756 Yes and . . .
757 . . . Why indeed . . .
759 . . . heads. . . .
761 . . . I—~~I have touched no weapon~~[?] who have had
762 . . . it unless indeed, . . .
763 . . . If it were that I . . .
764 but the Oracles as men have understood, they at least
765 Polybus has carried with him into Hades—
766 they . . . .
767 . . . since.
768 . . . did; but . . .
769 Lay those things to heart no more.
770 . . . words of thine were better, . . .
771 . . . have my
772 . . . to fear, and yet . . .
773 Your . . . a great sign to hearten us.
774 Great I know; but . . .
778 . . . you fear?
780 Lawful or unlawful for another to know?

781 Lawful, certainly. Loxias once said . . .

783 . . . home . . . Corinth: I have found good

784 fortune; yet still it is sweet to look upon the face of one's
parents.

785 . . . indeed because of this you . . .

786 in exile from that city?

787 And because I . . .

789 Then why have . . . from this fear? For I have come in
friendship.

791 . . . for this I

792 came. I think to . . . it.

793 . . . house.

796 How old . . . the gods' . . .

799 Yes, I . . .

801 your parents?

802 Even so, old man. This is the thing that frights me always.

803 Do you not know that all these fears are empty?

806 Because Polybus was nothing . . . .

808 No more than he who speaks to you—just so much as that.

810 him who is nothing . . .

815 ~~And yet he loved me dearly~~. How . . .

818 And you—had you bought me or found me by chance?

819 I found you in Cithaeron's winding glens.

822 What! A . . . wandering hireling.

823 But your preserver to this hour, my son.

824 And when you took me in your arms was I in pain?

825 Your ankles answer

826 that.

827 Why do you speak of that old . . .

828 I freed you when you had them pinned together.

829 The brand of shame I carried from . . .

830 It was such that it has given . . .

831 Oh! For the gods' love, was . . .

832 . . . father's. Speak!

836 . . . yourself.

841 . . . King . . .

844 . . . alive that . . .

846 . . . anyone . . .

847 . . . of? One . . .

848 . . . pastures. The . . .

849 revealed.
850–51 [Lacking]
852 ... ask ~~of~~ whom he spoke ~~?~~ of ? Do not think about
853 it—do not waste a thought on what he
854 said. It was idle.
855 I will not have it that with clues like ... hands
856 I failed to ... birth
857 ... you have any care for your own
858 life give ...
859 Be of good courage; though ... yes
861 ... base born.
862 Yet hear ...
864 ... but ~~finding~~ searching the ...
866 Yet I wish you well—...
868 ... advice vexes my patience.
869–70 O unlucky one! May ... are!
871 Go some ...
873 Alas! Alas! Miserable! That word is
874 ... can say to you. No other word than that for ever. (*Rushes*
into Palace)
875 ... Lady ...
876 ... will come a
877 ... sorrow.
878–86 ... what may. Be my race never so lowly I cannot help but
crave to learn it. That woman, perchance, for she is proud
with more than a woman's pride, is ashamed because of my
lowly birth. ~~But I who think myself fortune's well-favoured~~
But I, who think that i[t] was Fortune's very self that bore
me, fear no dishonour. She is the mother that I spring from,
and the months of the year that are my kinsmen have made
me lowly sometimes, ~~at others~~ sometimes great. Such being
indeed my lineage, I never will prove false to it, or fail to
search out the secret of my birth.
Chorus
887–94 [Lacking. No chorus is provided.]
895 ... never seen him, may ...
896 ... so, ~~naming~~ ******* I think that I can see that herdsman we
have so long
897 looked for: his ...
901 Yes: I know ~~him~~ the man ... coming he ...

902 . . . service; as trusted
903 as any among the shepherds.
  (*Enter Herdsman*)
906 This man you are looking at.
907 Old man! I would have you look this way and answer what I
  ask of you.
909 . . . was; not . . . slave but . . .
914 And in what region, mainly?
915 Sometimes Cithaeron—sometimes the neighbouring ground.
916 . . . remember having met with . . .
918 Doing what? What . . .
919 . . . man here—have you ever met him before this moment?
920 . . . cannot ~~remember it at~~ **** recall . . . at this moment.
922 . . . memory—I am sure that he remembers very well when
  we two were at
923 Cithaeron; he with two flocks, I, his comrade, with but one.
924 . . . half years . . . Spring . . .
925 Autumn, and for the Winter I would drive my flock into . . .
926 . . . he took his . . .   `
927 Tell me now, did this happen or did it not?
928 You have spoken truth; though . . .
929 Come tell . . . remember at that time giving
930 . . . to be reared as . . . foster son?
931 What! Why do you ask this
932 question?
933 That man there, my friend, is he who
934 then was young.
935 . . . you be
936 silent?
937 Do not ~~find fault with~~ blame . . .
939 . . . offended, noble master?
941 . . . ignorance—he is busy to no
942 purpose.
945 Do not for . . . God, misuse
947 Go someone; tie him up this instant.
948 Alas; wherefore? What . . .
951 . . . did, and would . . .
952 Well you . . .
955 . . . delay!
957 . . . it? From your own house, or from some

958 other's house.
959 ... my child ...
961 From whom of all those ...
962 ... any more ...
965 ... child then of from ....
967 ... the dreadful brink of speech.
968 ... hearing. Yet ...
969 If you must know then it ...
970 ... Lady ... can the best tell ... things.
971 How? She gave ... ?
972 Yes, O King.
973 For what ...
976 Yes; from ...
982 ... to another land that he himself had
984 ... says then have you been
985 born to misery.
986 ... truths ...
987 ... Light ... you! Having ...
988 ... bloodshed, in marriage,
989 ... my birth accursed! (*He rushes into Palace*)

Chorus

990–1004 [Lacking. This chorus is not supplied in this typescript.]
1005 [Lacking. Stage direction lacking.]
1006 What deed shall you hear—you that are ever honoured in this land! What deeds look ...
1007 ... sorrow shall you bear ... to your race ...
1008 ... house ...
1009–12 ... many are the ~~wing~~ misfortunes it covers, or is on the point of bringing to the light.
1013 Indeed the misfortunes that we know are lamentable things.
1014 What more than these do you announce?
1015 It is but a short ... telling: our royal Lady, Iocasta
1016 is dead.
1017 ... miserable one, how ...
1018 ... hand. The worst pain of it all comes
1019 not to you—for you have not seen what I have seen.
1020 Yet ... as memory helps, you shall know all. When,
1021 half-crazed, she had come to the vestibule, she ran
1024 chamber she dashed ...
1026 ... ~~long [?] since [?] begotten~~ who ... and begot upon

1027 . . . mother an accursed stock. And then she wailed . . .
1029 fold stock . . .
1030 child. And how after that she died I do not know, for
　　　Oedipus . . . in.

[End of typescript]

II

As with Yeats's *Sophocles' King Oedipus*, there is preserved in
the Script Room of the Abbey Theatre a bundle of typescripts
relating to Yeats's *Sophocles' Oedipus at Colonus: A Version for
the Modern Stage*.[14] In addition to scripts for various actors' parts
there exists a typescript of the whole play with manuscript corrections in Yeats's hand. This is the typescript presented here.

Here too Yeats used the Jebb translation as his point of departure,
consulting various other translations including the one in French by
Paul Masqueray.[15] In our book we intend to trace the development
of Yeats's version, using the following extant manuscripts: a corrected typescript among the National Library MS 8767 papers which
is full of echoes from Jebb; a "Prompt Copy," i.e. a corrected typescript (carbon) among the NL MS 8767 papers which represents a
further advance, possibly with some missing manuscript between;
and the Abbey Theatre corrected typescript presented here. This
typescript, badly singed in a fire (possibly the famous fire of 1951
which destroyed the original Abbey Theatre), is the original of
which the preceding typescript is a carbon copy. However, the
manuscript corrections on the two typescripts show that those on the
Abbey Theatre typescript were copied from the other and not vice
versa. There is some indecision in the earlier manuscript which has
vanished in the later. For this reason, because it is the original typescript, and because it is in the Abbey Theatre files, we hold it to
have better authority than the other manuscript, perhaps being the

14. First produced at the Abbey Theatre, Dublin, 12 September 1927. First
published in *The Collected Plays of W. B. Yeats* (London 1934), pp.
519–75.
15. Jeffares, p. 247. Cf. Sophocles, *The Plays and Fragments, with Critical
Notes, Commentary, and Translation in English Prose*, by R. C. Jebb,
Part II, *The Oedipus Coloneus* (Amsterdam 1965; reprint of the 1928
Cambridge University Press edition), hereafter referred to as "Jebb." Cf.
also *Sophocle*, Tome II, texte établi et traduit par Paul Masqueray (Paris
1924).

version actually used in the production of the play, 12 September 1927, at the Abbey Theatre.

The special interest of this typescript is that some of the manuscript corrections appear to advance the text of the play printed in *The Collected Plays of W. B. Yeats* (London 1952) and used as the basic text in *The Variorum Edition of the Plays of W. B. Yeats*. On the other hand, the typescript itself, as opposed to the manuscript corrections, is in turn advanced by the printed text. Many of the manuscript revisions bring the typescript into conformity with the printed text, although some provide slightly different readings. Sometimes the printed text advances the text of this typescript; at other times the manuscript revisions on the typescript advance the printed text.

The reader will be interested in Yeats's manuscript revisions of passages which, as typed, are identical with the printed text. These revisions are consistent with Yeats's stated aims. He wrote to Olivia Shakespear on 6 December [1926]: "My work on *Oedipus at Colonus* has made me bolder and when I look at *King Oedipus* I am shocked at my moderation. I want to be less literal and more idiomatic and modern."[16] Using Professor Alspach's line numbers from the *Variorum Plays*, we indicate below some significant manuscript revisions of the text which was ultimately printed.

The Collected Plays of W. B. Yeats (London 1952)	Manuscript Revisions on Abbey Theatre Typescript
262 have respect enough for a blind man to come him-	have respect
263 self?	
266 Your name has . . .	It has . . .
287 . . . now can hardly . . .	. . . now I can hardly . . .
599 . . . comes in its stead, and . . .	. . . comes, and . . .
742 . . . What do you	. . . You know
743 know of the fortune of that kingdom? But I know	nothing of that kingdom's future, but I know
744 it. My knowledge comes from Phoebus and his	My knowledge is from Phoebus and his
745 father God most high, aye, from truth itself, while	father God most high, aye from truth itself.
746 you have come with . . .	You have come with . . .

16. *Letters*, p. 721.

757	I am well content with your part in it, for	I am well satisfied with your share of it, for
766	And yours, ...	Yours, ...
773	These others will bear me out in what I have	These others know that I am right,
774	said, and . . .	and . . .
775	own kith and kin, if . . .	own kin, if . . .
835	. . . given yourself up to . . .	. . . given way to . . .
853	. . . taken by force the . . .	. . . taken the . . .
858	They hear both you and me, and they know	They hear my words and yours, but know
859	that my wrongs can strike, that my revenge shall not	that my revenge shall not be words, that my wrongs
860	be in words.	can strike.
885	My tale is finished.	His men have carried them off.
887	altars, . . .	altar, . . .
914	. . . wisdom, you have	. . . wisdom have . . .
925	. . . because I did not	. . . because it never came into my
926	believe that . . .	head that . . .
942	. . . borne, indeed, but by no . . .	. . . borne, from no . . .
955	. . . must,	. . . must.
956	whether I will or no— Misery! . . .	Misery! . . .
969	. . . that was how it	. . . is the way it
980	. . . Goddesses whom this	. . . Goddesses
981	land worships to . . .	to . . .
990	. . . if your men have carried them away.	. . . if already gone.
991	They will . . .	Your men will . . .
1023	O that I had seen it all mounted upon a cloud!	O would that I had seen it straddled upon a cloud!
1024	O that . . .	Would that . . .
1051	. . . again. Come closer on either side,	. . . again. Come to either side,
1052	children; cling to your father; rest, for you are tired	children; cling to your father, come close and rest tired
1054	. . . girls and so afraid . . .	. . . girls afraid . . .
1055	. . . a crowd as this.	. . . a crowd.
1061	. . . you all	. . . you and to this place all

1062 . . . wish, give it to you and to this land,	. . . wish,
1063 for through you and through you alone, and here	for here,
1064 alone, here . . . world,	here . . . world, and through you, you alone of men,
1092 . . . your countryman.	. . . your own countryman.
1141 . . . friend, that if this man comes hither	. . . friend, that neither this man
1142 neither he nor any other	nor any other . . .
1186 Say why you come, my unhappy brother, for	Tell him why you come; speak out of your heart, for
1195 . . . to those here, to those who . . .	. . . to these here, to these who . . .
1198 . . . been driven into exile, driven out of	. . . been driven out of . . .
1210 . . . or drive out my	. . . or put down my
1212 . . . allies.	. . . allies:
1213 Seven . . .	seven . . .
1214 . . . Thebes. Amphiaraus	. . . Thebes; Amphiaraus . . .
1227 . . . oracles, shall be with that	. . . oracles, goes to whatever
1228 party that you favour, and upon whatever side	party you favour, to whatever side
1233 . . . reigns as king, . . .	. . . reigns a king, . . .
1237 . . . you in your own house once more. . . .	. . . you once more in your own house. . . .
1241 Oedipus; say something, speak, speak to your son	Oedipus; speak to your son; say something
1245 . . . . But now he shall hear . . .	. . . . But now let him hear . . .
1267 . . . father. These are good, . . .	. . . father. My daughters are good, . . .
1283 . . . himself. Go, . . .	. . . himself to make my least word true. Go, . . .
1296 . . . be	. . . come
1297 fulfilled, and . . .	true, and
1307 So you would lead it again— why rage against	Why should you lead it again? why do you rage against
1362 . . . he can no more turn . . .	. . . he cannot turn . . .
1380 . . . altars . . .	. . . altar . . .
1385 Why this sudden clamour? Why am I called	[cancelled]
1386 hither, called as it seems by this stranger and by my	[cancelled]

1387 own people alike? Have . . .	Have . . .
1462 sacrificial hollow in the rock where . . .	basin of stone where . . .
1497 . . . never forsake	. . . never to forsake . . . .
1513 . . . seemed, to heaven . . .	. . . seemed heaven . . .
1528 . . . past, dread the future?	. . . past, dread what is to come?

It is possible, of course, that Yeats referred to this typescript when later revising the text for that finally published in *The Collected Plays of W. B. Yeats* (London 1934) and that he consciously rejected the revisions listed above. It is more probable that he forgot that he had made them, as he is suspected to have done even with printed revisions.[17] We cannot assert that Yeats would have included these revisions in the final printed text if he had recalled them. Although some of the revisions aim at a more natural speech than that of the printed text, it may be that Yeats would finally have chosen dignity and a high style rather than colloquial ease.

For example, in the typescript, one of Theseus' speeches (lines 875–78) reads:

> What is this quarrel? What is the trouble? Your high words have reached me at the altar of the Sea God, the patron saint of your own Colonus. Speak out—the uproar has brought me from the sacrifice with more speed than comfort.

The revisions in Yeats's hand bring about a more colloquial tone:

> What is this quarrel? What is all this noise? It has reached me at the altar of the Sea God, the patron saint of your own Colonus, interrupted the sacrifice and brought me with more speed than comfort.

The printed text sacrifices some of the colloquialism for dignity and yet is terse vigorous speech:

> What is this quarrel? What is the trouble? High words have reached me at the altar of the Sea-God, the patron saint of your own Colonus. Speak out—you have interrupted the sacrifice. (*Variorum Plays*, p. 879, lines 875–78).

It may be that many of the revisions in this typescript, which seem to advance the text beyond that in *The Collected Plays*, 1952, are

17. Cf. e.g., Robert O'Driscoll, "The Tables of the Law: A Critical Text," *Yeats Studies: An International Journal*, I (Bealtaine, 1971), pp. 87–118, esp. p. 99.

the result of a desire for more colloquial dialogue which Yeats later modified. A revision may, for example, have seemed a good idea during rehearsals, when he was perhaps trying to give the actors more speakable lines, and then seemed too low in style when he was preparing the printed text.

As before, the typescript is collated with *The Collected Plays of W. B. Yeats* (London 1952) using the line numbers and following other procedures of *The Variorum Edition of the Plays of W. B. Yeats*. Manuscript revisions are placed above the line, even revisions of punctuation. (The reader must be careful to distinguish commas placed above the line from apostrophes.) Some very trivial corrections have been made silently, but very few. In order to be as true as possible to the manuscript, we have included almost every peculiarity, including probable typos. (Why deprive the reader, for example, of what must be one of the most furious locutions in literature: "intermperate angaer" (line 1136)?) Exceptions to this rule follow: typed stage directions are italicized whether they are underlined in the original or not. Stage directions written in by hand are not italicized, and are underlined only if underlined in the original. Stage directions in the typescript are usually enclosed in parentheses while those in *Collected Plays* are enclosed in square brackets, introduced by one square bracket, or centred and with no brackets. We have not indicated these differences. Typed stage directions are not end-stopped in the typescript. This difference from *Collected Plays* is not indicated. With this exception, all differences of punctuation and of capitalization are indicated. Proper names have been normalized according to *Collected Plays*, since the variants are merely occasional misspellings.

OEDIPUS AT COLONUS

TITLE   Oedipus at Colonus
DATE   [lacking]
DRAMATIS PERSONAE   [lacking]
STAGE DIRECTIONS   [lacking]

1 Oedipus [Speaker indications so styled throughout.]

8 . . . passer-by and . . .

13 . . . singing. Sit

14 down therefore . . . stone, . . . for ~~as~~ an

22 . . . passer by . . . .

27 search. Somebody . . . .

29 . . . us, ask . . .

30   (*enter stranger, . . .*)

39 . . . dreadful goddesses, . . .

47 They are my . . . .
                    until I have
48 . . . force ~~without first~~
        reported   got
49 ~~reporting~~ to . . . and ~~getting~~ their . . . .
            my questions
51 . . . answer

54 ~~I will tell you all I know.~~ The whole . . .
                        protects
56 . . . seated keeps ~~guard over~~ Athens . . .

58 . . . Colonus, and . . .

62 So then there . . . ?

66 The king . . . .

68 Theseus son . . . .

70 To bring him here? Or with what object?

72 . . . service—

73 . . . he gain from . . . ?

78 . . . town but . . .

81 . . . (*the Stranger . . . .*)
        (Kneels)
85 Dreadful

88 ...~~for w~~hen he   [W above "for"]

89 my many sorrows, the God ~~Phoebus/said~~ that ...   [proclaimed above "said"]

91 ... hospitaliy, and death' ...   [t above i, comma inserted]

94 Furthermore he ...

103 ... Oedipus' upon this ghost for ...

(She leeds him into the wood) [Actually the d and the)
are fused!]

109 ... *E*
(~~e~~nter *the Elders of Colonus, the Chorus, as if searching
for someone*)

113 ... country; no ...

116 ... speak, a shrine ...

119 ... *hiding place* ...

120 .... see ~~you~~ with ...

129 ... been ~~miserable,~~ and ...   [accursed above "miserable"]

130 ... curse ~~upon the top of all~~ the others. ....   [to above]

133 .... ~~Go~~ back.   [Come above "Go"]

134 ~~Go~~ back. ....?   [Come above "Go"]

137 ... but ✱✱ keep ...

141 ... and' as far as we can' doing

146 ... me therefore that ...

149 ... *stops*)

153 ... Lady.

160 ... *edge of the* ✱✱✱✱)   [wood above]

Have I gone far enough?

162 ~~No further?~~⟨

165 Move *** sideways and crouch down . . . .

167 . . . work, father, step . . . .

168 . . . step, lean . . . .

170 Dreadful is the fate of the blind.

173 country are you come.

188 . . . you, come, speak . . . .

190 . . . (*Cry* . . .) And . . . .

195 . . .

      (. . . *away and cover* . . . *cloaks and give a great shout of horror*)

198 . . . land.

204 . . . deceit, ~~** you harm instead of ****~~.

216 . . . hope, and . . . .

219 . . . driven by a God, and who so

220 driven could do otherwise?

        the
223 . . . dread ~~that~~ anger . . .

233 . . . mother, you

234 . . . already; it . . . .

        and
237 self-defence, ~~but~~ I . . .

        a place
239 . . . promise ~~that seat~~ where . . .

248 . . . fulfill . . . .

DAVID R. CLARK AND JAMES B. MCGUIRE   *255*

249 . . . sacred for . . .

252 . . . rest see . . .

254 . . . awe;

255 understand ~~what you say~~ for they . . .

259 . . . who brought
      He set out when
260 . . . [lacking]
    you named yourself.
261 [lacking]
       come, that he will
262 . . . will⟨

263 . . . man ~~to come himself?~~

   It
266 ~~Your~~ name has . . .

267 . . . put inclination

270 . . . me only but . . . city. . . .

278 . . . is, she . . .

280 . . . here.
        [Stage direction lacking.]
        <u>xRise</u>
281 . . . . child?

283 . . . moment for . . .
<u>Ismene comes in</u>
285 Father and sister, I had ~~had~~ a . . .
         I
287 . . . world, and now⟨can

289 . . . come my . . . .

291 . . . here my . . . .

295 . . . sisters!

ing
314 . . . travel-weary

315 . . . places and always, that . . .

317 you my . . .

, ,
318 . . . bringing me unknown . . . Thebes

321 . . . terror do you bring? . . .

322 . . . empty handed.

327 . . . thought;. . . .

328 that our race has . . .

332 . . . youngest, . . .

son,
334 . . . elder/Polyneices

has been
335 . . . it is rumoured is in Argos

336 . . . there and plans . . .

337 . . . Argos. ~~Further~~ [=Father] I have . . .

Father
338 . . . tale/—when . . .

341 Yes father . . . .

348 So it seems that I am good

349 for something.

352 . . . nothing, am . . .

361 Explain what brings him, daughter.

363 border yet . . . .

enemy's es
365 If an ~~enemies'~~ country possess your bones they

367 That is the oracle?

375 . . . Thebes

376 A day—what day?

377 When they come in arms and you blast them

381 Apollo has . . . ?
And
388 ⟨Not to . . . .

389 . . . offending, they
              I blast them from the tomb
395 . . . till ~~I decide the issue.~~
                     raised
398 . . . neither⟨up their . . .

402 . . . day when . . .

409 . . . sons who . . . hindered

416 favour, yes they . . .

420 . . . I ~~have~~ meditated ~~upon~~ . . .

421 . . . brought and . . .

424 . . . But ~~str,~~ strangers, . . .

428 . . . daughters; and . . .

431 . . . me sir, . . .

434 desses for . . .

435 . . . stranger.

439 . . . do.

446 . . . olive tree

448 . . . say, that . . .

458 ters, you . . . them-

464 good-will, . . .

      When Ismene goes out
        Antig leads back Oed to Seat.

469 On . . .

473 turn.   (*she goes*)

483 everywhere I . . . .

489 . . . ignorance, I . . .

493 . . . me, I . . .

498 What is that that . . . ?

506 . . . me, my . . . .

      there was somebody
515 . . . tale, ~~who was it~~

    that you killed.
516 ~~that you murdered?~~

    killed
518 You ~~murdered~~ your . . . !

    You killed him!
520 ~~A murderer!~~ ⟨

521 Yes. ~~A murderer,~~ but I can plead

528 . . . comes summoned . . .

      (enter Theseus)
530 . . . say. [Stage direction lacking.]

    (Rise)
531 . . . by hear-

534 . . . Oedipus, I

536 . . . girl; and

541 . . . tomorrow . . .

542 today.

544 . . . words.

545 . . . me right and . . .

547 . . . I ~~want~~ ^{must} to and . . . .

550 . . . upon it . . .

563 do, it . . . .

568 . . . come, why . . . ?

569 [This line is underlined by hand.]

570 [<u>temper</u> is underlined by hand.]

574 . . . unheard of . . . .

593 . . . ^{Not} Even

594 . . . friends ~~cannot long~~ ^{can} keep . . .

597 . . . again it maybe turn . . .

598 . . . today . . .

599 . . . comes ~~in its stead,~~ and . . .

600 . . . trifle, ~~and when that day comes my~~ ^{My} body . . .

601 . . . buried ^{when they take to it} and yet ~~it shall,~~ though cold in death, ^{shall my body}

602 drink hot Theban blood, if Phoebus son of God

603 spoke truth and God be God. But . . .

604 . . . more; I . . .

612 . . . man, his . . .

613 . . . city and . . .

614 . . . asks, I . . .
             To   and to blast them from the ~~ground~~ ground
625 ~~The place where I shall~~ vanquish those that drove me out

626 [Lacking]

      w
630 Ķill . . . .

636 . . . come—

640 [<u>fear</u> has been underlined by hand.]

644 is a stormy sea between . . . .

            <u>Sit down</u>
647 . . . *out*)
              ' horses; and come praise
648 . . . Colonus ~~and its neighborhood,~~
               of the wood's intricacies,
649 The wine dark ~~ivy of the sacred wood,~~

659 . . . olive tree

667 . . . beauty drunken . . .

668 . . . olive trees,

674 . . . or paddled by . . .

677 . . . bit,
            (*Rise*)
686 . . . indeed.

691 you. I I can . . . eyes; why . . .

692 away, I . . .

693 . . . Greece, I . . .

699 . . . hither, and . . . chief because . . .

706 . . . penury and . . .

712 . . . land worthy . . .

        then
724 . . . remember͜that . . .

726 . . . away

729 . . . but'

730 when you needed neither' offered help and gift,

732 . . . me' and' therefore' though

734 . . . are; you . . .

735 [not is underlined by hand.] . . . home' but

739 [that . . . this is underlined by hand.]

740 [this is underlined by hand.]

    ~~noth~~
741 . . . in my

     You know
742 . . . . ~~What do you~~
   nothing of that kingdoms future, but
743 ~~know of the fortune of that kingdom? But~~ I know
        is
744 ~~it~~. My knowledge͜~~comes~~ from . . .

745 . . . itself, ~~while~~
   Y
746 ~~y~~ou . . .

747 . . . sword, and yet . . .

748 may you . . .

749 . . . words, no . . . you, get . . .
     my daughter
750 gone; ~~she~~ and . . . chosen, and *** |our life| no

751 . . . in͜so long . . .

754 Who has . . . ?

755 . . . , or I that . . .

            satisfied   share of
757 I am well ~~content~~ with your ~~part in~~ it for

758 . . . nor thee that . . .

        Y
766 ~~And~~ yours . . . .

769 . . . you, in my own

770 name, and in the name of these others to be gone. And . . .

                  know that I am right
773 These others ~~will bear me out in what I have~~

774 ~~said,~~ and . . .

775 own ~~kith and~~ kin . . .

777 . . . you, I . . .

781 . . . hence and . . .

789 man.

790 . . . you away, stranger, you

794 . . . am. Where

806 . . . stronger (*they . . . him threatening*)

815 . . . hold I . . . .

      (Calling off [?])
818 To . . . rescue.

822 . . . you my

828 . . . misery! (*exeunt guards with Antigone*)

833 [giving way is underlined by hand.]

834 [to anger is underlined by hand.]

        way
835 . . . ~~yourself up~~ to . . . [Whole line underlined by hand.]

836 . . . and ta that has [Whole line underlined by hand.]

837 [<u>been your curse</u> is underlined by hand.] (*he . . . guard*

842 . . . is it seems dearer . . .

848 . . . king . . . .

853 blind and . . . taken ~~by force~~ the . . .

854 . . . Therefore I . . .

855 Sun God . . .

know that
my words and yours, but my revenge shall not be words,

858 They hear ~~both you and me, and they know~~

859 that . . . strike, ~~that my revenge shall not~~

860 ~~be in words.~~

861 . . . threatened, alone . . .

862 . . . am' I . . . .

874 . . . with.
(*enter Theseus*)

all this noise
875 . . . is ~~the trouble?~~

It has
876 ~~Your high words have~~ reached . . . Sea

, interrupted
877 . . . Colonus. ~~Speak~~

the sacrifice and brought me with more speed than comfort.
878 ~~out   the uproar has brought me from the sacrifice with more speed than comfort.~~

off
His men have carried them ~~away.~~
885 ~~My tale is finished.~~

887 altars, . . .

888 cross roads, . . .

889 . . . rein for . . .

891 . . . away. (*turning to Creon*) As . . .

893 . . . would ~~have~~ already have had something . . .

894 . . . better I deal out to him law that

895 . . . Oedipus. (*to Creon*) You . . .

905 . . . nothing Thebes . . . this, her

906 . . . honourable, nor . . .

907 . . . me—nor . . .

914 . . . wisdom, ~~you~~ have

920 . . . stranger, you . . .

921 . . . race but . . . been tried and

923 ~~I have done~~ what I have done I did neither because I

924 . . . law nor men . . .

925 . . . ~~I did not~~ it never came

into my head

926 ~~believe~~ . . .

931 . . . then, but . . .

933 . . . anger

934 [anger . . . old. is underlined by hand.]

942 . . . borne ~~indeed, but~~ by from no . . .

943 . . . Gods, enraged it may be against my house and ancestors.
Set . . .

the gods
944 ... all ~~they~~/

945 have ...

946 house and ...

948 ... do, the oracle ...

own
949 ... his/son. ...

954 ... her seeing ...

.
955 ... must,

956 ~~whether I will or no.~~ Misery! Misery! ...

'
959 ... unknowingly but ...

961 ... teeth and ...

f   e
966 ... ~~is~~ he were, perchanc ...

is the way
969 ... that ~~was how~~ it

970 ... me, into ...

980 ... Goddesses ~~whom this~~

981 ~~land worships~~ to ... side and upon

985 ... words, the ...

already gone.
990 ... if ~~your men have carried them away.~~

Your men
991 ~~They~~ will ...

1003 ... peace, be satisfied ...

1007 man.

Go up back L & look ****
(*Exit Theseus, Creon, and attendants*)

1008 . . . face

1009 . . . shields Colonus in chase

1010 . . . strand or . . .
          the ever
1011 Where ****/blessed spirits . . .

1012 . . . know

1013 . . . snow

1014 . . . track

1015 . . . back

1016 . . . saddle   turn . . . call

1017 . . . fall

1018 . . . slain   many . . . slain

1019 . . . Colonus   terrible . . . .
     O
1020 I̶glitter . . . bit   O . . .

1022 Vowed   and . . . vowed

   would that   ~~straddled stradeled~~ | straddled |
1023 O ~~that~~/I had seen it ~~all mounted~~/upon a cloud

   Would
1024 ~~O~~/that . . . thither   a . . . wind

1025 . . . all in the eye . . . mind

1026 . . . say ;

1028 . . . home

1029 . . . finished'that . . .

1030 . . . deer'from the . . . this'

1031 . . . sister Apollo . . . Artemis

1032 . . . The men . . .

1033 . . . midst . . . .

1036 . . . might ~~look upon~~ see . . .

1037 . . . there.

1041 ~~Come to me,~~ chidren, let . . . .

1042 . . . though[t] to . . .

,also,
1044 We ~~come, for~~ we too long . . . .

1045 ~~Where are you?~~

1046 ~~Here, approaching you together~~.

1047 Oedipus   My darlings-
Oedipus
~~Antigone~~ Props of my old age.

to
1051 . . . again. Come ~~close~~/~~on either side~~

come close and
~~come close and~~
1052 children, cling . . . father, /rest ~~for you are~~ tired

1053 . . . all,

1054 . . . no you . . . girls ~~and so~~ afraid . . .

1055 . . . crowd ~~as this.~~

and to this place
1061 . . . you/all

1062 . . . wish, ~~give it to you and to this land,~~

1063 for ~~through you and through you alone and~~ here

and through you, through you alone of men,
1064 ~~alone,~~ here . . . world ⟨

1070 . . . me, no, no, . . .

1073 . . . favourable to me in the

1074 . . . as you are in . . . .

1075 What could be more . . . .

1076 . . . children, what . . .

from [typed]
1078 me. My . . . not/
They
1081 . . . nothing. ~~Your daughters~~ will . . .

1089 . . . the Altar of . . .

1091 Altar . . .

y   own
1092 . . . not ~~your~~⟨countryman.

1094 . . . thing, he . . .

1098 Altar . . . .

1105 . . . ask. me.

1112 . . . to *o

1125 . . . harm therefore can . . .

1132 moment and think . . .

1133 . . . mother and what

1136 termperate angaer? Give . . . [intermperate angaer? underlined by hand.]
1137 you, it is . . .

1139 . . . asked of me goes . . .

1141   ... that ~~if~~ /\ this man ~~comes hither~~
       neither (above "if")

1142   ~~neither he~~ nor ...

1146   ... master. (*exit Theseus R.*)

1154   ... song

1156   ~~Not~~ to ...
       Never (above "Not")

1157   ~~Not~~ to have ~~drawn~~ the ... life at all ~~or~~ looked ... day.
    Never   drunk   nor

1158   ... a ~~quick~~ goodnight
    gay

1163   ... Polyneices.
                (Oedipus seated during speech)
   (*Polyneices enters*)

1167   ... his clothing in [his clothing in is underlined by hand.]

1168   [Whole line underlined by hand.]

1169   ... wallet. [Heaven knows what and in that old wallet. are
underlined by hand.]

1174   ... and ~~whatever~~ [?] God ...
    whereever

1177   ... again. *(a*

1178   *pause)* Why ...

1179   ... away, will ...

1182   ... me, persuade

1184   ... Altar ...

1186   ~~Say~~ why you come, ~~my unhappy brother, for~~
    Tell him   ; speak out of your heart,

1190 Polyn~~e~~ces ⁱ I will say all, you . . .

1191 good advice. But first of all_/put . . .   ^I

1193 . . . Altar . . .

1195 . . . to those here, to those who . . .   ^{these}   ^{these}

1198 . . . been driven into exile, driven . . .

1200 . . . throne. Et~~o~~cles, though . . .   ^e

1201 . . . exile though . . .

1203 argument. He was able/so to prevail/against me by cajolery   ^{has}   ^{ed}
and intrigue

1204 because of . . . house, so

1210 . . . or drive/out my   ^{put down}

1212 . . . allies*   [:]

1213 Seven leaders, . . . spearmen   ^{seven}

1214 . . . Thebes. . . .   [;]

1217 . . . Capaneus who . . .

1220 . . . his but . . .

1222 . . . Argos, implore . . .

1227 victory if . . . oracles, shall be with that   ^{goes to whatever}

1228 party that you favour, and upon whatever . . .   ^{to}

1233 . . . reigns as King, and . . .   ^a

1234 . . . help I . . .

1237 and you~in your own house | once more/

1238 party all . . .

                speak to your son, Say
1241 Oedipus; ~say~ something, ~speak, speak to your son~

                let him
1245 . . . now ~he shall~ hear . . .

        (Rise)
1247 gone. Villain, . . .

1249 . . . hand'you . . .

                        rags
1250 nationless . . . these **** . . .

                but
1252 . . . tears, ~for~

1254 live and . . .

1260 . . . you, punishment begun,

1261 . . . until you army

1263 . . . fall
                        My daughters
1267 . . . father. ~These~ are . . .

1269 . . . curse if . . .

1272 . . . orphan begone . . .

1274 . . . country and your

1275 kin, . . .

1278 . . . of Thebe** And I . . .

1279 . . . night, . . .

1281 . . . such fearfu* hatred

                to make my least word true.
1283 . . . himself/ Go, . . .

1284 . . . ears and publish abroad among the men of

1285 Thebe* and among your faithful allies******that

1292 . . . plans, little . . .

1293 . . . Argos Misery, misery, . . .

1294 . . . any but . . .

        —you are
1295 . . . Promise ~~me this~~, my sisters,

      —   come
1296 though his daughters, that . . . ~~be~~
true
1297 ~~fulfilled~~ and . . . Thebes you . . .

    If you see to it
1298 . . . burial. ~~Promise~~ . . .

    you will be
1299 . . . dishonour ~~and~~ be . . .

1300 service, that . . . father, *** that . . . .

1303 . . . Argos, do . . .

1305 . . . impossible, I . . .

  Why should you   ?   do you
1307 ~~So you would~~ lead it again—why rage against

1308 . . . last how

      your
1321 So then, my brother! ~~Your~~ decision . . . ?

1322 . . . further, hence-

1327 . . . Goodbye sisters, . . .

1332 . . . death.

1334 No, no, hear . . . .

1335 A useless toil.

1336 If useless then . . .

1340 . . . it. (*he goes out*)

[Above the speaker-indication *Chorus* in the next line appears a large X and above that an illegible word.]

1341 I shudder in expectation of a birth

1342 Unnatural or supernatural

1343 From heavenly travail on the bed of earth

1344 When I behold that ragged beggar call

1345 Curses upon old cities and the great

1346 And scatter . . . estate
(*Thunder*)
1347 . . . uproar, God . . . us.

1355 . . . head

1356 . . . found

1357 . . . finished on . . . bed

1358 . . . sound

1359 Nor can . . . vain
cannot
1362 . . . end, he ~~can no more~~ turn . . . .
May the gods
Once more that ; God
1367 ~~Once more that~~ dreadful sound, ~~God~~ pity us

What ever happen
1368 ~~When all is finished~~ on . . . earth'
;
1369 . . . Oedipus'

1370 Whatever child maternal . . . forth'

1371 Pity Colonus'nor . . .

1372 . . . beggar man.

1379 Come King . . . land '

1380 . . . altars . . .

1381 . . . sacrifice or . . . hand ; [?]

1382 Come for the fearful rags that do God's will

1383 Have promised blessing on . . . us ;

1384 Come King . . . come King . . . .
(*enter Theseus*)

1385 ~~Why this sudden clamour? Why am I called~~

1386 ~~hither, called as it seems by this stranger and by my~~

1387 ~~own people alike?~~ Have . . .

1390 . . . you, king, good . . .
loud [typed]

1400 Prolonged/thunder

1402 . . . things and . . .

1407 . . . death and

1414 . . . daughters much . . .

1417 . . . successor and . . .

1418 bed that . . .

1424 . . . best governed . . .

1426 . . . you; the . . .

1428 place for . . . .

1431 . . . guide, come, come, . . .

1432 me, all . . .

1433 . . . tomb, Come . . .

1435 . . . time, O . . .

           my
1436 . . . people, best

1438 . . . mounts

1439 . . . tomb. (*He . . . Theseus and attendants*)

1447 . . . Tartarus.

1448 . . . call death, has . . .

1449 . . . Oedipus,

1450 . . . destiny,

1452 Fellow countrymen, . . .

1457 . . . God-appointed painless . . .

1459 . . . man set

1461 feet but . . . .

       basin of stone
1462 ~~sacrificial hollow in the rock~~ where . . .

1464 . . . there midway . . .

1466 pear tree, . . . Thoricus,

1470 . . . there and

1474 . . . feet as . . .

1475 . . . shades a . . . thunder and the . . .

1478 . . . said

1479 . . . father and . . .

1483 . . . all and . . . .

1485 ... go and ...

1487 ... another sobbing ...

1490 Oedipus and ... heads for

1492 ... times, "Oedipus, Oedipus" it said

1494 ... He knowing ... spoken called

        Theseus
1495 King Oedipus [struck over with *Theseus*] ... said "O ...

1496 ... daughters,

        to
1497 ... never forsake ....

1498 ... man pro-

1499 ... oath and ...

1501 ... sworn Oedipus ...

1502 ... said "My ...

1503 ... place for ...

1505 ... go but ...

1506 ... everything for ....

1508 ... a li little ....

1511 Then after a little he ...

1512 ... Heaven praying as

1513 ... seemed to heaven ....

1519 affirm and ...

        what is to come
1528 ... past, ~~dread the future~~?

1543 . . . he has no . . .

1552 earth, you . . . protection, ~~Do~~

1553 ~~not vex them with lamentation~~, and I . . .

1566 accomplished-

[*THE END* lacking]

Suggested Guidelines
for Catalogue of
Yeats Manuscripts

These guidelines have been compiled by the editors.

Categories of Manuscripts:
I. Manuscripts, including typescripts.
II. Galley and Page Proofs.
III. Copy texts.
IV. Printed versions with manuscript corrections unless they fall
into III (above).
V. Marginalia.
VI. Correspondence.
VII. Manuscripts not covered by previous categories.

Information required for all categories of manuscripts:
1. Custody.
2. Provenance (if known).
3. Short editorial title and terminal dates.
4. Mode of preservation and ordering.
5. Description in existing catalogue, if any.

I. Suggestions for description of individual manuscripts.

   A. Gathered.
      1. Was it gathered prior to use or after use?
      2. How is it gathered?
         a. bound notebook.

   b. sewn; type of thread.
   c. pinned; type of pin.
   d. stapled.
3. Cover.
   a. material (vellum, paper, cardboard).
   b. colour.
   c. dimensions (in centimetres).
   d. distinguishing marks by manufacturer.
      i. title (if any).
      ii. number of pages if specified by manufacturer.
      iii. other distinguishing marks.
4. Whether gathered manuscript intact or not.
   a. fewer pages than manufacturer's specification.
   b. remnant or torn pages.
   c. both covers intact.
5. Notations or distinguishing features on
   a. front cover recto.
   b. front cover verso.
   c. back cover recto.
   d. back cover verso.
6. Manner in which gathered manuscript is used.
   a. consecutively from front to back?
   b. consecutively from back to front?
   c. at random?
   d. whether the manuscript is used for one purpose, or for several purposes.

B. Gathered or ungathered leaves.
   1. number of leaves.
   2. pagination, if any.
   3. dimensions (in centimetres).
   4. character and distinguishing features.
      a. part of a notebook.
      b. torn from a notebook.
      c. lined or unlined.
         i. number of lines to a page.
         ii. distinguishing marks of lines (e.g. first line in red ink).
      d. watermarks.
      e. chain lines (horizontal or vertical).

5. kind of inscription.
   a. holograph (in whose hand?)
      i. pen.
      ii. pencil.
      iii. pen with revisions in pencil or pen.
      iv. colour of ink or pencil.
   b. typescript.
      i. original or carbon.
      ii. distinguishing features of typeface.
      iii. colour of ribbon.
   c. mixed (e.g. typescript with manuscript corrections).
      i. in author's hand.
      ii. other.

C. Contents.
   1. Work to which materials relate.
      a. unpublished work: skeleton description of kind and contents.
      b. if related to published work, state how, e.g.
         i. almost identical, i.e. fair copy.
         ii. radically different in certain respects.
   2. Sequence.
      a. gathered.
         i. sequence of contents, including intervening blank pages, if any, e.g.
            1ʳ to 4ᵛ—*On Baile's Strand*
            5ʳ to 5ᵛ—*Presences*
            5ᵛ to 6ᵛ—*On Baile's Strand*
            7ʳ to 10ᵛ—Blank
            11ʳ to 16ᵛ—*The Second Coming*
      b. ungathered.
         i. first and last words on each group of leaves.
         ii. if leaves of different kinds, note kind to which each leaf belongs.

D. Terminal dates on manuscripts.
   1. internal evidence.
      a. dates on cover or specific leaves of manuscript.
      b. manuscript in relation to date of published version.
   2. External evidence (reference in letters, autobiographies, etc.)

II. Galley and Page Proofs.
    A. Type of proof, with page or galley sequence if possible.
    B. Identification of work and edition to which proof relates.
    C. Nature of corrections and revisions and by whom.
        1. with relation to manuscript and printed version.
        2. with relation to printed version.

III. Copy Texts.
    A. Typescript used by printer.
    B. Manuscript used by printer.
    C. Previous printed version used as copy text for new edition.

IV. Printed version with manuscript corrections unless they fall into category III. Identify with relation to appropriate number in Wade-Alspach *Bibliography*.

V. Marginalia: manuscript comments by Yeats on his own or other printed works.

VI. Correspondence.
    1. Custody.
    2. Published or unpublished; if published where?
    3. ALS or TLS.
    4. Recipient.
    5. Date.
    6. If unpublished, subject matter, people, places, and publications referred to in the letter.

VII. Manuscripts not covered by previous categories.

Catalogue of Yeats Manuscripts in the Olin Library, Cornell University

Phillip Marcus

1. Unpublished; ALS; Mrs. [Roland] Crangle; 13 June [1916?]; the letter apologizes for a delay in answering one from the recipient, "shortly after" the arrival of which "this tragic Irish rebellion shifted my thoughts out of their serene course."
2. Unpublished; ALS; Mrs. [Roland] Crangle; 7 May [1914?]; accompanies a picture of WBY, probably that by Sargent (see item 5).
3. Unpublished; TLS; Mrs. [Roland] Crangle; 22 October 1924; courtesy note in reply to letter from recipient; reference to "Dr. Lappin" and to memories of lecture tours in America.
4. Unpublished; ALS; Mrs. [Roland] Crangle; 29 March [1922?]; refers to the death of his father, about which Mrs. Crangle has apparently sent him a notice; speaks of having "now taken" the 82 Merrion Square house; also references to Thoor Ballylee and Oxford.
5. Unpublished; TLS; Mrs. [Roland] Crangle; 30 March 1914; reply to a letter from the recipient; WBY promises to "write from England" and send the "Sargent picture."
6. Unpublished; telegram; Mrs. [Roland] Crangle; 18 February 1914; WBY says he will call to see recipient.
7. Unpublished; TLS; unknown; 7 January 1908; WBY asked about the authenticity of an alleged Blake signature in a book possessed by the recipient; reference to "acknowledged authorities on William Blake": Mr. Archie Russell, Mr. Eric Maclaghan.

8. Published (*Letters*, p. 803n); photocopy of memorandum relating to Irish Academy of Letters.
9. Published (*Letters of James Joyce*, II, 17); ALS; James Joyce; [? 25 November 1902].
10. Unpublished; TLS; James Joyce; 9 December 1902; advice about publishing in English periodicals; references to *The Speaker*, *The Academy*; Lady Gregory; D'Annunzio.
11. Published (with only minor variations, down through "It has distinction" in *Letters of James Joyce*, II, 23; at this point the Cornell version follows, with only minor variations, the fragment printed by Ellmann, II, 13–14, and identified there as a Yale MS. The remainder of the letter Ellmann gives on pp. 23–24 is *not* found in this Cornell item); TL (dictated) copy; James Joyce, 18 December [19]02.
12. Unpublished; TLS; James Joyce; 25 October 1911; concerns a translation of *The Countess Cathleen* by Joyce's friend Nicolò Vidacovitch (see *Letters of James Joyce*, II, 298); references to United States and Ireland.
13. Unpublished; ALS; James Joyce; 14 May 1912; concerns the translation of *The Countess Cathleen* referred to above; reference to Bernard Shaw.
14. Published (*Letters of James Joyce*, II, 363); ALS: James Joyce; 7 September [1915].
15. Unpublished; ALS (amanuensis); James Joyce; 8 November 1917; rejects *Exiles* for the Abbey Theatre; reference to Edward Martyn.
16. Published (*Letters of James Joyce*, II, 405); ALS; James Joyce; 26 August [1917].
17. Unpublished; TL (copy); James Joyce; 1 July 1924; invites Joyce to stay with WBY in Dublin for the Horse Show and Tailteann Games; references to Ezra Pound, the Marquis McSwiney, Lavery, Shaw.
18. Published (*Letters of James Joyce*, II, 388); ALS; Ezra Pound, 11 February [1917].
19. Unpublished; ALS; Wyndham Lewis; [possibly 1929 or 1930]; letter of introduction for Lennox Robinson.
20. Unpublished; ALS; Wyndham Lewis; [1914 or 1915]; concerned with WBY's efforts to help Lewis's friend William Patrick Roberts; references to Sir Matthew Nathan and AE.
21. Unpublished (but quoted extensively in *Letters of Wyndham*

    Lewis, p. 181n); TL (carbon or copy); [mid-1928]; praise of Lewis's novel *Childermass*; references to *A Vision, Gulliver's Travels*, and Olivia Shakespear.

22. Unpublished (but quoted extensively in *Letters of Wyndham Lewis*, p. 183n); TL (carbon or copy); Wyndham Lewis; [September 1928]; WBY gives permission to quote (with modification) his opinion of *Childermass*.

23. Unpublished; TLS; Wyndham Lewis; 5 November 1928; apologizes for having missed a meeting with Lewis; references to London, Ezra Pound, "Limbo."

24. Published (with a few slight variations in *Letters of W. B. Yeats*, pp. 762–63, from a typed copy belonging to Mrs. Yeats); ALS; Wyndham Lewis; 24 April [1929?].

25. Unpublished; ALS; Wyndham Lewis; n.d.; apparently accompanied a statement about one of Lewis's books.

A Note on Some of
Yeats's Revisions for
The Land of Heart's Desire

Colin Smythe

The Abbey Theatre archives contain a copy, with manuscript revisions in Yeats's hand, of the June 1903 issue of Mosher's *Bibelot* which contains Yeats's *The Land of Heart's Desire*. Some of these revisions were incorporated in the 1912 revised edition of the play; others were not and therefore represent an intermediate stage in Yeats's thinking. It appears likely that Yeats, when he undertook what proved to be a substantial revision of the play in 1911, first took a copy of the 1903 Mosher text and began to make the actual revisions on the text,[1] but finding this procedure inadequate he turned, most probably, to the blank pages before him on his desk.

I list below all of the revisions that appear in Yeats's hand on the 1903 text. These revisions are printed in italics and are arranged according to their corresponding line numbers in Alspach's *Variorum Edition of the Plays of W. B. Yeats*. If the revision was incorporated, with little subsequent change, in the 1912 edition of the play, I indicate this by placing "1912" before the appropriate line number in Alspach. If the revision was not incorporated in the 1912 edition, I place "Int." before the appropriate line number in Alspach to indicate that the particular revision represents an intermediate stage in Yeats's thinking; later Yeats either rejected these revisions

---

1. Compare his method of revising *The Tables of the Law* in 1925. See Robert O'Driscoll, "The Tables of the Law: A Critical Text," *Yeats Studies*, No. 1 (Bealtaine 1971), p. 99.

or forgot he had made them. My own interpolations are inserted in square brackets.

I am indebted to Gabriel Fallon for allowing me to study the Abbey volume.

1912	108	Colleen, they are the children of the *fiend,*
Int.	126a	*Has come* to beg a porringer of milk.
Int.	152	The wise priest of our parish to our *left,*
Int.	153	And you and our dear son to *right* of us.
Int.	198	Thinking that all things trouble your *dark* head—
Int.	235a	And seen a pale-faced *girl* with red-gold hair,
Int.	248a	Be happy too. *It is a girl that sings*
Int.	249	*She must be cold. I will bring her in*
Int.	257	*I'll crouch beside the fire,*
1912	259	*You have a comely shape.*
1912	265	*You have coaxing ways*
Int.	298	~~Because you are so young and little a child~~[2]
Int.	299	[lacking]
Int.	300	~~I will take it down.~~
Int.	320	Maurteen Bruin *sits at fire*
Int.	320a	~~It will buy lots of toys; see how it glitters!~~
		[replaced by 321–323]
1912	321	*Here are some ribbands that I bought in the town*
1912	322	*For my son's wife and she will let me give them*
1912	323	*To tie up that wild hair the wind has tumbled*
1912	325	*Do you love me?*— ~~I love you.~~
1912	326	*When the Almighty puts so great a share*
1912	327	*Of His own ageless youth into a creature*
1912	328	*To look is but to love.*
1912	329	And do you love me? *too?* [added at end of line]
Int.	330	~~I—~~I do not know. [I— deleted]
		You love that *young man* over there:
1912	337	You fear because of her *unmeasured* prattle;
Int.	342	*But when I put on womanhood I marry*
Int.	348	I am *the Spring's* daughter.

2. Yeats deletes this line and the succeeding one in the Mosher text, indicating that they were either superfluous or in need of revision, but the three lines that replaced them in the final text do not appear here.

Contributors

DOUGLAS N. ARCHIBALD   Chairman of the English Department, Colby College, Maine. Author of *John Butler Yeats*. Preparing a critical study of Edmund Burke and a book on W. B. Yeats.

DAVID R. CLARK   Professor of English, University of Massachusetts. Publications include *W. B. Yeats and the Theatre of Desolate Reality; Lyric Resonance: Glosses on Some Poems of Yeats, Frost, Crane, Cummings and Others*, (co-editor) *Druid Craft: The Writing of The Shadowy Waters*.

KAREN DORN   B.A. and M.A. at the University of Maryland. Has just completed a Ph.D. dissertation on "Play, Set and Performance in the Theatre of W. B. Yeats" for the University of Cambridge. At present she is preparing her thesis for publication.

DAVID FITZPATRICK   A student at Cambridge University, at present writing a thesis on the Social History of Ireland. He has tutored in twentieth-century history at LaTrobe University, Melbourne.

JAMES W. FLANNERY   Director of English Theatre at the University of Ottawa and producer of a number of Yeats's plays that have won critical acclaim. Publications include *Miss Horniman and the Abbey Theatre*, and a forthcoming book entitled *W. B. Yeats and the Idea of a Theatre: The Early Abbey Theatre in Theory and Practice*.

MICHEÁL MACLIAMMÓIR   Ireland's most distinguished man of the theatre and Founder of the Gate Theatre in Dublin. Author of several plays in Irish and English, volumes of autobiography, and books on Yeats, Wilde, and others.

PHILLIP L. MARCUS   Associate Professor of English and Director of Graduate Studies at Cornell University. Author of *Yeats and the Beginning of the Irish Renaissance* and *Standish O'Grady*.

JAMES B. MCGUIRE   Professor of English at Springfield College, Springfield, Massachusetts.

ROBERT O'DRISCOLL   Founder and first Chairman of the Canadian Association for Irish Studies, 1968–72. Founder and Artistic Director of the Irish Theatre Society and the Irish Arts Theatre, 1967–74. Professor of English, St. Michael's College, University of Toronto. Poems and articles on Yeats, Joyce, Synge, Lady Gregory, Beckett, and nineteenth-century Irish literature. Editor of *Theatre and Nationalism in Twentieth-Century Ireland*.

JOSEPH RONSLEY   Department of English, McGill University. Author of *Yeats's Autobiography: Life as Symbolic Pattern*. Chairman of the Canadian Association for Irish Studies, 1972–73.

COLIN SMYTHE   Publisher and Joint General Editor of the *Collected Works of Lady Gregory* and the *Collected Works of George Russell (A.E.)*. Author of *Guide to Coole Park*. Chairman of the Bibliographical Sub-Committee of IASAIL.

RICHARD TAYLOR   Department of English, University of Ife, Nigeria. Editor of *Frank Pearce Sturm: His Life, Letters, and Collected Work*, and author of articles on Western and Japanese drama. Now writing a book on Nō drama.